The Consultative
Real Estate Agent

D0829833

The Consultative Real Estate Agent

Building Relationships that
Create Loyal Clients,
Get More Referrals, and
Increase Your Sales

Kelle Sparta

American Management Association

New York • Atlanta • Brussels • Chicago • Mexico City • San Francisco
Shanghai • Tokyo • Toronto • Washington, D.C.

333.33
S73c

Special discounts on bulk quantities of AMACOM books are available to corporations, professional associations, and other organizations. For details, contact Special Sales Department, AMACOM, a division of American Management Association, 1601 Broadway, New York, NY 10019.
Tel.: 212-903-8316. Fax: 212-903-8083.
Web Site: www.amacombooks.org

This publication is designed to provide accurate and authoritative information in regard to the subject matter covered. It is sold with the understanding that the publisher is not engaged in rendering legal, accounting, or other professional service. If legal advice or other expert assistance is required, the services of a competent professional person should be sought.

REALTOR® is a registered collective membership mark that identifies a real estate professional who is a member of the National Association of REALTORS® and subscribes to its strict Code of Ethics. AMACOM uses these names throughout this book in initial capital letters or ALL CAPITAL letters for editorial purposes only, with no intention of trademark violation.

Library of Congress Cataloging-in-Publication Data

Sparta, Kelle.
    The consultative real estate agent : building relationships that create loyal clients, get more referrals, and increase your sales / Kelle Sparta.
        p.   cm.
    Includes index.
    ISBN 0-8144-7321-0
    1. Real estate business.   2. Real estate agents.   3. House selling.   I. Title.

    HD1379.S64   2006
    333.33′068′8—dc22   2005015275

© 2006 Kelle Sparta.
All rights reserved.
Printed in the United States of America.

This publication may not be reproduced,
stored in a retrieval system,
or transmitted in whole or in part,
in any form or by any means, electronic,
mechanical, photocopying, recording, or otherwise,
without the prior written permission of AMACOM,
a division of American Management Association,
1601 Broadway, New York, NY 10019.

Printing number

10   9   8   7   6   5   4   3   2   1

To my mother:
This one's for us.

University Libraries
Carnegie Mellon University
Pittsburgh PA 15213-3890

CONTENTS

LIST OF EXHIBITS

ACKNOWLEDGMENTS

This book would not have happened without the input of many people along the way. The first person I want to thank is Christina Parisi, my acquisitions editor, who met me at a National Association of Realtors® Expo, and asked me to write this book. I had no idea how much work it would be at the time or what was entailed in the process, but she coached me through the process beautifully. Thanks also to Robyn Mellish who was kind enough to come to the expo with me and work the booth even though she knew nothing about real estate. I would have never had the time to even talk about this book if it weren't for her.

Next I want to thank Stephanie Machell, my partner in crime in our writing group. She was very helpful in editing chapters along the way (specifically the Life After Divorce chapter where her expertise as a therapist was invaluable). Samantha Schack was my saving grace when, one month from my deadline, I realized I still had to write about 200 pages. In my panic, I was close to shutting down completely. She looked me in the eye and said, "I know you went to college. I know you wrote tons of papers. Think of this month as finals week and write a whole bunch of twenty-page term papers." With that thought in mind, I was able to buckle down and get it done. Thanks, Sam.

When the time came to copyedit this book, my editor passed me along to Niels Buessem. I got my first (and my most treasured) compliment from him about the book. He has assured me that it will be a winner. Thanks for the encouragement and the great comments along the way, Niels.

Then there are the people at ERA Key Realty Services who got my resume a couple of years ago and saw that I wasn't quite a match for the position they had, but didn't want to let me go. They created a position especially for me as Director of Recruitment and Training for all of their then nine offices. They gave me the foray back into the industry that I needed that took me where I am today. Thanks Nelson, Bruce, Cheryl, and Mike for believing in me. To all of the real estate agents I ever co-broked a deal with—thanks for the learning experiences and the laughs.

To Ludwig Pulaski, my friend, my former business partner, and occasionally my knight in shining armor, I love you. And finally thanks to Daniel Singer, who dragged me kicking and screaming into the one thing that would make me truly happy. I am in your debt.

INTRODUCTION

In today's real estate market, we agents need to find a way to distinguish ourselves from the rest of the agents out there. We need to find a way to add value to the transaction. Buyers can find information about listings on the Internet. Sellers can list their homes on ISoldMyHouse.com and other FSBO sites. More and more, the primaries in a transaction are asking themselves why they need us.

As any good real estate agent knows, buyers and sellers need us much more than they realize. We may be a line of defense between them and the parties on the other side of the deal. Or perhaps we are a hand to hold through the stress of the process. The fact is we do much more than simply putting buyers and sellers together in the same room. The best of us are one part entrepreneur, one part expert negotiator, one part problem solver, and one part counselor. But how do we get this idea across to our potential clients?

We need to shift our focus away from the houses that we help transfer and onto the services that we provide to our clients. We need to focus on the intangibles in the industry. Anyone can find a home for you, but how many people are capable of keeping you on an even keel all the way through the process, no matter how choppy the waters get? That takes patience, skill, good problem-solving abilities, and true compassion.

In this book, we focus on developing these coaching skills. Whether you are a new agent just coming into the industry, or an experienced agent looking to improve your people skills, this book will help you find your way to a relationship with your client that transcends just the transaction. You will learn to help your client not only through the transaction itself, but also through the major life transitions they are facing that cause them to decide to move in the first place. And, as you learn to create those relationships, you will also learn how to transform those clients from happy past customers into raving fans who continually send you referrals.

For new agents in particular, learning these skills is primary. The single most important factor for converting a lead into a client is people skills. Agents need to have confidence in themselves and their abilities, and they need to be able to convey that confidence to the client. No amount of memorization of scripts and dialogues will give you that confidence. Some people think you have to be born with it. I disagree.

This book teaches confidence. It accomplishes that task by offering insight into the emotional side of the transaction. You'll learn about the feelings that buyers and sellers are experiencing and how to develop rapport through effective listening skills. You'll learn how to handle yourself, your clients, and other agents to keep the deal on course. Every agent knows that if you can connect with the client, then you'll get the deal. Here, you'll learn how to connect.

This is the practice for the new millennium. *Here* is the value-added proposition that many of us are looking for. Get closer to your clients. Get to know them on a more significant level. Let them know that you understand their wants, fears, desires, and dreams. When you understand these things about your clients, you are in a better position to be able to help them reach the goals that are real estate related. Get to know your clients and you will never worry about losing them again. They will come back to you and they will bring their friends.

This is how I worked with my clients for over six years. This is how I teach my students to work with their clients. Overwhelmingly, I have had a positive response from the clients and the agents. The clients report having felt cared for and understood throughout the transaction. The agents get more repeat and referral business. Everyone has a better transaction. It worked for me, it works for my students, and it will work for you too.

Kelle Sparta
May 2005

PART I

RELATING TO BUYERS AND SELLERS

THE PROCESS OF CHANGE

Welcome! This book will be different from any other book you will read about real estate. We will be looking not just at the real estate transaction itself, but also at the emotional issues associated with the major life transitions that your clients go through that cause them to move in the first place. As such, we will be exploring the relationship we have with our clients on a deeper level than ever before.

Before we can begin to talk about the problems that individuals face in real estate transactions, we first need to understand the process of change itself. It is through the understanding of this process that we will be able to better coach and educate our clients on what they can expect throughout the transition period. It is this sort of information that makes us stand out from the competition and puts us in a position to create loyal, lifelong relationships with our clients.

Understanding the process of change is the foundation to the work we will do in the rest of this book. In order to best explain this subject, I'm going to explore it first through our personal experience as agents and people rather than relating it to the real estate transaction initially. Hang in there. I promise I will bring it home to the practice of real estate before we get to the end of this chapter.

Why Understanding the Process Is Important

When we go through the process of change, there is a series of distinct and measurable steps that we take each time. Each step has its own indicators, pitfalls, and issues that come with it. In understanding each of these steps, we give ourselves a sense of control. It is the knowledge of the steps and what each one is about that allows us to be more comfortable with what is a very uncomfortable experience.

Fear

Before anyone can begin to make changes in his life, he must first get past the fear that holds him in place. Fear is the biggest stumbling block for most people. Ninety percent of the population is motivated to move away from what they don't want, while only 10 percent is motivated to move toward what they *do* want. This makes us a society of fear-mongers. We use fear in advertising; we use it in movies; we use it in relationships. Threats, ultimatums, warnings—all are ways in which we try to control our environment. But what are we afraid of?

Many people will tell you that they do not make changes in their lives because they are afraid of the unknown. If they make a change, they don't know what will happen and they are afraid of that. I suggest that this is not quite the unvarnished truth. I believe that it is not the unknown that we are afraid of. I believe that what we are truly afraid of is losing what we have—no matter how unsatisfactory what we have may be. Our current reality is where our comfort zone lies. And in this comfort zone, we feel at home. It doesn't matter how miserable that "home" feeling is—it's ours and we know what to expect from it.

This is why so many people stay in bad relationships, bad business partnerships, bad living circumstances. They are afraid of what they will get if they let go of them. They fear that what comes next will be worse than what they left behind, or that they will not know how to deal with the new things that show up.

Also, we instinctively know that when we change one aspect of our lives, we run the risk that everything else in our lives will change with it. We are afraid that we will lose the things we have worked so hard to put in place. We know that every aspect of our lives plays into every other aspect. When we disrupt one, the others get shaken up as well. We are afraid of losing what we have that we like.

The problem with this thinking is that it makes us forget about choice. We often fall into the trap of thinking that everything happens *to* us, rather than it being the result of us acting upon the world. We forget the causal relationship between our choices and the changes that they result in, so we feel out of control, victimized by circumstances.

Consider how you felt when you were a new agent in the business. When I do trainings, I often ask the groups I teach how long they waited before they got into the business. How long did they think about becoming an agent before they actually went out and did it? I get answers from a few days to as much as twenty years. On average, I find that my students tend to think about getting into real estate for about five years before they actually make the move. Why does it take us so long? Fear. We are afraid to give up a steady income. We are afraid to test ourselves and see if we can do it. We are afraid that we will fail. We are afraid that we will succeed. Whatever the fear, it's there. If it weren't, we would all get into the business the first time we think about it.

When people don't change, it is fear that stops them. We all know people who talk about needing to make a change, but never quite seem to manage it. We may think it is laziness or lack of motivation, but that is not the case. Fear is an insidious creature. It lurks in our subconscious minds, distracting us from making changes. It suggests that we are tired, or that we need to go do something—that this other thing over here is far more important. These factors are not laziness or lack of motivation, they are *fear* distracting us—dragging us away from a decision that will change our lives.

We faced many of the same issues when we were new in the business. We were overwhelmed by the amount of information that we needed to absorb. The feeling of being overwhelmed quickly turned into a sense of helplessness or even hopelessness and we became afraid that we wouldn't ever be able to learn it all. Our fear manifested as shut-down and we stopped working. We found ourselves slogging through emotional molasses trying to force ourselves to go out and meet people, see properties, learn the Multiple Listing Service (MLS) computer system, etc. We found it hard to get out of bed in the morning. We started coming into the office later and later, and sometimes not coming in at all.

Many agents leave the business when they hit this barrier, but we slogged on. Eventually, we got an understanding of the industry, of what was expected of us, and of our clients. In short, we eventually got a sense of comfort in our new surroundings. And, as we developed this sense of comfort, our fears dissipated and life got easier. We showed great courage in not giving in to the subconscious and conscious fears that threatened to stop us in our tracks with self-sabotaging habits. We ignored our impulses to shut down. We moved through the feelings of inadequacy and incompetence. We reassured ourselves that we *could* do it. And because we believed it, it was true.

Breakdown Before Breakthrough

As we discussed above, any time we make changes in one aspect of our life, the rest of our life is affected as well. This is true both on a physical, obvious level, and on a more subtle one. When we move from one location to another, we change how we commute to work, we change where we shop, we change the people with whom we interact on a day-to-day basis. These are the obvious physical factors. The less obvious ones are the psychological factors. If we move into a nicer neighborhood, we begin to redefine ourselves as someone who lives in a nicer neighborhood, someone who interacts with a higher social strata of people, someone who has "made it." This affects the way we carry ourselves, the way we interact with the world around us, who we are.

If we have friendships with people who have not "made it" the way that we have, they may begin to feel slighted. We have left them behind. We have abandoned them. They may tell us that we are conceited, full of ourselves, too big for our britches. They will try to emotionally drag us back down to their level since they are comfortable with us when we are there. When we fail to conform to their preconceived notions of how we should behave, they will break off the friendship. They will do this not because we are bad people, but because we have changed. And because we have changed, they feel threatened. They feel as though they either have to change with us or they have to stop being friends with us. It is easier for them to stay in their comfort zone than it is for them to come with us on the journey, so they break off the relationship.

This is *breakdown*. When we see this kind of breakdown occurring in our lives, then we know that we are on the right track. We are making real changes in our lives.

We need to be careful when dealing with this process, not to take things too personally. It is natural that there will be some fallout as a result of the changes we are choosing. We should expect it. It is sad to see people we have been close to fall by the wayside, but it is a natural consequence of growth. The harder we try to hold onto these relationships, the more we hold back the progress of the changes we are making. We need to let go. People will make their own decisions about what is best for their lives; we cannot take those decisions personally. Just like our decision to change our lives had nothing to do with them, the same is true for their decisions *not* to change *their* lives having nothing to do with us.

Another form of breakdown can occur as a result of our internal changes. Many of us can remember back to when we first started in the business. Some of us held other jobs as we transitioned into the business. When we did this, there came a point in our jobs when we realized that we were no longer mentally there. We were invested in our real estate practice, not in our day job, and it was starting to show in our work. Some of us quit our day job at this point, others stuck it out. Some of us may have gotten fired because we stayed too long physically at a job we had left mentally months before. This is one type of breakdown that can occur as a result of our mental shifts.

When we change our minds about something, it shows in everything we say and do. The more significant the shift is in our perceptions, the more far-reaching the change is in our interaction with the world around us. Moving into the real estate industry is a significant shift, and doing it physically at a speed that is slower than our mental shift runs the risk of affecting our lives strongly by losing our jobs due to inattention and lack of commitment.

Oddly enough, I've noticed that breakdown usually occurs before we begin the actual conscious process of change. It is an indicator I use to see what is moving in my life. When I broke up with my boyfriend, I knew my business was about to take off to a new level. When it was time for me to buy a new car, but I was still avoiding it, I hit a pothole coming home from the office that took out my tire. It was the final straw in the long list of needed repairs. It was time for me to buy a new car. Ironically, the pothole was next to a sign for a junk removal company called "Get Rid of It." There's nothing like an unsubtle message.

Placing Your Furniture Order: A Metaphor

The best metaphor I have found to describe how the process of change works once we begin it is that of ordering custom-made furniture. When we order custom-made furniture, we have to first decide what it is that we want. We search through all of the showrooms looking at the style of sofas available. Do we want a high back or a low back? Do we want the legs to show or do we want a more tailored look? Should the cushions be attached to the frame or free-floating? Do we want buttons? What color do we want? What fabric? Rounded arms or squared? Wood? Sleeper sofa or plain? There are so many options to think of. And once we've decided upon the styling, then we need to decide what other pieces of furniture we want in the room with the sofa and we have to decide whether those pieces should match exactly or be complimentary in nature.

This process of deciding what we want is the same as what we think of as "goal setting." We do this each year when we decide how many houses we want to sell in the next year or where we want to go on vacation. Regardless of what we are choosing for ourselves, we are placing that custom furniture order.

Getting Rid of the Old Furniture

Once we have placed our order for our new, custom-built furniture, we have some time before it comes in. During that time, we need to clear out the space where we will be putting the new furniture. That means getting rid of the old furniture that we already have sitting in our living room—the worn-out, stained, shabby, out-of-date furniture that we are so accustomed to. Sure it's ugly, but it's like an old friend.

I recently traded in Ruby, my old Honda Civic, a car I bought as a statement of my independence when I got divorced in 1998. Over the years, I had put 207,000 miles on her. She had been cross-country with me twice, and camping with me more times than I can remember. I had moved with her, lived out of her, and had great times with her. She was a good friend. I couldn't imagine letting her go (especially since she was paid off). I didn't see exactly how shabby Ruby had become over the years. I looked at her through the eyes of memory and love.

When I finally traded her in for my new Honda Element, it was hard on me. I went to clean her out and remove all of my personal items. As I did so, I said goodbye to this faithful friend who had taken me through so much in my life. When the last of my things were gone and I took one last look, I was stunned. The car was a mess. The seats were stained, the back carpet was disintegrating from the bleach I had spilled there years before, and the dash was tired looking. My precious Ruby was a beater car. I had no idea.

I had been so proud of the fact that I had taken her so far with me. I reveled in every scratch and ding. I knew the history of all of her little imperfections. But when I looked at her in the cold light of day, I realized that she just didn't fit with my new life. I needed to let her go to make room for my new car, which reflected my new life. I love my new car, Tigger. I spend lots of time showing him off to people (Honda should pay me a commission). But I'm still getting used to him. He's not the old, comfortable Ruby.

Whenever we make a change and place an order for something new, we have to let go of something old in our lives. This doesn't mean that what we are letting go of isn't any good or that it was a mistake to have had it in our lives in the past, it simply means that it is time to move forward. Ruby was a great car. She was exactly what I needed to take me through that part of my life. But it was time to move on. I needed to let her go.

We need to get rid of the old before there is room for the new to come in. I could have given Ruby to a friend, or kept her as a backup vehicle. But I knew the importance of letting go in a way that I couldn't go back. I traded her in. I have no idea where she is now, but I know I can't get her back. I have to move forward. "Getting rid of our furniture" needs to work the same way. We need to get rid of it in a way that says that we can't go back. If we hedge our bets, then we tell our subconscious mind that we aren't really serious about the change. So when we empty that room, we want to put the furniture out on the street—free to any takers—or sell it in a yard sale, or give it to charity. If we give it to friends or store it in the basement, what we are saying is that we don't trust our decision to let it go. We might want to go backwards and we want to keep that option open.

I have this conversation often with new agents. I ask them if they have an alternate plan for what they will do if real estate doesn't work out for them. What they don't realize is that the ones who have an alternate plan are *less* likely to succeed than the ones who don't. They have told their subconscious minds that there is a chance that they will fail. Since this is the case, their subconscious minds have that as an option and they may take it (depending on what other tapes they have playing in their heads). The ones that don't have an alternate plan *have* to succeed. They have given themselves no other option.

The "getting rid of the furniture" stage is where we find out exactly how committed we are to the change we are making. If we hedge our bets, then we're not very committed. If we don't, then we know that we will follow this through to the very end.

Sitting in the Empty Room

To continue with the metaphor, once we have managed to get rid of the furniture, there will be a period of time when the room will be empty. We will be sitting in that empty room waiting for the new furniture to arrive. This is the most uncomfortable part of the process because we have nothing to look at but ourselves. It is when we are sitting in the empty room that we begin to question ourselves most critically. We berate ourselves for making bad decisions. We lament the loss of the old furniture. We question the wisdom of the order we have placed. We are alone with our thoughts, and those thoughts may not be pleasant.

If we are going to change our minds, this is the time when it is most likely to happen. This is the reason that I recommended *not* putting the furniture someplace where we could get it back. When the gaping void of the empty room becomes too much for us, we may be tempted to put the old furniture back into the room and cancel our order. We slide back into our comfort zone forgetting why we had tried to make the change in the first place. It will be months before we get up the courage to try again and then it will be even harder since we remember giving up before and we will try to convince ourselves that it is just too hard to change.

We must stay strong in this stage. We need to reaffirm our commitment to the process. We need to give ourselves pep talks, telling us how good we are at this, what a good decision this is, and reminding ourselves of the reasons we chose to make the change in the first place. If we can make it through this stage, everything gets easier from here.

Receiving Delivery of the New Furniture

Once we have sat in the empty room for a time, eventually the doorbell rings and we see the delivery van in the driveway. We are excited and nervous because we placed this order a while ago and now it's here. It's intimidating to think that we will have a room full of new furniture shortly. And, we're not really sure whether we even remember exactly what the furniture will look like. What if they deliver the wrong furniture? What if we picked the wrong color? What if it doesn't look good in the room? What if we hate it?

The last of the fear comes out as we see the truck pulling into the driveway, but we know that it's too late to turn back now. The driver comes up to the door and asks us where we want it. We show him the living room and he heads off to the truck to unload our order. When the last of the furniture is in the living room, we sign for the pieces and he drives off—leaving us alone with our new furniture.

We stare at it for a few moments aware that it is here now and we are stuck with it. Eventually, we pull out a set of scissors and begin to carefully cut away the wrapping around the pieces. As the true color of the furniture begins to emerge, we realize that we have a problem. The furniture does not go with the wall color. We're going to have to repaint. Well, there's nothing to be done about it now, so we keep cutting. Eventually we have all the wrappings off.

We appraise the furniture with a critical eye. Did they manufacture it properly? Did it get damaged in shipping? Is it the color, fabric, style, and size we ordered? Is it what we expected? (It rarely is.)

Now that we have revealed it and inspected it, it's time to place it in the room. We try several different layouts looking for the way that feels right to us. After all, we're going to be living with this new furniture. It needs to be arranged in a way that is comfortable to us. Eventually we find an acceptable layout and we leave it. We know that we need to redecorate, but we need to get used to the new furniture first before we can face any other changes just yet.

We "receive the delivery" when the things we are working for finally start to fall into place. We don't always know what the final outcome will look like (in fact we rarely know what the outcome will look like), so we are often surprised when it finally shows up. It's something that we have to wrap our brains around and get used to before we can totally accept it.

When I first started selling real estate, I wanted to sell a lot of houses. I didn't know what my life would look like when I was selling a lot of houses, but I knew that I wanted to. So when the deals started to roll in, I found myself overwhelmed by the amount of work to be done. I had no systems in place to keep me organized (half the time I wasn't even sure what I was supposed to do). I flew by the seat of my pants and prayed that I didn't miss anything. My life, on the other hand, took a beating at the same time as my business took off. I worked long hours, took little time off, and didn't spend much time at all with my loved ones. I was so busy trying to be successful that I forgot that part of success is having time to enjoy it. Eventually, I started putting some systems in place so that I could take some downtime. And finally, it all fell into place in the most comfortable way as I got used to my business and arranged it to my liking.

Decorating

Once we have finished arranging the furniture and taken a little down-time to relax from the stress of the change, we will begin to feel dissatisfied with the decorations. We will want to make the room feel "done." This will require a little redecorating. The walls that don't match the furniture will need to be painted. The accessories that matched the old wall color will have to go and be replaced with ones that match the new theme. Perhaps we'll put up tapestries where there were once prints. We may add a little texture to a room that had been hard lines before. It's our room (our life), we can decorate it however we like.

Taking a little time between receiving the furniture and decorating is a good thing. It lets us get used to the idea of having new furniture. It lets us get used to being the type of person who would have this kind of furniture in her home. It gives us a chance to consider what we might like to do for the decorating part of the project. We need to consider who we are in this new space and how we want to reflect that in our decorating style.

In real life, this is the time when we add in the extras that make life worth living. We make new friends. We choose hobbies we want to pur-sue. We find ways to be creative. We create a love life that is fulfilling to us. These are all things that cannot and should not be rushed. Taking our time in this process is a good thing. Making conscious decisions about these choices is an even better thing. Once we have let go of the past, the world is our oyster. We can choose whatever we want. Being cognizant of making those choices and perhaps choosing differently than we have in the past is a way to create a richer experience of the change we have wrought.

Renormalization

Everything is delivered, arranged, and decorated the way we want it. The room has come together nicely. Every time we walk into the room we are reminded of how much it has changed and how lovely it looks now. Over time, we think this less and less as we become accustomed to this new reality. And, eventually, one night we get up in the middle of the night and walk through the room without turning on any lights and without stubbing our toes on anything. What had been new and different and stress-inducing, is now normal to us. It has become our new comfort zone.

When we reach a new comfort zone in life, we find that many more options open up to us mentally. Where we felt limited in our old space, we feel more free to move in the new one. We have reached the summit and we can see to the next horizon. What had seemed unreachable before is now commonplace. If we make enough changes in our lives, we start to get used to the process. We begin to see how anything is possible if we are willing to pursue it.

Translating These Ideas to Clients

When we begin the process with our clients, we embark on a journey with them. They don't know what to expect out of that journey, but we do. We can help them feel more comfortable with the changes they are facing by helping them to understand the process as a whole. We can use the metaphor of the new furniture to explain the process of change to them. When they understand what to expect, they are not so stressed when these things occur. They know that this is a normal part of the process and that this is only a stage. The stage will end eventually and they will stop feeling so disoriented and out-of-sorts. Sometimes just knowing that there will be an end to the feeling is enough to help them through it.

Here's a quick look at how this process manifests itself with our buyers and sellers:

- *Fear.* We will usually engage this stage with sellers who are "thinking about" selling, but aren't quite sure. (They're not sure if they are willing to risk uprooting their lives and letting go of their comfort zone.) We'll also see it in sellers who know they need to start packing away items, cleaning up their property, and getting it ready to put on the market, but can't quite seem to manage to get started on the project. (They're stuck in fear and it's winning.) The easiest way to help these sellers is to explain how their fear gets in the way. Encourage your sellers to focus on what they will get out of moving rather than on what they might lose. If they can't get started packing, go over and help them, or hire a personal organizer to get them started. Usually, if you can get them past the first hump of work, then they can keep going on their own.

- *Breakdown Before Breakthrough.* Buyers and sellers usually reach this phase before they get to us. We can reference back to it to help explain the process to our clients. If we tell them about a stage they've already been through, then they are more likely to believe us when we tell them about the stages to come.

- *Placing Your Furniture Order.* For both buyers and sellers, it is important for us to help them create a visual of how they want the process to go and what they want things to look like when they are done. We can help them with this by asking questions like, "If everything went perfectly in the transaction, what would that look like?" or "Imagine that we've just closed on your home—what do you want that to feel like?" Our job is to get our clients to create a clear idea in their heads of what they want and then help them to remember that vision whenever they get off track. In this way, we help them order their new furniture.

- *Getting Rid of the Old Furniture.* Remember, this stage is a test of our clients' commitment to the process. Our goal is to help them commit fully. For buyers this means turning in their notice to their landlord as soon as the home inspection is complete. For sellers this means removing the contingency for them to find the home of their choosing before selling. When sellers commit to moving, they will find the home they want. If they're not committed, then they may use not finding the "right" home as an excuse to slide back into their comfort zone and not move after all.

- *Sitting in the Empty Room.* Buyer's remorse is a function of sitting in the empty room. Buyers, especially first time buyers, have a long wait from the time they put in their offer until they close. They will question their decisions mercilessly. But, if we warn them of this stage in advance, they will recognize it when it happens and it will hold less power over them. We can remind them to keep their thoughts toward the positive and to solicit positive input whenever possible. We can also help by offering positive comments about their purchase decision whenever we talk to them.

- *Receiving Delivery of the New Furniture.* For both buyers and sellers this stage comes when they close on the home and finally move. They will feel overwhelmed and exhausted by the sweeping changes taking place in their lives. Our best suggestion to them will be to take some downtime and to pamper themselves a little along the way.

- *Decorating.* Remind your clients that the sooner they can get one room completed, the sooner their stress levels will reduce immensely. But also remind them not to make too many "decorating" decisions too quickly. Remind them that they have time to settle in to their new place before they choose to add social activities, clubs, friends, etc. They should stop and consciously choose what they want for their new lives rather than simply trying to replace what they left behind. Encourage them to take their time in this process.

- *Renormalization.* We normally don't get to see much of this stage with our clients. This stage usually comes long after we have left the scene of actively working with them. But we should still tell them about it. It provides them with a sense of comfort if they know that someday soon, they will feel comfortable again.

Summary

Understanding the process of change is the key to knowing where your clients are in their emotional world. If we can also translate that information back to our clients to provide them with an emotional roadmap of the process itself, we can help them to reduce the amount of stress they will experience along the way. Anytime we can reduce our clients' stress levels, we increase their appreciation of us. It is through understanding our clients that we create stronger, longer-lasting relationships that will feed us business for years to come.

CHAPTER 2

PROBLEM-SOLVING EMOTIONAL ISSUES

Death, divorce, and moving are the most stressful times in a person's life. In real estate, we are always dealing with at least one of these issues, if not two. We never know what will be waiting for us on the other end of the line when we pick up the phone, so we need to know how to deal with anything that arises. When we know how to handle a situation, then our stress levels go down significantly. There are several steps inherent in dealing with any emotionally-based problem.

Step #1: Determine the Actual Problem

The first thing for us to keep in mind is that the actual problem is often *not* what the client raises as an issue. A buyer may call and say that the sellers are being unreasonable about the home-inspection response. He may tell us that he suddenly wants the seller to do two more things on the list that he hadn't asked for before. Likely, his real concern isn't the home inspection. He's probably feeling buyer's remorse. He did the math again and he's starting to play out scenarios in his head about the mounting costs of unforeseen repairs. The projected costs of running the home and the fears around major problems are combining to form a wall of panic. Before he completely melts down, he looks for an outlet for his panic and he finds it in addressing the home inspection issues again with us. We need to be detectives to find out if there's really a problem with the home inspection or if it's just his panic talking. If it is his panic, then we need to deal with his fears, not the home inspection.

Step #2: Find Out if She's Just Venting, or if She Actually Wants Help

There are times when the buyer or seller will call up and vent. It won't necessarily be clear from her comments what she wants you to do about it. If you try to identify the actual problem, she may become more and more vague. It's possible that she is just blowing off steam—relieving the pressure of the stress of the move.

When someone is venting, there is no solution because there is no actual problem. We can ask the client if she is venting or if there is a problem that she wants us to solve for her. If there isn't a problem, then all we need to do is listen. We can nod and make murmured comments at the right times, but otherwise we're just there as a sounding board. If the client seems distressed that she is having these feelings, then we can reassure her that the feelings are completely normal and to be expected. Beyond that, our job is done.

Step #3: Ask Permission to Help

If, however, there is an actual problem in the mind of the buyer (like the home inspection, for instance), then we need to deal with it—solve the problem. It's time to get the buyer out of his house and over to our office where we can talk to him face to face and calm him down. But we can't do that until we can get his permission to help.

Some people are very protective of their problems and will not let us help them. Others want to drop the problem on our doorstep at every opportunity. Regardless of the type of person we are dealing with, getting permission to help is a critical step in the process. When he says "yes" to help, he removes many of the defensive barriers he has in place to keep people out of his business. If we try to enter into that world before we've obtained permission, we might find ourselves surrounded by brick walls.

So when we speak with our buyer, the scenario will go something like this.

"I can hear you're upset. What's the problem, Doug?"

"It's the home inspection—we didn't ask for enough."

"We covered all of the major issues. Is there something in particular you're worried about?"

"Yes, the gutters never got cleaned. Who knows what we'll find under all those leaves. They may be rotten."

"Ah, so you're concerned about things we might not be able to see right now. Is that right?"

"Yeah, you never know what you're going to find when you get into things. I had a friend who bought a house and the thing was a total money pit. He never really dug out from under it."

"And you're worried that this will happen to you too."

"Absolutely. You should be looking out for me here! That's what I'm paying for isn't it?" (Be careful here—if we don't put ourselves on his side *right now*, he'll take off after us instead of the home inspection.)

"I am looking out for you, Doug. I can hear that you're very upset. I'd like to help you get through this. Why don't you come into the office and we'll sit down and talk this through. Would that be OK?" (Asking permission to help.)

"Yeah, I guess. I don't understand why we can't deal with it over the phone."

"I want to be able to talk to you in person. I'd like you to bring your monthly budget with you too. If this really is going to be too much for you to handle financially, then I want to know now so we can try to get you out of this deal. Bring everything you need with you so we can look at the budget and make a determination. When can you be here?"

"OK. I'll be there in half an hour."

"All right. I'm going to cancel my 3:30 appointment so we have enough time. I'll see you when you get here."

By canceling the other appointment we are showing Doug that he's a priority. We'll tell the other client that our buyer is having a meltdown and we need to be there for him. We'll reschedule for another time. We should wait a good ten minutes to make the call canceling the appointment, though, because Doug may call back and cancel. Oftentimes, simply the fact that someone is willing to sit down and go through the math with them will make people come to their senses and realize that they are not being rational. They usually talk themselves down from the limb before they ever get to the office. So we may not have to cancel that other appointment after all.

If Doug calls back to cancel with us, he will feel silly and foolish. It is important for us to provide him with a way to save face. We need to tell him that his feelings are not unusual. It is soothing to a client to know that they are not acting in a way that is out of the norm. If we can convince him that it is a normal course of events that happens all the time, then he will be less stressed about having gone through it.

Buyer's Remorse

Buyer's remorse is a very emotional issue. Buyers question themselves, their decision, our advice, everything. Sometimes they even start to regret having decided to buy a house at all. The stress is getting to them. Buyer's remorse happens when people are sitting in the empty room in the process of change. It's not about paying too much for the house, or the house being in bad condition, it's about questioning their choices and wondering whether they are really ready for this change. Buyers will put all kinds of window dressing on this issue, but at the core, that is the actual issue.

The best way I have found to deal with buyer's remorse is to avoid it altogether. Whenever I took buyers out, I made it my habit to point out all of the flaws in a home. I wanted them to go into the purchase with both eyes open. I pointed out everything from cracks in the foundation to the steepness of the driveway and the problems they might have getting in and out in winter. I played devil's advocate. I was *not* Ms. Doom and Gloom, I wasn't negative about the house. I simply made a point of being sure that the buyers were aware of all of the drawbacks to the property. Every time I made a comment, it was in a neutral tone. My comments would be something like this: "Now, Carla, this house is going to be a thirty-minute commute to work for you. You said you only wanted fifteen minutes—are you OK with making that change?"

My goal wasn't necessarily to talk the buyers out of the house (although this *was* occasionally the result of the questions). It was instead to give them the opportunity to make a completely informed decision based on all of the facts. I can't remember having a single buyer with buyer's remorse because I pointed out all of the things that they could second-guess themselves on up front. I never wanted a buyer to "settle." If she wasn't thrilled, then I told her it was time to move on.

Another way to circumvent this process is to explain the process of change to our clients. When they can identify the empty room and the emotions associated with it, then they can feel a little more comfortable in the space. Also, we can provide them with the tools they need to get through the process (supporting themselves with positive self-talk and focusing on being excited rather than worried). Between these two techniques, buyers don't often experience remorse.

I find that many agents avoid this process because they don't want to blow the sale. The problem with this approach is that one of two things happens. Either the buyer blows the sale later in the process thereby wasting a lot of our time along the way. Or, they buy the house and are unhappy with it and blame us. Either way is a bad result. I've talked many buyers out of buying homes. And each buyer I did this for (with cause of course) has been a staunch advocate for me, sending me many referrals over the years.

Step #4: Getting Unstuck

If Doug does come in for the appointment, then we need to work with him to get him out of his panic. He will need to be handled gently and carefully since he is volatile as a result of the panic he's feeling. Once he's in the office, we will ask him to tell us the problem again. It helps to have people who are overwhelmed cover all the issues multiple times. They have so much going on that they are unclear on where to start. We will write down each problem as he lists it so that we can both see it on paper. It is much less intimidating when the problem is on paper. The problem seems smaller, less intimidating.

If we determine that money is the issue and not the home inspection, then we need to go down that path. But there is another possibility here: He may just be questioning his decision to purchase the home altogether. It may be that he doesn't trust himself to make a good decision. We can explore this option by questioning that path.

"So, Doug, tell me how you're feeling about choosing this house."

"Well, I'm stressed about it. What if it's a money pit like my friend's house?"

"I don't think that's likely. The home inspection came out well. I know the home inspector and he doesn't generally miss stuff. Actually, I think you made a great decision in choosing this house." (We want to give him validation on his decision.)

"You think so?" (With this response, it's clear to us that he was actually questioning the wisdom of his decision.)

"Absolutely. I've seen a lot of houses in my career and this is a good one. It's a great location, both for living in and for resale. It's a good floor plan. The home inspection came out well. We got a good price on it. Overall, I think it's a great deal for you." (Here we're providing evidence to support our assertion of his choice being a good one.)

"Yeah, I guess that's true."

"You've done a great job. I think you're just panicking a little. Totally normal response. I see it all the time. In fact, do you remember when we talked about how you would feel when you were 'sitting in the empty room' in the process of change? Doubting yourself and your decisions, questioning the wisdom of your move?"

"Oh, yeah. . . . "

"I'd wager that this is how you're feeling right now. Am I right?"

"Yeah, I guess it is." (He says with a sheepish grin.)

"No problem, I'm used to getting this response. Take a few deep breaths and remind yourself of what a great house you've picked out. Run through your mind all of the fun things you're gong to do in the house. Focus on the positives and try not to entertain the negatives. It's easy to get stuck in a negative spiral going through 'what ifs' in your mind if you're not careful. Just focus on the positives and you'll be fine. And of course, you can always call me to remind you when you forget." (End the conversation with a smile. During these comments, we're focused on offering a solution to the panic situation, a way to avoid it in the future. Having a way to avoid the panic gives the buyer a sense of security that he won't have this problem again. It also provides closure to the conversation.)

"Thanks."

"Anytime."

This conversation went well. It flowed easily into resolution. But it isn't always this easy. Sometimes our clients aren't ready to let go of their issues so quickly. Sometimes they go into an endless stream of "yeah, buts." We need to learn how to get them past this stage.

Step #5: Calling Our Clients on Their "Yeah, Buts"

When we offer a solution to a client and he refuses to take it, we get a "yeah, but." For example, the conversation with Doug might have gone like this:

"We addressed all of the major issues on the home inspection."

"Yeah, but we didn't have them do the gutters. We could have gotten more out of them."

"We can't focus on 'could haves' or 'should haves,' we need to keep our eyes on the goal here and now. The time for negotiation has passed."

"Yeah, but maybe they'd do it if we went back and asked."

"Or, the sellers could tell us to go away. We could lose the house over that question."

"Yeah, well, if they did that, then I wouldn't want the house anyway because I'd know they were hiding something."

"Look, Doug, I'm hearing a lot of 'yeah, buts' in this conversation. It seems like you're looking for a way out of this deal. Is that what you want? Or are you just feeling uneasy and you want me to find a way to make you feel better?"

"Well, I want the house, but I don't want it if it's going to be the money pit."

"I know that you're concerned about that. The home inspection looked good. We have no reason to believe that there is anything wrong with this house. I've seen no red flags that made me stop and wonder if the sellers were trying to hide anything. In fact, they seem to have been completely reasonable and above-board with us. I don't see a problem here. But it's obvious that you're upset. Are you maybe panicking about the purchase?"

"No. That's not it."

"Are you sure? Because from here it sounds like you're freaking out a little. It's OK if that's the case. Every buyer goes through this at some point or another. It's that moment when you think to yourself, 'What am I doing? Am I crazy? I should never have bought this house!' I've seen it lots of times. It's nothing to be ashamed of. It's a natural part of the process. So natural, in fact, that if you think back to the presentation I did for you on buying, you'll remember that the last thing it said was about not panicking. Do you remember that?"

"Yeah, I do remember that."

"So, do you think that maybe that's what we've got here—a little panic?"

"Yeah, maybe."

"Don't worry about it. Let's talk about why this house is a great choice for you."

Once we have gotten him to admit that he's panicking, then we can move on to helping him feel better. Many buyers are out of touch with their feelings. They are so overwhelmed by the process that they have lost sight of what's going on inside. They are overwrought and they don't even know it. We need to provide them with empirical evidence to support our assertion that they are panicking. We can do this by pointing out the ways in which they are behaving irrationally, or the ways in which they are blowing problems out of proportion. When viewed with a critical, objective eye, these actions will be proof to the clients that they may be under more stress than they realize. Once they have accepted that, then and only then can we begin to help.

If you were paying attention, then you're realizing that this step is turning out to be the same thing as getting permission to help. It's just the next layer down in the spiral. Doug didn't know he needed help with his panic because he didn't realize he was doing it. Therefore when we asked permission to help him, he said 'yes' without having that apply to the panic. We need to get him to acknowledge the problem before he can give us permission to help solve it.

Step #6: Patiently Sitting in Silence

When a client is trying to figure out what his actual issue is, we need to give him the space to do that. If he is being irrational, then we need to point out the places where he is being irrational and then ask him to resolve his concerns into something coherent. Obviously, how we present this to the client is critically important. If we confront him using an aggressive tone, then we have basically guaranteed that we will be on opposite sides of this discussion. If, instead, we approach it with a compassionate tone explaining that we are trying to understand the issues, but he is contradicting himself and we need clarification, then we can get a better, more positive response.

As a general rule, we need to meet the client's remarks with a quiet resolve. We need to stay grounded, meaning that we don't want to escalate the conversation by being loud or aggressive in our tone. In our minds we picture every comment that is angrily thrown in our direction hitting a force field in front of us and sliding down to the floor before it ever hits us. Above all we need to remember that none of this has anything to do with us. Any comments that are made or fingers that are pointed in our direction have nothing to do with us. They are simply the client trying to find an outlet for his fear.

And when there is nothing more to say, no more roads to go down, we should be silent. There has been a lot of energy thrown around the room. It needs time to settle before we can be calm again. We must be patient. The silence gives time for reflection, and puts distance between the comments made and the present moment.

When all else fails, we call a break. We suggest that each party takes the rest of the day to think about things. We sleep on it. The next day, when tempers have cooled and reason has set in, it is often easier to get through to the other side.

Stress-Reduction Techniques

One of the ways that we can help our clients avoid meltdowns is to teach them some simple stress-reduction techniques. Obviously, getting a daily massage would be a great way to reduce stress, but not everyone can afford either the time or the money for such luxuries, so we need to offer our clients another option. The first technique, and the one I use most often, is deep breathing. Anytime one of my clients is beginning to stress out, I tell them to breathe. Some clients hear it so often that they think it's a standard phrase, like "Hello." I refuse to continue the conversation with them until I actually hear them take a deep breath, sometimes two or three depending on how upset they are.

Deep breathing reduces stress levels by increasing the oxygen to the brain and providing a trigger to the body to relax. When we are stressed, our bodies tense up, our breathing becomes shallow, and our bodies dump adrenaline into our systems. This is part of the fight or flight defense mechanism. When we breathe deeply, we trigger our brains to relax our muscles and bring our adrenaline levels back to normal.

By telling our clients to take deep breaths, we are telling their bodies to stand down from red alert. They can relax and slow down. Since it is impossible to relax and panic at the same time, we reduce the panic levels as well. When a client is past all reasonable thought and fully into panic mode, having her focus on her breathing for a few minutes is a great way to break the panic cycle and bring the stress levels down at the same time.

Another form of stress reduction is stretching. We can suggest that our clients take a moment to stretch. Just a few minutes of focused attention on the muscles and stretching them out go a long way toward lowering the tension levels. Add to this the fact that most people breathe deeper when they are stretching and that their focus is taken away from what is upsetting them, and we get a really relaxing experience.

Exercise is the final technique I suggest. Getting out and walking is the easiest form of exercise. It requires nothing more than a good set of shoes. When clients are really at wit's end, I suggest that they take a walk around the block (or several blocks). Getting the blood flowing and giving their bodies a way to use up the extra adrenaline helps tremendously in bringing them back into balance.

All of these techniques are great ways to help our clients reduce their stress levels. Providing these options as solutions for our clients is a great way to add value to the service that we offer. (It also doesn't hurt if we practice these techniques ourselves. Our clients aren't the only ones under stress.)

Transitions

When it comes to major life transitions, some are more major than others. Someone who gets a promotion is less traumatized than someone who is getting a divorce. Someone who is investing in property is less emotionally invested than someone who is buying her first home. Each type of transition has its own special requirements and tools. In this next section, we will discuss in detail some of the more common life transitions that come into play in our industry and how to handle them.

Some agents may consider the option of specializing in these marketplaces. With the information contained in these pages, we are better prepared than the average real estate agent to deal with the circumstances surrounding each transition. This is a value-added proposition that allows us to differentiate ourselves from the competition.

If these niches are something you think you would like to specialize in, then check out our website at www.spartasuccess.com. We offer certifications in each of these specialties. And, over the course of 2005, we will be developing targeted products for each of these markets to support those who are engaged in working with these niches.

CHAPTER 3

LIFE AFTER DIVORCE

Of all the reasons we get listings and sales in this business, the one that is often the hardest to deal with is divorce. The people involved are usually not done with the divorce process, and the house can become the site of a battle designed to inflict maximum pain on the combatants. If we are not careful, we can get caught in the crossfire. In understanding the process itself and the emotions of the people involved in it, we can find a way to walk through the minefield without getting blown up.

In this chapter, I am going to talk about some very intimate emotional issues associated with divorce. While we are not counselors and our job is not to provide therapy to our clients, it is useful for us to understand the process that they are going through. We shouldn't kid ourselves that any part of the proceedings is irrelevant to us. This isn't true. Everything is relevant because it could be the trigger that blows up our deal tomorrow and if we don't know what's going on, then we're not clear on what the actual issue is to be able to resolve it.

Loss of Self-Definition

When people are going through a divorce, tensions are high. They are feeling defensive, hurt, angry, depressed, and lost. When they got married they both began to define themselves in terms of the relationship. She became "wife" and possibly "mother." He became "husband" and possibly "provider" and "father." They both started to build their lives differently, making some compromises in order to build a life together. They probably pooled at least some of their resources and began to think of some things as "ours" rather than "mine and yours." They made decisions based on mutual benefit.

Now, as the marriage begins to disintegrate, those changed definitions of self are also breaking down. They have to deal with the fact that they will no longer be "wife" and "husband." They may be dealing with feelings of inadequacy. They are certainly overwhelmed. They may find themselves adrift without a sense of purpose or direction. If they have given up a lot of what they wanted in their lives to stay in the relationship, then they may have serious problems defining who they are now that the relationship is over. And without a sense of self, it is difficult for them to know what they want. Decision-making abilities can be impacted as they scramble for a hold on their respective realities.

What We Can Do About It

When a client tells you that he is getting a divorce, it is a sensitive time. He will be feeling vulnerable talking about the failure of his relationship. He knows that there are certain things that you need to know to sell his home, but he will want to get through those questions quickly. You can offer him the opportunity to talk about it by making sympathetic comments along the way and leaving a small space in the conversation in case he wants to open up. If he doesn't take the chance you offer, then let it be. He may not want to talk about it. In that case, your job is just to get the information you need as quickly as possible without prying more than is absolutely necessary.

A typical conversation might go like this:

John: "I need to sell my house."

Agent: "OK, I'll be happy to talk to you about that. I just need to get a few questions answered first." (Cover the details of where the property is, the condition, etc., and then ask:) "Why are you selling?"

John: "My wife and I are getting a divorce."

Agent: "I'm sorry to hear that." (Pause—allow time for him to respond if he chooses.)

John: "Yeah, me too."

Agent: "I take it that this wasn't your idea then."

John: "No."

Agent: "OK. Well, I'll need to cover some details with you. How far along are you in the process? Have you filed the paperwork yet?"

John: "Yes, she served me this morning."

Agent: "OK. Are both of you listed on the deed?"

John: "Yes."

Agent: "Is your wife—what's her name?"

John: "Ellen"

Agent: "Ellen. Is Ellen in favor of selling the house too?"

John: "I don't care what she wants. The house *is* getting sold."

We have a BIG problem here. If Ellen doesn't want to sell the house then we could be wasting our time. We need to get John to find out from

Ellen whether she will sign off on the sale of the house. It will probably take weeks if not months for both of them to sort through this as the attorneys get involved in the discussion. John is way too early in the stage to really be doing this. He needs to talk to his wife first. Here's how we deal with this.

> Agent: "OK. I can see that you have made up your mind. I have one snag though. If Ellen doesn't sign the listing agreement with you, then I can't list the house for you. Perhaps you should discuss this with her before we go any further. It will only save time and hassle later. What do you think?"

It is very important NOT to say that you know how John feels. There is no way you could possibly know how he feels. And he will call you on it. John is angry right now. He's just been served with his divorce papers. Even if he knew they were coming, it's still a shock to see them in person. He may be looking for someone to yell at. You need to keep your tone even and your voice smooth and calming throughout this conversation. If John detects even the slightest hint of condescension, you're in big trouble.

If John is further along in the process (attorneys have agreed to sell the house), then we can make an appointment to meet. Then we will need to cover the questions on the Seller Interview Sheet (see Exhibit 7-7 in Chapter 7) and the following Divorce Worksheet.

Divorce Worksheet.

Client Name _____

Property Address _____

Are both parties on the deed? ❑ Yes ❑ No
If no, then who is on the deed? _____

Are you agreed on selling the house? ❑ Yes ❑ No

Who is currently living in the house? _____

Is this person prepared to move out when the house sells? _____

Is there a timeframe that we need to keep to in dealing with the sale? _____

How far along in the divorce process are you? _____

Has the court ordered the sale of the house? ❑ Yes ❑ No

If yes, does the court need to review the sale before you can accept an offer?   ❏ Yes   ❏ No

If yes, how long will the court need to review the documents? _____

Do you need an appraisal for the court?   ❏ Yes   ❏ No

Are there any financial difficulties related to the divorce that will impact your home sale? _____

If yes, what are they? _____

Would you prefer that I do my presentation to you separately or together? _____

Are you going to be buying another home(s) when you sell this one? _____

_____

Attorney for Client 1 _____ Phone _____

Attorney for Client 2 _____ Phone _____

If there anything you need from me to smooth this process for you? _____

_____
_____
_____
_____

We need to find out as much about where they are in the process, whether it is a friendly or acrimonious divorce, and how long until the courts settle the details if the sellers can't agree on what to do with the house. If the sellers can't agree, then we should check in with one of the attorneys to find out how long it will be before the court decides. We will need to account for this in the timing of putting the house on the market.

Discovering the Legal Requirements of the Divorce

Sometimes we're coming into the situation at the end of the process. The divorce is complete and the house is being sold as part of the settlement. When this is the case, we need to know what the divorce decree states is to happen in terms of the house and the disposition of funds upon closing. This way there are no surprises along the way. We should ask to see the divorce decree.

Dealing with the Emotional Issues

This is a very stressful time for our clients. They may be on the brink of tears or angry outbursts often. They are going through a lot, and there isn't a guidebook to tell them how to get there. They will be dealing with a lot of feelings that they aren't sure how to process.

Our clients may or may not ask our advice on these matters. If they are dealing with a therapist through this time, they may not need information from us to help them process the shift. In that case, we would focus solely on getting the sale done and keeping the parties moving forward. But there will be other times when our clients are not working on their feelings with a professional. Occasionally we will find them leaning on us for support and guidance. Without stepping into the role of therapist (which it is important for us to avoid), we can offer some assistance in the process.

One of the best things we can do for clients in this situation is to explain to them that these feelings are common and that they will eventually fade. There is great comfort in knowing that something is normal. It gives them a sense of belonging, a sense of not being alone.

The next thing we can do is to encourage them to find the positives in this shift. Suggest that they look forward rather than back. If they can find something exciting or fun to work toward, it often takes their minds off of the problems they are dealing with now. These people are "sitting in the empty room" for the entirety of their divorce process. It is a long, drawn out, unpleasant experience. Often they just need a shoulder to lean on, a friendly ear to listen, and someone to tell them that everything is going to be OK.

Grief

One common experience that most divorcing people go through is a deep sense of grief for the loss of the life they were trying to build together. Before the divorce, they had an idea of what their lives would look like in ten and twenty years. They had built a sense of security based on the belief that the other person would always be there for them. Now, they are feeling lost, alone, and totally bereft. They need to grieve the loss of the life they were hoping to build and the person that they were in relation to the marriage.

What We Can Do About It

Grief is a tough process. In *On Death and Dying* (New York: Scribner, 1997), Elisabeth Kubler-Ross talks about the five stages of grief. They are as follows (and usually in this order):

- Denial
- Anger
- Bargaining
- Depression
- Acceptance

When people get divorced, that relationship and the resultant life that they were building together die. This is a death no less significant than the death of a person. The same feelings result. Even the person who was the initiator of the break will go through many of these stages. Whether they are happy about the change or not, the future that they had been building together has been lost and it is necessary to grieve it.

But how do we help them with their grieving? Again, acknowledging the issue is the first step. Explaining the process to our clients helps them to understand what they are going through. When they know that there are discrete stages and that they will get to the other side, it lets them relax a little as they process their feelings.

Denial

At each stage, we can offer our assistance. Sellers experiencing denial will often simply refuse to sell. It doesn't matter that her husband has moved out. It doesn't matter that the house isn't being maintained. It doesn't matter that she may be close to foreclosure. In her mind, if she doesn't sell the house, then the divorce didn't happen. She is holding onto that idea as her one safety line to keep her from having to acknowledge that her life has fallen apart. It is not easy to get someone out of denial. The best we can offer is a reiteration of the facts, in a calm and comforting tone.

> Agent: "Alice, I know this is a difficult time for you. I know you don't want to leave your home, but the courts have ordered that you have to sell the house. You don't want to have to go back to court again, do you? Wouldn't it be better if you focused on your future now? I'd really like to help you through this, but you have to help me out. What do you think? Do you think you could manage this move if I helped you? I can make some calls to some movers for you. Does that sound like a plan?"

Offering emotional support and understanding often goes a long way. Offering to help move the process forward by getting the movers in is often helpful too if the seller is overwhelmed in addition to being in denial. But if she is stuck in denial, it is not our responsibility to shift the seller out of it. It will be up to the court and her attorney to accomplish that task. We can only be supportive along the way as we state the facts simply, clearly, and with compassion.

Anger

Unfortunately, this is where we usually come into the situation. The parties have each accepted that they are getting a divorce and now they are intent on blaming each other for it. The anger phase has begun. Our task in this stage is to get each person focused on the future.

Our only goal in this process is to get the house sold and (if applicable) to get the sellers into their new homes. The best way for us to effect this result is to keep the sellers focused on their expected futures and the positive aspects of that. The more we can keep them from getting involved in arguments and blaming, the better off everyone is in the long run.

When a seller starts to get angry and spiral into a tirade, we need to break the cycle as quickly as possible. We must stay neutral in the process though. We need to be careful never to agree with one person that the other person is a problem, since we do eventually have to deal with both of them. We need to say something like: "I know you're upset, but we really need to focus on this issue right now. Can you put aside your anger long enough to get through this or do we need to take a break?"

Usually, if the divorce is a bitter one, the couple will opt to meet separately (and you will actually prefer this as well since it keeps them from bickering). But occasionally, they think that they can keep it together for the appointment and they fail. If this happens, the simple thing to do is to raise your hand in the air like you did in school when you were waiting for the teacher to call on you. Be quiet. Don't say anything until they acknowledge you. Then, don't acknowledge the argument, simply move on with what you had been saying. Do not indicate any irritation or frustration (even if you are frustrated), simply move on. Any emotion you add to the equation is only likely to set them off again. If they continue to bicker and cannot seem to get through the appointment, do not hesitate to ask to reschedule the appointment. If it's bad enough, you may suggest that you are willing to have this meeting with them each separately if they would prefer. (Let it be their decision though, otherwise they may take it as your passing judgment on them for their fighting.)

Sometimes it is better to take a humorous approach when things are getting out of hand. You might say, "Hey guys! Help! I'm getting flashbacks to my divorce here!" If you are meeting with one of the sellers and she starts getting upset and yelling at you, you can ask her, "Am I really the one you're angry at?" Or something like, "Hey, I'm just the messenger here, please don't shoot me." Or even, "I'd like to help you, but it's difficult to do when you're yelling at me." It's important that you set your boundaries and not let people take out their anger on you.

But it's also important that all of these comments be delivered in an appropriate tone. If they aren't then you risk escalating the situation. The appropriate tone is lighthearted for the humor and deadly calm for the other comments. Don't throw a comment back in anger or one-upmanship *ever*. It will blow up in your face every time.

Bargaining

In the bargaining stage, the person is likely to try to work things out with his spouse. He will promise the moon and the stars if only he can get her back. He will seem completely rational and reasonable, but he is feeling extremely needy and clingy. He is seeing his life slipping away and feeling powerless to do anything about it. This is the stage where people are most likely to lose it. They can get violent or abusive—emotionally and physically. They are literally fighting for their life. This is the most dangerous stage for us because our client can become unpredictable in his actions around the sale of the house. He will have agreed to something and then change his mind about it a minute or a week later. He will fly off the handle about something minor and then give in on something major. He may yell, throw insults, plead, cajole, debate, etc. All are panic reactions designed to manipulate the situation back into a place where he feels in control again.

The problem is that he isn't in control. His spouse is refusing to stay with him. There's nothing he can do about that. And there's nothing that we can do about it either. The best thing we can offer him is a focus on the future. Remind him to think about what he has to look forward to rather than what he is losing. If he has nothing to look forward to, then help him find something. Surely there is a class he wanted to take or a vacation he wanted to go on or a car he wanted to purchase that his wife would not allow him. There must be something about his freedom that he can celebrate.

It is a judgment call on your part as to whether or not you want to engage this conversation with your client. Some people will have this conversation with us, others will not. The only reason I suggest having it at all is that this can help him to accept that he can move forward in his life and this acceptance will get him to stop making wildly irrational decisions. If he doesn't want to engage this conversation (or you don't), remember that referring the client to a licensed therapist is always a good option. In fact, you can do it via form letter, like the one below.

> Dear Client,
>
> Thank you for trusting me with the listing for your home. I will do my best to get your house sold quickly and for the highest price possible. I know this is a stressful time for you in your life. Rest assured that I will do everything in my power to keep the stress levels associated with the sale of your home to a minimum.
>
> I have often found that my clients going through divorce can benefit from a little outside help as they go through this process. I have included the card of a friend of mine who is an excellent counselor who specializes in helping people who are getting divorced. Her services are covered under many major health insurance policies and her advice is invaluable.
>
> If there is any other way I can be of service to you through this process, please do not hesitate to ask. My goal is to help you get through this rough time in your life and move on to the next stage with as much ease and grace as possible.
>
> Sincerely,
>
> Sally Sells

By offering this information to both clients in a form-letter format, your clients are not likely to take it personally that you have given them the name of a therapist. (They will compare notes on this so make sure you send one to each of them.) Again, I used the word "counselor" to reduce the impact of the comment.

Depression

This is the point at which the people involved have given up hope of reconciling. They are resigned to the fact that the divorce is going to go through. This is when depression most often sets in. We need to be aware of our clients at this stage. Most will be fine, but a little down-trodden. Keeping them focused on the future and concentrating on a point of hope in their world is the best approach.

Failing that, getting them up and moving around—physically active—is a good salve for depression. Physical activity increases serotonin levels in the brain, which provide a sense of well-being. If someone is getting too down, then we can offer to pick her up and go for a walk for the meeting. The exercise is good for her in reducing her stress levels *and* good for us too. Especially if the divorce is taking place in the middle of winter when the light levels are low, we should get her outside and into the sunshine as much as possible. Fresh air and sunshine are great dispellers of depression. If she has a fireplace, then a fire is a great idea. It creates a sense of warmth and comfort. Massages are particularly good for the spirits since one of the things that we lose in a divorce is a regular form of physical contact with a loved one. Regardless of what we recommend, it should be something that pampers the client during this time.

In rare instances, people will become dangerously depressed. We need to recognize the warning signs and know what to do about them (see Exhibit 3-1).

Exhibit 3-1. *Warning signs.*

Warning signs are changes in a person's behavior, feelings, and beliefs for a period of two weeks or longer and are considered to be maladaptive or out of character for the individual.

Early Warning Signs

- Difficulties in job/school
- Talking about suicide, death
- Depression
- Neglect of appearance
- Increased substance use
- Dropping out of activities
- Changes in sleeping habits
- Isolating oneself from others
- Feeling that life is meaningless
- Loss of interest in activities
- Hopelessness
- Restlessness and agitation
- Helplessness

Late Warning Signs

- Feelings of failure
- Sudden improvement in mood
- Overreaction to criticism
- Preoccupation with one's failures

- Overly self-critical
- Collecting means to kill oneself
- Anger and rage
- Making final arrangements
- Pessimism about life, the future
- Ending significant relationships
- Giving away possessions
- Inability to concentrate
- Having a suicide plan
- Preoccupation with death
- Taking unnecessary risks

SOURCE: U.S. Public Health Services, *The Surgeon General's Call to Action to Prevent Suicide*, Department of Health and Human Services, © 1999.

If in doubt, we should always be prepared to call in outside help. Any suicide hotline number can give us the contact information for the appropriate authorities if we are afraid for our client's life.

Acceptance

Once a client hits this stage in the process, it is much easier for us to deal with her. She has accepted that this is the way of things and is prepared to move forward. We hope that all of our clients reach this stage during the process, but that will not always be the case. We do the best we can with them and we try to help them move forward.

Betrayal

Along with this sense of loss, there is often a feeling of betrayal. No matter why the marriage is ending, one partner or both may be feeling betrayed. When we marry in our society, we promise to love, honor, and cherish until death do us part. Since neither of the parties has died, they are both breaking their vows and betrayal is the ultimate emotional consequence of that action for some people.

Betrayal often triggers other emotions in people such as feelings of guilt, anger, worthlessness, inadequacy, etc. People feeling betrayed often ask themselves, "Why me? Why wasn't I good enough, smart enough, sexy enough, strong enough, etc.?" The feelings of inadequacy are often overwhelming.

What We Can Do About It

Remind the person that sometimes things just happen. It doesn't have to be about him. It may simply be that they grew apart or that they were incompatible to begin with. It may be a midlife crisis that has nothing to do with the spouse who is left behind. It is important for the client to remember that each person does things for their own reasons. Those reasons may have absolutely nothing to do with the other person. Once again—get the client focused on the future. Moving forward is the best solution.

Spite

Sometimes our clients can, in an effort to stop feeling victimized, put the house in the middle of a power struggle. She may put her foot down over price or condition or terms, not because it is important to her, but to be able to have control over something. Sometimes, it is simply to make her husband miserable by not letting the deal happen. It is during this time that we need to be able to adequately shift the person's attention onto another focus. Pointing out that getting in the way of progress doesn't serve the person's ultimate goal will occasionally be helpful. But we need to tread lightly here. She is already feeing threatened and abused. We need to make it clear that we are on her side. If she perceives that we are working in anyone else's best interests (including our own), then she will dig in and never come around. She may blow up the deal just for the satisfaction of making someone else as miserable as she is.

Our goal is to keep her focused on what is in her best interests long term. Remind her that part of her discomfort is from being stuck in "the empty room" and that each step she takes forward brings her closer to getting out the other side. Make it clear that you are there for her and that you feel for her. Commiserate with her:

> "I know this is terrible for you. I know it hurts. And I really don't want to see you hurting like this. I think that blowing up this deal is only going to make you feel bad for longer. Wouldn't it be better to just be done with it now? Is it really worth putting yourself through this just to make him miserable? Can't we just let it be? Wouldn't that be better for you in the long run?"

Place yourself clearly on her side and then point out what is in her best interests. Trust her to be reasonable.

Overwhelmed

The most obvious factor we will notice when dealing with clients in the midst of a divorce is their sense of being overwhelmed. They are beyond their knowledge base. They feel totally lost. They have no sense of direction. They are acting entirely on instinct. They have lost their ability to see and think clearly.

The symptoms of being overwhelmed are often similar to those of depression. People who are overwhelmed tend to be easily irritated and just want to be left alone. When alone, they do things like watching TV for hours on end, eating or sleeping excessively or not at all, or drinking themselves into a stupor. They are looking for a release, if even for a moment, of the stresses associated with their out-of-control life.

What We Can Do About It

The easiest way to get someone out of this stage is to give them some structure and a plan of attack. When we get overwhelmed, we feel that we can't handle anything. Having someone else walk us through a plan of attack, give us our responsibilities and then gently hold us accountable for those responsibilities, we can begin to get back on track again.

If a client is feeling overwhelmed, you need to give him a plan—a discrete series of steps that he needs to take. Do this in small pieces since he is already overwhelmed. For instance, if he isn't getting his paperwork together for the mortgage application, then you can say something like, "I need you to send me your tax returns for the last two years. Can you have them for me by the end of the day? Great!" Then at the end of the day, follow up. Are the tax returns there? If they are, then ask for the next item—pay stubs. Give a deadline for those as well. If the tax returns aren't there, then offer to come over and help him find them. Point out the importance of getting this information in to the mortgage officer.

Lack of Trust

When clients are in the midst of their grief, they can often lash out. We are sadly the recipients of much of that anger—not because we deserve it, but because we are the person closest to them when they are feeling this way. We may find that our clients don't trust us as readily as they might otherwise because their trust has been betrayed recently by someone they trusted implicitly and they are therefore having issues with it in general.

Our clients may also try to get us on "their" side, or they may occasionally feel that we have taken the other spouse's side over theirs. First, we need to be particularly careful not to take sides. We must be Switzerland in this transaction—completely neutral. We *must* be able to explain all of our actions to *either* client in terms of what was in the best interests of both of the parties involved. If there is a conflict about what is in the best interests of the parties, then we leave that to the attorneys to negotiate.

We need to remember that our client's process isn't about us. We need to be able to allow whatever they say in the heat of the moment to roll off of us like water. We don't have to own or accept the criticisms thrown in our direction. If we keep in mind that the client is hurting and is merely looking for an outlet for her grief, then we are better able to let the things she says not affect us.

Listen, but Don't Repeat

It can be challenging to work with two clients who are at odds with each other. Each may, in their own time, confide in you. You must be clear in your conversations with them that you will not share confidences. Tell them that you will listen to both spouses, understand both sides, and perhaps even act as the arbitrator of problems related to the house, but you will *never* use the information given to you to give one spouse an advantage over the other. Anything said in confidence remains there.

Also, keep in mind that you should try to keep track of what each spouse has said to you in the past. You don't want to accidentally reference something said by one spouse about the other. If in doubt, don't reference past conversations at all. It's safer than inadvertently sharing something you shouldn't have.

Judgment

We must keep our perspective throughout this process. We need to remember that there are always three sides to the story—what each person says, and the truth. The more we can simply accept that what a person says to us is true for that person even if it may not be empirically true, the better off we are. Staying away from making value judgments (this person is right or wrong, good or bad, etc.) allows us to maintain our sense of objectivity and our role as arbitrator. The minute one spouse feels we have made a judgment or taken a side, we are done. We have just lost the trust of the person who feels slighted. If we maintain our objectivity we preserve our ability to be effective.

CHAPTER 4

THE EMPTY NESTER, THE RETIREE, AND THE WIDOW

Each of these categories—the empty nester, the retiree, and the widow—would seem to be a distinct type of transition, but they all have common issues, which is why I am addressing them together. In each of these instances, we are usually dealing with a person who is leaving behind a home that they have lived in for many years. When we live in a home for a long time, we begin to associate our lives with that home. We begin to identify that home as being an integral part of our lives. When we face the task of leaving that home behind, it is as though we are leaving a part of ourselves behind with it. It can be a heartbreaking task for people, especially when it is combined with other large-scale life transitions like retirement, children leaving home, and death.

Grieving for the Home

In each of these instances, we will need to help our clients grieve the loss of the home and the life that they lived in it. For each type of transition, that grieving process will be slightly different, but the tools we offer will be the same in each instance. In each case, the sellers need to find a way to mark the passing of the home from their lives and a way to honor that home for the role it played in supporting that life.

We need to be aware that when someone is attached to their home, making decisions about leaving it may take time. They may need to sleep on an offer when it comes in. They may want more information about the buyers than they really should have. They want to know that their happy home is going to good people who will care for it as they have—after all it is a piece of them and they want to leave it with people who respect and honor the gift. These sellers are the ones most likely to give gifts to the buyers moving in. It is their way of passing along the good energy from their life to the new owners. They leave the darndest things. I've even seen a seller replace carpeting for the buyers without being asked to. She wanted them to have a nice place to move into. It was her surprise to them when they came to the walk-through. Each person has her own way of processing through this time. We need to be patient and gentle with her, and let her move at her own pace.

Tools

When people move into a home, they hold a housewarming party. This ritual is designed to bring the light and love of friends into the home (and get some good gifts along the way). When people leave a home that has been an integral part of their lives for so long, they also need to be able to mark that passing. We can suggest to our clients that they hold a "good-bye party" for their home. If we want to increase our chances of referrals, we can even offer to host the party for them. Here's a sample invitation we might send out to their friends:

You're Invited!

Help Joe and Susan say good-bye to their trusted friend, confidante, and protector—their home!

We are hosting a good-bye party on:
Sunday, May 16 at 3:00 P.M.
At their home at:
315 Maple Street
Anywhere, USA 12345

Please join us for light hors d'oeuvres, drinks, and fun. Bring a story of some time you spent in the home to share with the group. A videographer will be on-site to record your memories for the owners.

This party is hosted by Sally Sells of ABC Realty for the owners.

The owners get a gathering of friends to acknowledge the importance of the event (after all, our friends always come to the important events in our lives). Plus they get the video of their friends telling great stories about the house. It's a good way to create memories and to mark the passing of the home for the owners. And it's a great way for us to meet their friends and potentially get more business.

If our sellers don't want a party, then we can suggest that they do some journaling to record their memories of the home. They can also create a scrapbook to go with their writings that will contain pictures of the home and each of the rooms, and perhaps even a piece of the wallpaper from behind the refrigerator in the kitchen or from the back of a closet. No matter what they do, it should be focused around acknowledging the past, stating clearly in the present that they are leaving, and creating memories for the future.

Here are suggestions of other ways you can encourage your client to grieve for the house and refocus on their new home:

- Remind them of their goals and the things they will be able to do once they move.
- Encourage them to take a video of walking through the house so they have the entire house on tape.
- Take a small piece of the property that the new owners won't miss (such as wallpaper that is behind an outlet, an extra tile from the kitchen, or pressed flowers from the garden). If the clients are especially into gardening, they may want to take seeds or graft their favorite plant from the garden to plant in their new home. That way they are not really leaving their garden behind—they are taking it with them.
- Encourage them to begin a scrapbook of things from their old house with a section on things they will have in the new house. This will help them focus on the continuity of moving their memories from one place to another.
- Have them begin planning how they will be active in their new community. If they've always been active in local politics, get them to find out how they can participate in their new area. Perhaps get them local newspapers of their new town. If they like to golf, find out not only where the nearest courses are to their new home, but what upcoming events or tournaments they might participate in. If they like to read, get them a calendar from their new local library. These items start to make their new life feel real. They will start to envision what living there will be like and what their new role in that community will be.

The Empty Nester

Empty-nest syndrome is most often felt by women, but it applies to whoever the caregiver of the family has been. The parent has defined herself in terms of her children for the last eighteen to twenty-five years. She has put much of the rest of her life on hold often to take care of the children and provide for their needs. She has done this for so long in many instances, that she has forgotten what life she wanted to lead and has enmeshed herself in being wife and mother. When her children leave the nest, she loses her sense of self. She doesn't know what to do with herself anymore. She feels lost, alone, useless, used-up. She no longer has a purpose for her life.

This process can be extremely disorienting, especially for women who have prided themselves on being "Super Mom." These women have made an art out of parenting. The carpool list, the kids' activities, school events—these were all the central focus for these women's lives. When these events cease to be a factor, they are left without a rudder, without a focus. There is nothing left to drive their days.

Add to this the fact that in order for Mom to move forward, she needs to find something new to do in her life and she's really got a lot to deal with. Everyone has fears around doing anything new. Mom's got it coming from two directions at once. She needs to learn to let go of her kids (and her house) at the same time as she finds something new to occupy her time and her attention. There are two big changes at once, both resulting in a fundamental shift in how she sees herself—that's one big wallop. And we wonder why midlife crises can be so extreme at times.

As in all change, the key is in understanding the process itself. If we can point out to the seller that she needs to redefine herself, that she is re-creating herself in a way, it will help her through this very difficult time. Giving some suggestions about how she can explore her interests is often helpful too. Because with all of the change going on, she may also be feeling overwhelmed. And when we're overwhelmed, coming up with solutions to our problems is more work than we can bear at times.

As with all of the grieving that we have looked at so far, it is important to keep her focused on the future and aware of the positives that are associated with the change. Point out that she will now have time to pursue her own interests. Tell her that she can go away for the weekend now without having to worry about leaving the kids at home alone. She doesn't have to plan her life around school vacation anymore. She never has to pick up the bratty kid down the block for carpool again. And PTA politics are a thing of the past—it's time to celebrate! There are many positives that come as a result of the kids leaving home; sometimes we just need to be reminded what they are.

And then there's the possibility for the future. Get your seller to dream. See where her dreams take her. How far can she go? What amazing things can she do now that she is no longer fettered by responsibilities? Has she always wanted to backpack across Europe? She can go now (and stay in B&Bs rather than hostels—she's earned it). How about a trip to Niagara Falls or a cruise to the Bahamas? Anything is possible. My father tells of the day my stepsister (the youngest) moved out of the house, when he stripped naked and ran around the house yelling, "It's mine, it's mine, it's all mine!" However our seller wants to celebrate is up to her, but we need to help her see that it is a change worthy of celebration as well as sadness.

Here are some ways that you can encourage your client to celebrate their new life in their new home:

- Have them dedicate a part of their new home to a hobby that they've been ignoring.
- Encourage them to think about how a smaller space will be less home to heat, less home to clean, and less home to light.
- In addition to spending less on their home, they are likely spending less on their kids, unless they are paying for their children's education. If they will have more money, encourage them to think of things they've sacrificed over the years that they can now afford.
- This transition, like most other transitions in life, deserves a celebration, like a party or special trip.

The Retiree

Retirement is also a time of mixed emotions. On the one hand, we plan our entire lives to be able to stop working and enjoy life when we get older. On the other hand, we spend our entire lives defining ourselves in terms of what we do for a living. This creates its own unique challenge when the time comes to actually retire. Add to this the disruption that comes with a significant and lasting change in one's daily routine and we're really in a pickle.

Let's look at an example, we'll call him Charlie. Charlie worked for thirty years in business. He retired from his position as CEO of a Fortune 500 company at age sixty to enjoy the good life. His wife, Darla, had focused her life around attending the "right" events and throwing parties for the "right" people to support Charlie's career. They spent much of their time apart doing their various jobs. When Charlie first retired, they took a trip around the world to celebrate their independence from the work-a-day world. Now that they are back, Charlie is home all the time. Darla, on the other hand, is still participating in her social calendar. She is still high up on the social charts, but her status is waning a bit as people begin to realize that Charlie no longer holds the influence he once did.

Charlie is spending time at the golf course and country club. He's meeting his old friends as often as possible, but he's finding that they are not available often. Charlie is realizing that he has more time on his hands than he had thought and is beginning to miss the excitement and authority of running a large company. He's also noticing that his status is declining as well. He isn't sure of what to do with himself. As someone who is used to being in charge, he's lost without something to run.

Charlie is encouraging Darla to sell their current home, which is far too big for them now. They don't hold the social functions that they once did and the cost of maintaining the property is high. Charlie wants to get them a nice condo in a gated community where they will have a built-in social circle to spend time with.

Darla doesn't want to move. She's happy where she is. Isn't it bad enough that the changes Charlie has made in his life by retiring are affecting her? She has her social circle. The last thing she wants is more change. But Charlie is the money guy in the family and he insists that it's necessary. Darla reluctantly agrees.

This is an all-too-common theme. I could have used the example of a plumber retiring and it would not have been much different. When we also consider that retirement usually comes with a loss of self-definition and a disruption of the family schedule and we add in those stressors too, we find exactly how taxing the retirement process can be.

The couple who comes to us during this time is leaving behind the home in which they were members of the working world. They may have raised children there. They certainly have many memories associated with the home. They will need to grieve not only the loss of the home, but the fact that they are leaving behind the people they were when they lived there. Plus, they may be moving into a retirement community, which will force them to think of themselves as "old people," which won't help matters either. Today's retirement communities aren't what they once were, but there is still a shift in perspective that comes with entering one.

Much like we discussed with mothers and empty-nest syndrome, we have a loss of purpose, a change in the way that the person defines himself. He needs to find a new purpose, a new direction for his life. If he has retired and she hasn't, then he may also need to deal with feelings of inadequacy as she becomes the primary breadwinner for the family.

The final piece of the puzzle is that life is a continuum. Many people think of their lives as a line: We are born, we grow up, we work, we retire, and we die. For these people, retirement is the phase right before death. Our clients may be dealing with issues related to facing their mortality. They may be concerned with the fact that they may not always be self-sufficient. They're worried about becoming infirm or about being a burden to their loved ones. They may be depressed. They may lack motivation. They may drag their feet in the moving process—especially if they believe the home that they are moving into will be their final home, the place they will die. It's often hard for our clients to move into that new space—to acknowledge their mortality.

Tools

We can help our clients through this transition by again focusing them toward the future. Ask the person who is retiring questions about the things he has always wanted to do, hobbies that he now wants to pursue, volunteering that he might wish to participate in. Get him to think about what he will be doing in his retirement. Point out that it is common for retired couples to experience challenges during the transition, as one spouse's change in status and routine affects the other. Suggest that he try not to interfere in her routine or in aspects of their lives that have historically been her domain.

If he is dealing with feelings of inadequacy, we need to NOT address those directly. Men can be very touchy when it comes to these types of issues. Instead, we should help him realize how important he is to her life. Help him to find a different way to define his contribution to the household. Point out how important his emotional support is to her. Compliment him on the beauty of the yard and explain how important it is to women for things to look nice and what a positive affect it has on their attitudes. Coach the wife to express her gratitude for these things as well. It will go a long way toward making their lives happier.

If the issues revolve around dealing with their own mortality, there is not much we can do to help with this. One thing we definitely should NOT do is to address their age. They know how old they are—us pointing it out can only be insulting. There is a *Judging Amy* episode where Maxine (the mother) is thinking about renting out a room in her house, and the real estate agent is trying to talk her into selling instead. The agent keeps saying "a woman your age . . ." and Maxine keeps getting more and more angry, until finally she says something like "if you say 'a woman my age' one more time, I'll throw you down the stairs." This is not a common response that we would get, but it would certainly be a common thought that would go through our clients' minds if we make their age an issue.

Instead, we can keep them focused on the gifts they are still offering to the world. Helping them create a purpose for their life is helpful here as well. There are many volunteer organizations that would welcome help from them if they need some. I used to be on the board for my local Habitat for Humanity affiliate, and they were always in need of people to coordinate volunteers for them. This was a job that could be accomplished by anyone with a phone and time on their hands. So if they have always linked their self-esteem and self-worth to their job, make sure they know that, just because they aren't working anymore, doesn't mean they have to lie down and die. They are still contributing members of society. Keeping them focused on the positives helps to keep their thoughts off of dying and, for those who are afraid of this passing, that can be a godsend.

If they are truly concerned about becoming a burden to their children, then we will want to refer them to an attorney who can set their minds at ease. They can set up trusts, wills, durable powers of attorney, living wills, etc., that will make the process of their illness and/or death easier for the loved ones they leave behind. Some people avoid this process because it scares them. For other people, it is a comfort for them to know that they have handled the details so their loved ones don't have to. If they are truly concerned about this, then recommending a good estate and wills attorney can be a gift of peace of mind.

Here are some things you can do to help your clients focus on the positives:

- Offer them information about their new community such as volunteer organizations, local parks, and events that are coming up.
- Urge them to start visiting their new community. For example, mention a good restaurant in their new town that they can try out before they move in, or a store that is unique. The more they visit their new area, the more at home they will feel when they move.
- Pick up some guidebooks for their new area. Give these to them as an early closing gift.
- Talk to them about hobbies or activities that they never had time for before and point out that they could do them now.

The Widow

The one group that has no option but to deal with the concept of death and mortality is the widow(er). Usually, we are dealing with the woman in this instance since women tend to live longer. She is dealing with many issues in her life. She has lost a spouse and is grieving that loss. She is feeling lost and alone. Her sense of security may have been shattered. She may feel unprotected. She may be in a low-level state of constant panic even though she seems calm. She is certainly overwhelmed.

In addition to dealing with the loss of her spouse and her way of life, she is also selling her home and dealing with the grief of letting that go—the place where she and her husband resided together. She probably didn't want to sell the home, but is left in a financial position where she has no choice. She may feel victimized as well as traumatized. She may feel out of control and not know how to stop it. She may be angry or short with us. She may seem emotionally shut down. She may wear a happy face, even when it seems inappropriate. These are responses to stress—coping mechanisms. When things happen too quickly, we often shut down in an attempt to be able to get used to the idea of the new ways of things before we can deal with the emotions that show up as a result of those changes. We should not force her to confront these emotions too soon. Let her keep her coping mechanisms in place—she needs them for the moment.

There are some special issues that we need to deal with when we deal with widows, especially when we are dealing with people who grew up in the depression era. If the person who passed was the person in charge of the finances, the primary decision-maker for the couple, then we have some special issues to address. For depression-era couples, it was common for the man to be in charge of the finances and to make the decisions affecting the financial aspects of their lives. Often, the women made few decisions of financial consequence. Therefore, when the husband dies, she is left without a compass. She has no one to guide her on these issues and she has little to no experience making her own financial decisions. She has been told her whole life that she should not make these decisions on her own and therefore, she doesn't trust her own judgment. She will look to us to make the decisions for her.

We must avoid doing so at all costs. It is not our place to make decisions for our clients. Our job is to advise our clients, make sure they are completely educated about the subject, and then follow their instructions. We cannot become the person who makes decisions for our clients. Aside from the fact that it is putting us out on a legal limb we don't want to be on, it is also detrimental to her eventual adjustment to this new way of life. We don't want to enable her in thinking that she can delegate her decisions to other people for the rest of her life. If we do so, then we may be participating in helping someone in the future to cheat her out of her money.

We want to help her to understand that she is capable of making good decisions. We can coach her. During the process of putting the home on the market, we want to educate her. Ask her to make small decisions along the way. We tell her that neutral colors are best for selling the home. We ask her to pick a neutral color to paint the walls. She will pick a bunch of colors, then ask for our advice. We need to refuse to give it— encourage her by saying that we're sure she'll pick a good color. Then we tell her what a good decision she made, thereby reinforcing in her mind her ability to decide. We should offer many opportunities for her to make decisions along the way. In doing so, we are training her to make decisions for herself. This way, when the time comes to decide on taking an offer on the house, she will feel competent to do so.

Occasionally, someone will refuse to step up to the decision-making plate. We will know this relatively quickly when we ask, "Who will be involved in deciding to list this property?" If she answers that she will be the only one, but then when we get to the appointment, she looks to us to make the decisions, then we need to get her family or children involved in the process. Usually, we will not be the ones to initiate this conversation since she is likely to call her children herself once we make it clear that we won't make the decisions for her. If she has no children or seems disinclined to take their advice, then we can encourage her to enlist the help of a friend or attorney. We do not want to be the decision-makers. If she refuses to do it, then we need to bring in someone who can.

If we are going to get the children, friend, or attorney involved though, we want to do it up front. They need to understand the role that we are playing in the process. We need time to develop trust with them as well as the seller. They should be there from the initial listing presentation through closing. If we didn't find out this problem until the listing appointment, then we should walk the new person through the presentation as soon as they are involved so that they are up to speed. If different children have different opinions of what should be done, then we need to serve as the objective voice of reason always advocating for our client.

In all of these cases, we are dealing with people who are letting go. They are letting go of the past, letting go of a home that once served as the center of their lives, letting go of a definition of self that no longer applies. They are having to move forward, to create a new definition for themselves, to find a new purpose in their lives. These are not easy changes to make. They require a lot of work and they are emotionally draining. The more support we can offer, the more information we can provide, the more perspectives we can shift, the better off our clients will be in the long run.

Here are some things you can do to help widow(er)s:

- Get the family involved. Even if they are not involved in the decision-making process, encourage them to spend time with the widow(er). This is a difficult time in your client's life and he or she needs family.
- Encourage your client to start spending more time with groups of people. She needs to start building a new support group.
- If she's moving to a senior community, take her there for events or for tours. The more she sees it, the more comfortable she'll be when she moves in.
- Offer lists of services that might help her—free financial services, government services, and hotlines that she might need.
- Provide her with the contact number of a handyman and a personal organizer. She may need help preparing her house to sell.

CHAPTER 5

THE FIRST-TIME HOMEBUYER

Fear is the catchword of the day for the first-time home buyer. They are afraid of not getting their mortgage. They are afraid of getting in over their heads financially. They are afraid of all the little expenses associated with homeownership. They are afraid that they will make a bad choice for a house and end up with a money pit. They are afraid that they will choose unwisely and not be able to sell their house for a profit when they move. In some cases, they are afraid of buying a home because it represents growing up and they don't feel ready to do that.

These buyers need help. They need to understand the process. They need someone to give them back their sense of control. They need to be walked through the process and allowed to make decisions in their own time. They are looking for someone to parent them through the process.

First-time buyers come in all shapes and sizes. They may be in their twenties or fifties or anywhere in between. No matter what age they are, no matter what their backgrounds, they all have a few items in common.

Fear

Buying a home is an intimidating prospect. It represents putting down roots, being stable, and being a grown-up. It's responsibility incarnate. It's also the biggest purchase most people will ever make in their entire lives. It can be a very scary process.

I remember sitting down at the closing table with my husband. I was twenty-three and he was twenty-seven. He had been intent on buying a house. I had never thought about it before, but I went along because it seemed like a good idea. We had been living in temporary housing in anticipation of buying, and for two months we had been dragged all over the place looking at homes. And then we sat waiting for the deal to go through. We were finally at the finish line. No more temporary housing. No more living out of a suitcase. I was ready. When it came time to sign the mortgage, I signed with vigor. My husband, on the other hand, paused with his pen in mid air over the papers and sat there staring at the page. I asked him what was wrong.

He said, "If I sign this, I'm six digits in debt."

Frustrated, tired, and not at all amused, I responded, "If you don't, you're divorced."

He signed the papers. All it took was a little perspective to make him see that he was indeed making the right decision.

The point is that even though he was the one who had wanted the home, had insisted on it actually, he was also the one to have second thoughts at the last minute. He knew it was the right thing for us to do, but it still scared him. In his mind, he was solely responsible for that debt and it meant taking on a lot of responsibility he had avoided thus far.

Shame

Another common fear that buyers face is the fear of shame. They are afraid that the mortgage company will deem them not worthy of a loan. They are convinced that their credit report will reveal them to be terrible people who don't pay their bills and don't deserve a house. The most ironic part of this fear of shame is that it is often the people with the highest credit scores who have the biggest fears around this issue.

Disappointment

Once first-time buyers have determined that they can get their loan then they are worried that they won't be able to find a house they like for the amount of money they can spend. They are certain that they are going to have to settle for something terrible. This is just another indication of them being concerned that they are not good enough to merit a nice home. They may also be concerned that their friends or family will think less of them because their first home is not large or in perfect condition.

The Cure

The cure to fear, shame, and disappointment is information. Fear can run rampant if left unchecked by facts. It is easy for buyers to convince themselves that they cannot possibly get a home if they never take steps to find out. If buyers begin to panic, the best thing you can do is to put them in touch with the facts. Get them in touch with a mortgage officer to find out what they qualify for and how their credit stands. Have them get a pre-approval letter for a mortgage. This not only gives the client confidence when buying, it puts them in a better negotiating position when they are ready to make an offer. Then get onto the MLS to see what kinds of houses they can afford. When they know the facts—what their financial position will allow them to buy—then they can begin to get accustomed to it. Until then, they are stuck on a mental rollercoaster where they will assume the worst.

The Money Pit

Now that they are armed with the facts, they will begin to worry about finding the right home. They will be afraid that they will accidentally purchase "the money pit." In order to get past this particular issue, you need to explain the home inspection process to them. They need to understand that it is the home inspector's job to identify which houses are sound and which are money pits. They can rely on an expert to make that determination so they don't have to do it themselves. Also educate them on the types of home issues that are likely to cost a lot of money and be dangerous, and what types of repairs are cosmetic. This will prepare them for when they get the results of an inspection. They will already know which repairs are expensive, which ones would need to be done immediately, and which ones are minor. For example, when buying a home it's important to make sure there are no:

- Structural or foundation problems
- Pest problems that might affect the integrity of the home (such as termites, carpenter bees, or wood bees)
- Dangerous poisons or materials that would need to be removed (such as asbestos, oil tanks, or lead)
- Heating issues
- Plumbing issues
- Faulty wiring
- Leaky roof

These are major structural problems, but even these can be negotiated with the seller most times. Things like doorknobs that are loose, rooms that need repainting, etc., may be signs that the owner hasn't kept up with the house; however, these are really minor issues and you should tell them that before they start looking so that they don't blow a deal later over these items.

Analysis Paralysis

If we've done our interview process well, then we know what a buyer wants when she goes out looking at houses. If there are certain items that are deal breakers, then we should know that too by now. We should only be showing the homes that fit the buyer's criteria. If we show her a series of those homes and she still can't make a decision, then we know that she may be stuck in analysis paralysis.

Some buyers may feel as though they can't trust themselves to make a good decision on which house to purchase. Some are afraid of giving up the other houses by choosing just one to buy. They are certain that they will make the wrong decision and the house they should have bought will be gone. They're afraid of being stuck with a house they hate.

These buyers will avoid making a buying decision. They will go out on many showings, never quite deciding on a house—finding some minute detail wrong with each property. Or they will make a long list of properties that they have seen, prioritizing the list from house one through house twenty-seven, but never writing an offer on the first house on the list. These are the people who say that they really need to get to know the market before they make a decision. They will look for six months, a year, two years, and never buy anything. They're suffering from analysis paralysis. They've got too much information.

For these buyers, it's important to reduce the field of choices.

I had a client with this issue. She was a bright woman in her early thirties buying her first home. We had looked at fifteen properties—many more than my average buyer would see. She had still not decided upon a house. She had a binder with all of the properties she had seen in it, prioritized from one to fifteen. At the end of the showings for the day, I sat her down with her binder. I asked her to take the pages out of the binder, so I could see them—I promised not to get them out of order. I sat next to her, my arm touching hers so she could feel that I was supporting her as I had this conversation with her.

I asked, "So let me see if I've got this straight. If you had to make a decision today on what house to buy, you'd pick this one," indicating page one on the pile.

She replied, "Yes."

"And if, for some reason, you didn't get this house, then you'd buy this one, right?" indicating the second house in the pile.

Again, she said, "Yes."

"And if, in the rare instance that you couldn't get either of these houses, you'd buy this one." indicating the third house in the list.

"Yes."

"OK, good. Let me tell you that in my experience, no buyer has ever lost three houses in a row. So if we have your top three, then we don't need the rest of these." I took the rest of the pile and started to throw them away. She reached for them in a panic, not yet ready to let go of the other options. I stopped.

"If you buy something now, you're going to buy this one (the first one) and if you can't get this one, then you'll buy this one (the second one), and if you can't get that one, you'll buy this one (the third one). I guarantee that you can get at least one of these houses. So why do you need the rest of these?" I let her think for a moment, putting the pages down in front of her so that there was no imminent threat that they would be thrown away.

"I guess I don't," she replied slowly.

"I want to throw them out because they are getting in your way. They are keeping you from being able to make a decision. OK?"

She nodded quietly and watched with a slightly pained look on her face as I threw the sheets into the garbage.

"If by some fluke of nature you don't get any of these three houses, the others are still in the MLS system. I can find them again. Don't worry."

She relaxed a little more.

"Now, let's look at the top three houses. Here's your top choice. Tell me, is there any reason why you wouldn't want to buy this house?"

"No."

"There's nothing about it that you don't like?"

"No."

"So you like it."

"Yes."

"Enough to buy it?"

"Yes."

"OK, then why don't we write an offer on it right now. How's that sound to you?"

"OK."

"Good!"

We wrote the offer and she bought the house. It was a great house for her—new construction on a lot of land for her dog, wooded so she didn't have to do a lot of lawn maintenance. It was perfect, but she couldn't make the decision to buy it until she had cleared away the extra properties muddying the waters.

After I went through this process with this buyer, I instituted a new policy with all of my buyers. At the end of each showing, we would go back to the car and decide whether or not the house was an option. If it wasn't, then I would have them ball up the paper and throw it into the back seat of my car so they couldn't take it with them. If it was an option, then it would get put in the pile of possibilities. At the end of each day of showings, we would prioritize the list and keep only the top three. I would ask them to buy their number one choice and if they refused, then I would ask them to throw it away. If they weren't willing to buy it, then they shouldn't have it in their pile. They would either leave the car for the day with a copy of the offer we had written, or nothing in hand other than the properties they were to drive by the next day to prepare for additional showings. That way, they couldn't get stuck in analysis paralysis.

Obviously there will be exceptions to every rule. I couldn't usually get away with this when I was dealing with engineers. They like to put everything on a spreadsheet for comparison purposes. But if I provided them with the sheets in advance, they could spreadsheet the info and give up the MLS sheet at the end of the day. It was a good compromise.

Feeling Out of Control

Buyers will often feel out of control. It is especially difficult for those buyers who are usually extremely competent and well informed to walk through an unfamiliar process. Education is the best remedy for feeling out of control. The more information they can integrate on the subject, the better they will feel about their purchase. Each buyer will have their own level of information that is good for them. For some (engineers and the like), they will love us if we bury them in paperwork. For others, they just want us to explain things to them as they get uncomfortable, but they don't want to have to read anything at all (auditory learners). Still others want a combination of written information and verbal explanations. We need to ask our buyers what will make them happy and then give them the information in that fashion.

We need to be prepared to repeat ourselves often. People only retain about 20 percent of what they hear. That means that 80 percent of what we say will pass right through and out of their memories. So we will have to repeat ourselves, sometimes as much as five times (to get to 100 percent) to get them to retain the information. We need to be patient. When I begin to lose patience with a buyer, I just remember what it felt like for me to have to learn all of this real estate stuff from scratch. I remember how overwhelmed I was and how much my brain shut down on a regular basis from it. It's then much easier for me to be patient as I repeat myself for the fifth or sixth time.

Panic

Buyers who feel overwhelmed or out of control will often panic. As agents, we spend a great deal of our time peeling clients off the ceiling or scraping them off the floor. It comes with the territory. But we want to avoid this whenever possible because it's exhausting for the client and for us. One simple way to avoid this is to tell buyers that we are in charge of the panic button. In our buyer presentation books, we put in a page about not panicking until they are told that it is time to panic. This is helpful when they do actually begin to panic because we can use it to break the cycle.

The client calls in a panic. It doesn't matter why, just that they are panicked.

"What's the rule?" we reply.

"What?" They stop. They haven't processed the question yet, only that it wasn't related to what they were panicking about. This is where we begin to break the panic cycle.

"What's the rule?" we repeat.

"What rule?" Now they've stopped panicking for the moment and are trying to remember the rule.

"You're panicking. What's the rule about panicking?"

"Oh", they laugh, "We're not allowed to panic until you say it's OK."

"Right. Have I given you permission to panic yet?"

"No."

"Right. No panicking. It's not time yet. I promise I will tell you when it is time to panic. This is not that moment. OK?"

"OK."

Now that we have broken the cycle of panic, we can begin to solve whatever the problem is. The buyers will now be calmer as they discuss the subject and having gone through this process sets the idea again in their minds that there is no need to panic. It also reminds them that we know what we are doing and the fact that we are staying calm indicates that we are in control of the situation, even if they are feeling out of control. That provides an added layer of comfort.

Financial Details

The buyers are worried about their finances. Even after the mortgage officer has told them that they qualify without a problem, they will still be afraid that the loan won't come through until they have a commitment letter in their hands. They will also be afraid that they will not have enough funds to close. This is when it is most useful to have a complete list of expenses that buyers can expect to pay and when they can expect to pay them. Giving this list to the buyers gives them a sense of security about the issue and allows them to relax a little. They will still worry about not getting the loan, but at least they know they'll be able to cover the other costs. Exhibit 5-1 is a sample of this type of list to give to buyers.

Exhibit 5-1. Sample cash flow of a real estate transaction.

Money Due For:	Amount	When Due
Application Fee for Mortgage	$ 49.	Due immediately—apply for mortgage now
Initial Earnest Money Deposit	$ 1,000.	When you write the offer
Home Inspection Fee	$ 350.	Within 10 days of offer acceptance
Appraisal Fee	$ 300.	Within 15 days of offer acceptance

(continues)

Exhibit 5-1. (Continued.)

Second Earnest Money Deposit	$14,000.	(5 percent of purchase price less $1,000) Due upon signing purchase and sale agreement (14 days from acceptance of offer)
1-Yr Homeowners Insurance Policy	$ 600.	One week prior to closing
Closing Costs	$ 3,000.	(Rough estimate—see Good Faith Estimate from lender for complete cost breakdown.) Due at closing.

Dealing with First-Time Buyers

We need to remember how uncomfortable our buyers feel during their first home purchase. We should speak in soft tones, and give simple, clear-cut directions. If our buyers are overwhelmed, then we need to give them one thing to do at a time and have them call us for the next direction when they are done. They will only be able to keep one thing in their heads at a time when they're overwhelmed. We should give them information in writing and instruct them to put it on their refrigerator for easy access. That way, if we have to give them multiple instructions as once, they have it in writing when they forget. We should remind the buyers often that we are in charge of the deal—we have it under control—they can stop worrying. And we need to keep them informed not only of what is happening now, but of what they can expect so that they can't panic.

Give Them Permission to Hate the House

One final note about first-time buyers—give them permission to hate the house. First-time buyers don't want to hurt your feelings. They are afraid to tell you what they think about a house that they don't like, so they keep quiet. Give them permission to tell you both the good and the bad about each house. They need to understand that this house is not your house. You don't care if they hate it. In fact, you want to know exactly what it is that they hate about it so that you never show them a house with those attributes again.

I had just finished walking through a listing that was horrible. The tenants obviously were not happy about having to move and so they had allowed the house to become a pigsty. They had covered over the windows with blankets, and garbage and clothes were strewn across the floor. Also, they would not leave the house when we showed it, so it was even more uncomfortable for the buyers walking through. When we came out of the house, one look at the husband's face told the story. I looked at the wife and said, "Well, Laurie, Bob hated it. What did you think?" The two of them stopped cold in their tracks, stunned that I had just made that comment. I looked at them both and said, "Look, the place was terrible. We all know that. What I need you to tell me is exactly what it was about the house that you hated the most because I never want to show it to you again." They smiled with relief. They started talking immediately, giving me the details about what they had hated. I never had to prompt them for their feedback again.

CHAPTER 6

MOVE-UP BUYERS

Out of all of the owner-occupied categories, this is the least emotional of the bunch. Move-up buyers often have the same goals of making a good investment as do pure investors. They are making a business as well as an emotional decision, and we have to deal with them in a different way.

Move-up buyers are an odd bunch. On the one hand, they have planned effectively enough in the past that they have equity built in a prior home and they are trading up as a result. This makes them money-conscious because they don't want to lose the equity they've built in the past by making a bad investment now. On the other hand, they feel a little entitled and a lot needy. They put up with a home that wasn't big enough, nice enough, or in a good enough neighborhood for many years. Now they want their dream home, or at least something much closer to it.

They Don't Have to Move

Move-up buyers don't *have* to move. There is usually very little that is forcing the decision to move. The only exception to this rule is families that have outgrown their current homes and need more space. These families behave much more like first-time buyers than like the move-up buyers indicated in this chapter. Most move-up buyers are making their move as a statement of their success or as a reward for their past sacrifice.

It's Not Just Status—It's Business

They may be moving to keep up with the Joneses or they may be making the move as part of a business political move. For many move-up buyers, the next move is as much a business decision as it is an emotional one. Location, location, location. It's not just a rule in real estate sales, it's also a rule in networking. The best networking is accomplished in places where the powerful people congregate. Many of our move-up buyers are acutely aware of this fact. This may be one of the factors fueling their move. If they can get closer to the movers and shakers in the world, then they can get further along in their careers.

Business Brain Meets Denied Emotions

Because this move may be partly business-related and because these people have shown themselves to be keenly aware of the financial investment their house represents, they will attempt to make this purchase much like an investor would with investment property. They will try to keep their emotional distance from the purchase so as to keep a sound business head throughout the deal. However, this is still an emotional decision for them. They have those feelings of entitlement that come from doing without for so long. They have the desires for their dream home. They have their wants and needs like any other owner-occupant purchaser of property. But when it comes time to make the purchase, they will try to deny them and make the purchase as a business purchase. They will rationalize their emotions with logic.

Sales Contingencies

Part of their feelings of entitlement will come out in the form of their approach to the sale of their home. They will want to find their new home first. They will want to make the sale of their current home contingent on them finding a new home of their choice. They will want to be in total control of the transaction. They feel like they settled last time they bought, so the buyer on their current home can wait and settle for what he can get from them. Because they have no actual motivation to move other than their personal desire (and they are mostly denying that), we are in a weak negotiating position with them. These are the sellers who are most likely to put a house on the market and then change their minds months later after we've spent a lot of time and money on advertising the listing.

Identifying the Dream Home

Before we get too far into this process, we need to do a quick reality check with our potential clients. Are they being realistic about what they want in a home? Remember, they are feeling entitled. They put in their time in the small, cramped home they settled for, now they feel it's time to make the leap to their dream home. This doesn't mean that their dream home is within their reach. We need to know whether they have realistic expectations. If they do, then great—we'll move forward. If they don't, then we need to address that issue up front.

If we fail to address it now, it will only come back and haunt us later as we try to find a home for them to buy. By then we've put in a lot of money and effort on marketing their home and they may decide not to sell. We want to give them a realistic perspective of what they can hope to afford in a new home. If they can't afford their dream home, then they need to decide whether they are going to adjust their expectations or whether they will wait to move. Once again, it is their decision, not ours. Our only job is to educate them about the market and then ask for a decision.

Getting Them to Invest in the Move

The way to get these people to invest in the process is to get them to acknowledge the personal desire to move. Get them to admit that they feel entitled to something better, that they settled for the last home and they want something new. Get them to see the value of moving up—both financially in terms of better appreciation of property values in better neighborhoods and in terms of networking potential with the higher-end marketplace residents. We give their logical brains something to cling to and give their emotions a voice. When we do this, we have much more leverage in negotiating with them. They are invested in the move.

Mining for a Client's Investment Level

Ask them questions to evoke an emotional response like the following:

- What are you looking forward to in your new home?
- What will you not miss about your current home?
- Is this your dream home? Isn't that exciting!?
- What does this move mean to your life? What advantages does it offer your family? What goals does it represent achieving?
- Is this the location you wanted to be in when you bought before? Isn't it exciting that you finally made it!?! That's awesome!

When we have gotten them to admit that they have an emotional as well as a financial investment in this next purchase, we are off to a good start. We must be aware that they are effectively dealing with a split personality in their brains about the transaction though. So we will need to allow them to process their decisions emotionally at some times and logically at others. Let them lead in this regard. However they are approaching the particular decision, we will make our arguments to that side of the brain. We can make the cross-over if necessary, but we want to respect their wishes by addressing the issue in the way they have chosen first.

Educate, Educate, Educate

Once again, as with most of the issues we discuss in this book, education and understanding are at the core of solving these issues. We need to educate the sellers about how buying before they have a contract on their home negatively impacts their negotiating position for the purchase and the sale. They will not want to disrupt their lives by taking a chance of not being able to make the transition directly from one home to another. It is one more sacrifice that they do not want to make. It is entirely up to them how they want to go about their negotiations, but we are duty-bound to explain the consequences of their actions to them.

It's never our first choice to put a client into temporary housing. It's a lot of trouble all around. But the cost of temporary housing and storage of their household goods may be a couple thousand dollars and some inconvenience. The difference in the prices they get for both their sale and their purchase when they don't have contingencies on them could be tens of thousands of dollars. In a hot market, it could mean the difference between getting that dream home and not getting it.

These people have proven themselves to be conscious investors in the past. If we can show them that by insisting on making their purchase and sale on their timetable rather than allowing for the other parties' needs, they are damaging their investment potential, then they will usually see reason. In the event that they don't, that's fine. It's their decision. We can't make it for them. As long as the decision is an informed one, we have done our job.

Overwhelmed

Just like other people who are moving, these sellers will feel overwhelmed. They will say "No" to everything as a default because it keeps them from having to add anything to their plate. We need to be aware of this fact. We need to put them back in a position where they feel as though they are in control again. If we ask them to make a decision about something, then we need to have done all the legwork necessary to address all of their concerns. For instance, if we want them to sell their home not contingent on them finding another home, then we need to have information on interim housing available—with pricing—so they can see what they would be getting into.

If they choose to purchase without a contingency to sell their current home, then they need to realize that they will have to acquire a bridge loan. Our mortgage lender should contact them with this information and the associated costs. If they are unwilling to deal with a bridge loan, then we need to give them a reality check about what happens to sellers who look for homes before they have theirs under contract. The conversation will go something like this:

> "I understand that you want to find a home you like before you put your house on the market, but let me tell you what my experience has been with other sellers who have done exactly that. These sellers went out and found a home they loved. They had to have it. But one of a few things always happens at this juncture, and none of them are good for the sellers. Either, they will fall in love with the home and put in an offer contingent on the sale of their current home, only to discover that the seller of their dream house will not accept their offer. Then they have to decide between taking the contingency for the sale of their home out (meaning that they will need to get a bridge loan if their home doesn't sell in time), or they will need to wait to make an offer again until their home is under contract. If they wait, it almost never fails that their dream house gets sold while they are waiting for their home to sell. It's logical to assume that this will happen since the average days on market for homes in similar marketplaces will be similar. Since that seller's house was on the market first, it will sell first. It's the law of averages. I would hate for this to happen to you. The last thing I want to see is for you to fall in love with your dream house and then have it sell out from under you. There's nothing more heartbreaking than that. And then there are the sellers who can't stand the thought of losing that dream home. They drop their price to a level far below market just to guarantee their house will sell and they won't lose their dream home. Instead they lose thousands of dollars in potential profit on their current home. I wouldn't want to see that happen to you either."

> "OK, so we'll wait to look for a home. Then we'll need to make the sale of this house contingent upon finding our home of choice."

> "Well, there are issues with that too. I know that you may want the option to stay where you are if you don't find anything that suits you.

But buyers want to know before they spend money out of pocket for inspections and appraisals that you are actually going to move. They are leery of putting out that kind of money with the very real chance that you may decide not to sell them the house after all. I'm sure you can understand that."

"Yes, I can see that."

"So what happens is that you get the buyers who are willing to take risks. These buyers are the ones who will negotiate the hardest with us. They will try to get money off the price at every turn. They are risk-takers. They will risk losing the deal to get a better price. It puts us in a very bad negotiating position—especially since we have eliminated the buyers who aren't risk-takers, so we don't have a lot of other options. Do you see what I mean?"

"But that means that we may be out of a house without finding something we like."

"Yes, it is a risk you take. But, based on what you've told me about what you want for a home, I believe we can find it in your price range and with the amenities you've requested in the areas you've requested. I don't think we'll have a problem with it. And the benefits of taking the risk are substantial. It is your call, ultimately. I just want you to be making an informed decision when you make it."

"OK, we won't make anything contingent. But we'll have to really get busy looking when we get an offer."

"Absolutely. I have a great track record with buyers. I can usually find the home in six houses or less—sometimes in the first three houses they see. We'll get started the minute we have an accepted offer."

Finding the Dream Home

Move-up buyers will be looking for a combination of a good investment and the feeling of their dream home. We need to walk them through the buyer interview process to learn about their wants and needs in a home. Then we need to take into account neighborhood, market, and resale values in determining where to look. For the move-up buyer, their definition of a dream home includes good resale value and a good investment. Unless they are that special breed of people who are handy and like to work on homes, they will probably want something that is really close to move-in condition. These people generally either have busy work lives or kids or both. They don't have a lot of time to work on their homes.

Pricing a Move-Up Home

This is why, when we price houses in the move-up market, we need to take condition into account so strongly. These people don't generally want to work on their homes. First-time buyers will do work on a house because they think it's fun. It's the first time they've been allowed to make changes in a property in their lives, they're excited. Move-up buyers, however, have been through that once. The thrill has worn off for them. Therefore move-up homes need to be in good shape or they need to be steeply discounted to allow the buyers to pay professionals to do the work.

Status Issues

Some move-up buyers have issues around status. They want to be seen as being successful, and the home they live in is an indicator of that success. These people often have self-esteem issues around being good enough. We need to be careful that we don't accidentally trigger their issues. The self-esteem issues may come out as Know-It-All syndrome or as an intense sense of self-deprecation. For the Know-It-Alls, we remember that the rule was that when we explain how the process works, we want to say things like, "I'm sure you know" and "but you probably knew that already."

For the self-deprecating people, we want to be soft and supportive in the presentation of our information and patient in awaiting a response. We need to give them the space they need to make a decision. It will be easy for us to railroad these people, and that's the last thing we want to do.

Remember to Breathe

Move-up buyers have stress on both ends of their transaction. They have to sell and buy at the same time. We cannot underestimate the amount of stress associated with this process for them. Teaching our clients some of the stress reduction techniques that we learned in earlier chapters will be greatly beneficial to them. When they begin to panic (and they will), we can remind them to breathe. Breathing is the technique I used most often to calm my clients. It's common for someone walking past my office to hear me patiently and calmly saying the words:

> "Breathe. (Pause as they start talking again and I cut them off.) No. Breathe. I know you're upset. I'm happy to listen to you as soon as I hear you take a few slow, deep breaths first. OK, do it with me. Deep breath in. Hold it. And out. (Pause as they start to talk again.)

Nope, not yet. Take another one. Breathe in. Hold, and out. Once more. Breathe in. Hold. And out. OK. Feeling a little better now? (Pause as they say 'yes.') Good. Now tell me what the problem is."

Panic is the biggest emotional grenade we deal with in this business. Having tools to disarm it is critical. If we can teach our clients to recognize the signs of panic and just interrupt their patterns long enough to breathe a few times, we can provide them with tools that will help them for the rest of their lives (not to mention helping us now in this transaction).

CHAPTER 7

RELOCATION CLIENT

There are many issues unique to the relocation client. They have a short time frame for moving. They have to get settled quickly in their new space. They are likely to need to sell again soon, so they need to purchase something with good resale value. Yet they know nothing about the area they are moving into. They need to work with an agent who can look out for them. These buyers definitely need a buyer's agent on their side—and they know it.

Nothing is better than working with a relocation client, or relo client. They are motivated, they acknowledge that they need our services, and they are usually very practical about their choices of homes. They take all the good advice we can give them because they know they are out of their element. Often, these people have made multiple moves, so while they are still experiencing the overwhelmed stage, they have learned to function well within it. They melt down less often than other clients, they make decisions that are more practical than emotional, and they have clearly defined goals for the process. These buyers and sellers are gems.

Since these people are so easy to work with as a whole, we owe them more in the way of services. In order to provide these clients with all they need to make their move, we have to provide them with a good bit of information. Schools, services, commute information, houses of worship, these are just a few of the things that these people want to know about. The biggest challenge that we as agents face in dealing with this market sector is how to provide them with the information they need without accidentally violating fair housing laws.

Fair Housing

We can direct local clients to make inquiries on their own about anything that falls under Fair Housing. Relocation clients, however, are usually only in town for a weekend at a time. They have very little in the way of free time to do research. We know the information that they desire, but we are precluded from offering it due to fair housing regulations. Some of us ignore the restrictions and give out the information anyway. Others don't give out the information and instead provide poorer service while upholding the law. It's a Catch 22 that no one wants to get involved in. But we can't avoid the issue here—it's something that we deal with every time we have a relocating client.

I polled several of the agents in my area about what they do when this sort of thing happens to them. The general consensus of agents seems to be that they will acknowledge that they are forbidden to give this information by law to clients. Then they suggest other locations for the client to find the information such as websites for the local Chambers of Commerce and for the Town. If the question is one of "Is this a good neighborhood?" we do a similar side-step answer—usually saying that the definition of a "good neighborhood" is relative to the person's individual definition of "good," but that we either would or would not live in the neighborhood ourselves.

With sellers, however, I take a slightly different tack. Since as agents we cannot take a listing if the seller is placing restrictions on who it can be sold to based on protected class issues, I believe that we have nothing to lose by challenging their beliefs on this issue. We have two options: walk away from the listing or talk the seller into being reasonable. I have been known to argue with bigoted sellers to get them to agree to list their properties without restrictions. My basic argument is "What do you care who buys the home? You won't be living here anymore. Everyone's money is green—take it." If we consider the options, we really have nothing to lose by taking this perspective. We can't take the listing anyway, so what difference does it make if we anger the sellers by challenging their beliefs? And who knows? Maybe we'll get the listing and make another house available to the general market.

Emotional Issues

As wonderful as relocating buyers and sellers can be to work with, they still have emotional issues associated with the move that we need to address. These issues begin with whether they will be able to get the move done in time to start their new job. They worry about having to split up the family for the sake of getting all of the details taken care of. They worry about how their children will survive the move, not to mention the added stress of starting work at a totally new location in a place where they have no friends. Relocation buyers and sellers truly are changing almost everything about their lives all at once. It's a daunting task. No matter how used to the process they are, they still have a lot of stress to deal with. The one thing that relo clients want more than anything else in the world is a sense of control over the process and a designated end point at which they can settle in and get back to the job of living their lives.

I was a military child and a military wife. I've moved almost thirty times in my life. I've lived in nine different states. I know what it is like to be one of these nomads who move often. We get our routines. We know what to expect from the movers, what we need to pack separately, when we can expect our household goods to arrive in the new location, etc. Unlike other people, we hold the emotional content of our lives in our household furnishings rather than in our homes.

I didn't realize this was the case when I was younger. In fact, I found out the hard way that I stored my sense of safety and security in my household items. I thought I was footloose and fancy free—boy, was I wrong. I was getting married, but my husband was getting transferred to Hawaii just before we got married. This meant that if I wanted my stuff to go with the movers, it had to fit into his barracks room. I couldn't take any of my furniture. I didn't figure this to be a problem. After all, I'd moved without my furniture before when I went into the dorms on campus. What I didn't realize was that I had brought a variety of personal effects to my dorm room. This time, I left behind almost everything I owned with the exception of my clothes and toiletries.

When we got to Hawaii and unpacked, I was living in someone else's home. I had nothing familiar to me to put on the walls or to sit on a dresser. There was nothing of me in the home. I felt completely ungrounded. I was lost without my things. I'd done without them for short periods of time in the past, but always with the promise of their returning. Now I knew that I had let go of them forever. I was a rudderless ship. The sense of disorientation was intense. Combined with the move and the fact that I was getting married, I was at my wit's end. It took me many months to get past this feeling. I wish that I had had a kindly soul to suggest that I take a few choice items of importance with me. They would have made all the difference in the world.

When we work with relocating clients, we need to understand where they are coming from. They have convinced themselves that they are used to this moving thing. They think that they have the process under control. And, in terms of the details, they probably do. But what they are really saying to us is that they are used to operating in a constant state of chaos. They have become adept at moving forward through the overwhelmed stage. It does *not* mean that they are OK. They are still stressed. They are still feeling out of control (although not as much as people who don't move often, since they do know what to expect). They are still disoriented.

These people need the same coaching as we have offered our other clients. They want to be kept in the loop about everything that affects their transaction. They want to know what they can expect as part of the transaction. They want as much information about the community as we can legally offer. They need to move in and feel at home quickly since they may have very little opportunity to feel that way for long before the next move.

Time Zones

Just a quick aside. When I was living in Hawaii and we were moving to Connecticut, we worked briefly with a real estate agent in the Connecticut area. I say briefly because I hadn't been terribly impressed with her to date. The final straw was the day she called me at 6:00 A.M. wanting to talk to me about the upcoming move. Needless to say, she woke me up. When I told her this she sounded surprised. I pointed out that there was a six hour time difference between Connecticut and Hawaii. She said "Oh, I totally forgot there was a time difference." I told her that her services were no longer required. At the time, I figured that if she couldn't manage to remember that calling someone who was a quarter of the way around the world included a time difference then she probably wasn't someone I wanted to trust with my home purchase.

Now, we all make mistakes from time to time, and perhaps I was hasty in my response (she did wake me up and I'm always grumpy at those times). But the fact of the matter is that our clients expect us to understand what is going on in their lives. They expect a response from us that takes their personal situation into account. Details make all the difference. If you're working with a client from out of state, note the time difference. Write it on the file if you think you won't remember it. It could save a deal for you somewhere down the road.

Work Relief

We can offer some respite from this arduous task by offering to take some of the burden of the move off of these clients. We can offer to schedule hotel rooms, flights, etc. We can handle turning utilities on and off. We can arrange for an interview with the local schools to help them determine which area to pick. We can provide a list of things that every relocating client will need to handle before leaving the area (see Exhibit 7-3 at the back of the chapter). Anything we can do to lighten the load will be gratefully appreciated by these clients.

Helping the Kids Move

My mother was the military person in my family. She was a nurse in the Public Health Service (that's the same service that the Surgeon General heads). We moved roughly every couple of years. This was hard on me as a child since I was always the new kid in school. But my mother was very good at setting my perceptions for me. She pointed out that every time we moved, I had the opportunity to change my personality, to try on a new me. No one but she and I would know that I hadn't always been that way. If I was labeled the cry baby at one school, I could be the bossy kid at the next. It was great fun.

Then there was the issue of *where* we were moving. My mother felt it was important to have a positive attitude about each move we made (and I totally agree). When we were slated to move to Boston, my mother took me skiing. She wanted to get me excited about the prospect of being up north. Every time we went out on the slopes, she talked about how wonderful having the snow around all winter would be. She painted a beautiful picture of the wonderful things that life would have to offer in Boston.

Then, as is sometimes the case in the military, they changed my mother's orders to New Orleans. She quickly changed tactics and contacted friends in the service who lived in New Orleans and had them send up beads and doubloons from the floats in the Mardi Gras parade. She got home movies from these friends as well and we watched them, getting excited about being part of the crowds. We lived in New Orleans only long enough to see one Mardi Gras before we were off again. This time it was Maryland. My family was from Maryland, so she reminded me of the blue crabs and the oceans, and the hospitality of the people there.

The point is that kids are really flexible creatures. The key is to get them to buy into each move. If they can focus on the amazing things to come, then letting go of what is already here is much easier for them. (This is also true for adults, but we tend to be a little more stubborn and jaded, so it's harder to get us to invest in a new place before we get there.)

If we as agents can provide something to help the kids get excited about the new location, it will go a long way toward making our clients lives easier in the long run. If we are listing the home for sale, then we can work in concert with the agent on the other end to get this information from them. If the buyers are coming to us, then it's our job to find things for the kids to be excited about. It doesn't matter what it is, as long as there is something. I live in Boston now and I have not been skiing since I moved here. But I still love the snow, so it doesn't matter that the skiing wasn't relevant to my stay.

One more added benefit to helping out with getting the kids (and sometimes even the spouse) on board with the move is that we can become the confidante for these people. We can help smooth the way for the person who is being transferred. Often, family members can become angry at the person who is uprooting their lives. It is a natural response to having their lives thrown into turmoil. As the coaches for this group, we can allow family members to vent their frustrations to us, rather than taking them out on the person responsible for the move. We can remind them that they are angry about the move—not necessarily at the person who is being transferred. By placing the blame for their stress where it belongs, we can reduce the levels of intra-familial stress while still providing a sounding board for those who need it.

Education

Relocating clients will need a lot of education. Not only do they need to know about the area, but they also need information about how the process of buying a home works in the new location. Rules and regulations as well as standards of practice and customs vary widely from area to area and state to state. The more information we can provide to our clients up front, the easier will be the transition for them. Send everything in writing. It will give them something to read while they are on the plane and it will keep us from having to spend valuable time covering that information when they arrive.

Not every relocating client is an old pro. We should have a lot of information on hand to help people for whom this is their first major move. They will need to be coached through the process. Basic information about buying and selling will be appropriate for these people as well as information about relocating.

The Relocating Buyer

We begin working with a relocating buyer by interviewing them about where they are in the process of their move. Exhibits 7-1 to 7-6 at the end of the chapter are some forms we can use to accomplish this goal. Talk to them also about Buyer Agency.

Market Education

Once we know where the family is in terms of their move, then we can move on to providing education on the market. They will need the property sales statistics for each area they are looking at. If they have children, then we should provide them with school reports for the towns as well. Crime statistics are also useful if they are available, and we should always recommend that they cross-reference to the Megan's List website for registered sex offenders if they have children.

We can provide them with copies of contracts and disclosures for the area so that they can review them prior to having to sign them. And we should offer some written explanation of closing customs and occupancy issues for our local area. A copy of "Sample Cash Flow of a Real Estate Transaction" (see Exhibit 5-1 in Chapter 5) is also useful since the timing and cost of these items vary from state to state.

Travel Information

Our buyers may need information about where they can stay while they are in town. Some of the companies transferring people offer housing for their transferees. Others do not. If our buyers fall into the latter category, then we will need to locate affordable housing that can serve both short term for the househunting trip as well as longer term in the event that they are moving before they shop for their new home. Short-term furnished rentals are often appropriate for these buyers.

While they are in the area, our buyers will probably need a rental car. We should arrange this rental for them and see if we can manage to get a corporate discount as well. Perhaps by coordinating with their relocation company or the local office of their company, we can arrange for a better deal than they would have gotten themselves.

Relocating buyers also have to eat. We should give them a list of good restaurants in the area along with indications of the prices for each of the restaurants we recommend. We may also want to give them the number of a good massage therapist in the area as well. A good massage can do wonders for jet lag and stress reduction.

Relocation Package

We should create a relocation package with brochures on area attractions, Chamber of Commerce and Town info (from websites), and more. Once again, the more information we can give, the better. Remember that these buyers will be sitting in their hotel rooms twiddling their thumbs while we are home having dinner with our families. A map of the area is essential. Many of these buyers will map out the properties that we have sent them and will have a plan for previewing the area before they meet with us. At the very least, they will be using the map as a point of reference for the conversations we will have over the phone.

Once They Are in Town

Once the buyers actually arrive in town, there is a whole host of details to be handled. First, we need to clear our calendars to deal with them. They will need to see houses quickly and in a short period of time. Often relocation buyers will not leave the area without placing an offer on a home, so we need to add the time to write the offer into our schedules.

A welcome package in the hotel is a nice way of greeting our clients. We can arrange for this with the concierge at the front desk. A nice fruit basket is appreciated by buyers. It provides snacks in between meals as well as some much-needed hydration after they get off the plane. It also sets the stage with them that we have placed a priority on meeting their needs while they are in the area.

Each time a new relocation client comes to the area, we should provide them with a tour of the towns that we will be showing property in. Each tour should last about fifteen minutes per town. We should point out the shopping, amenities, town services, etc. In each town, we should also point out what the commute times are for them to get to their new job. We're not trying to teach them everything about the town in this quick tour, we're just trying to give them a flavor for the town.

After the first day's tour of the area, we will start fresh on the next day with showings. We want to be careful not to overwhelm the clients with more information than they can process at once. I have found from experience that keeping the showings to about six per day is the best way to keep people from getting confused. Sometimes we will have this luxury, other times we will not. If, due to time constraints, we have to show more than six houses each day, then we need to help the buyers create ways to remember the houses. At the end of each showing, we need to coach them to label the house with a name. This house is "the house with the ugly bathroom" or "the blue house" or "the house with the great family room." However, it doesn't matter how they label the house to remember it. What does matter is that everyone has the same labels for all the houses so that we can talk intelligently about them later.

Once more, we need to remember that we need to help these buyers weed out properties. If they come out of the house and they don't like it, then we don't need to label it—we need to throw the listing away. Too much information is the pitfall here. They can easily become overwhelmed, so let's narrow the field as quickly as possible.

When we drop the buyers off for the evening, they will have nothing to do. They will go out to dinner and then will go back to the hotel room and begin poring over the listing sheets. Don't be surprised if they call the next morning with a ton of questions. While we were busy setting appointments for the next day, they were busy reviewing the ones from yesterday. They may even have been out touring other neighborhoods. We need to be prepared for course corrections along the way.

But we also need to make certain that we have set their expectations properly. They need to know how long it takes to get into a house. If it takes twenty-four hours' notice, then they need to plan for that. We can't have them thinking that they will be able to get into each place immediately (unless that is the norm for our area). We need to set their expectations at a reasonable level. If we know that we will be looking at houses all weekend and will need second showings on short notice, then we should tell the listing agent this at the time we schedule the first showing. This way they can tell their sellers and they can plan appropriately in terms of scheduling their time and keeping their houses a little cleaner than usual. This way we can meet our clients' needs without unduly inconveniencing the sellers.

After Offer Acceptance

Once the offer has been accepted, our clients will need to know what is expected of them from there. They will most likely be heading right back out of town again and will need to have some way to keep track of their responsibilities from there. Below is a letter and a checklist that I give to my clients to keep them up to speed on their responsibilities in regard to the purchase of their homes. It is much easier for buyers to keep track of this information if they have it all on one page in front of them. Attached with these two forms is a utilities list that gives the buyers the contact information for all of the utilities that service the home they are buying. If we are going to take care of these details for the buyers, then we simply modify the letter and the checklist to reflect that.

Furniture Layout

One way to give your relocating buyers a sense of control over the move is to provide them with something constructive to do from their current location. Every time my mother and I moved, we put together a complete house layout. We spent days drawing out the rooms on grid paper, cutting out each piece of furniture and placing it into the rooms. We rearranged the new house endlessly until we had everything where we wanted it. That way, when the movers arrived, we knew just where to have them put everything.

This is an activity that everyone in the family can participate in. It's fun and it's useful. There is an inexpensive book, *Room and Furniture Layout Kit* by Muncie Hendler (Mineola, N.Y.: Dover Publications, 1981), that can help your clients with this process. This is a great "congratulations on getting your offer accepted" gift. Send the kit along with exact room measurements for their new home. Your clients will spend hours putting their new home together and they will thank you for it on moving day.

At Closing

When we give closing gifts to clients, we often end up giving something rather impersonal. We never know what to offer. With buyers though, it's an easy task. We can create our own "Basics Box" (see Exhibit 7-3, "What to Do Before You Move Out of the Area") and provide it to our buyers as a gift at closing. If we take the basics box and remove the towels and electric drill, what remains is a fairly inexpensive (less than $50) package, which can serve as a really useful gift to those just moving into a new home.

If the buyers have already created their own basics box, then a good idea is to have pizza and soda delivered to the house on the day of closing (if you know they'll be there) or to give your clients a gift certificate for dinner. This way they have something to eat while they are unpacking. There's nothing that's appreciated more than when we can reduce the hassles associated with the stressful first day of the move.

Strong After-Sale Follow-Up Program

It is absolutely critical that we keep up with these buyers after closing. If they were transferred for work once, it is more likely that they will be transferred again. We want to be the first name to mind when that happens so that we can get the listing when they leave. We discussed keeping in touch before, so I'm not going into it again here. Just suffice it to say that we should be extra vigilant with our relocation buyers. They are the guaranteed sellers of tomorrow.

Relocating Seller

Relocating sellers are even easier to deal with than the buyers. These people are motivated to move. They know that they have a limited time frame in which to get their house sold and they are prepared to make whatever deals are required to get the job done.

We will want to interview the seller to determine the details of their personal situation. We need to know if there is a company buyout that will take place if the house doesn't sell by a particular date or at a particular price. We need to know when the seller needs to move to their new location. Is this going to be a short-sale (will the house sell for less than the seller owes on it), and if so, will the seller or the company be making up the difference; or will we need to negotiate with the bank on that? Will the seller do any repairs? Can the seller hold any financing? What will the seller do if the house doesn't sell by the time he has to leave? Would he like us to handle the utility shut-offs? Has he hired a landscaper and/or snow removal company to care for the house while he is out of town? If it is winter, will he be winterizing the house or keeping it heated to avoid the pipes freezing? If he's keeping it heated and the house has oil heat, has he set up an automatic delivery from the oil company? How would he like to be kept updated—e-mail, phone, letter, or a combination? Will he be in town for the closing on the home or does he need to talk to his attorney about setting up a power of attorney for someone else to close for him? All of these are valid questions and we need to ask all of them. Below is a copy of the forms I used to get this information from my sellers.

We will need to keep in touch with the buyer's agent in the clients' new location. This agent will need to know when our listing goes under contract so that she can direct their efforts in earnest at that time. She will also need to know the proposed closing date so that she can coordinate that closing with this one. We can also help each other in terms of keeping the client on an even keel. If the client is upset with their buyer's agent, we can give that agent the head's up and let her handle it. Sometimes, we can even offer the client a disinterested third-party opinion, explaining why the agent is doing what she's doing. This often helps in keeping clients happy. The agent in the other deal is a great partner for us. We need to keep her in the loop and help each other out.

Before They Leave the Area

Before our clients leave the area for their new location, we will want to take care of the details for their sale. We will need to get checks for any seller-paid inspections, final utility bills, or condominium document acquisition fees. We will want to check in with them to see whether they will need to be in touch with a junk removal company or if they are doing that work themselves. Will they need a referral to a housecleaning service to do the final cleanup after the movers leave? How will we get in touch with them when they get to their new location? Do they have a fax machine available or can they receive faxes via e-mail when we need to send offers to them? Anything that has to be handled prior to closing should be discussed at this time.

As an added bonus to sellers (and a great advertising opportunity), some agents have preprinted yard sale signs that they loan to sellers. These signs have "Yard Sale" and "This Sign Provided Courtesy of Company Name and Agent Name" printed on them. They serve as a great way for sellers to advertise their yard sales as well as being good advertising for the agent and company. If we have these signs, then now would be a good time to offer to loan them to our relocating seller if they are planning on having a yard sale.

Offer Accepted

Just like with the buyers, we should have a letter and checklist for our sellers when they accept an offer on their home. In addition to the standard documentation, we will also need to know how and where they would like their documents related to the sale of the home delivered. Exhibits 7-7 to 7-10 in the back of the chapter are the standard forms I used for most sellers.

Included with both the buyer and the seller letters is the Performance and Service Evaluation. Exhibit 7-11 is the version that I used. This form is useful not only for improving our service level, but for acquiring compliments from clients that can then be used in advertising.

After-Sale Follow-Up Program

Don't think that just because a seller has moved out of the area that this is a good reason to remove her from our mailing list. That seller still has many friends and family in the area. They still have connections here. Plus, if we are training all of the people on our list that we can offer referrals anywhere in the world, then that seller can even offer us business in her local area. We should keep in touch with *everyone*. We never know when that person may be able to offer us a referral. Plus, who knows? Perhaps she will hate it in her new location and decide to move back. We want to know if that happens. We don't want her to think that we abandoned her just because she moved out of town.

*Exhibit 7-1, Part 1. **Buyer interview questions.***

Buyer Name: Date:

1. When do you get to the area?_____

2. When do you have to start work?_____

3. Are you making a househunting trip prior to your move? _____
    If yes, when? _____

4. When do you want/need to be in a house? _____

5. What are your goals for buying a home? _____

6. How long do you intend to live in your new home? _____

7. How does buying a home fit into your financial picture? _____

8. What relocation support and/or services is your company offering?
    _____

9. Do you have a house to sell? ❑ Yes ❑ No
    a. Do you have to sell in order to buy? ❑ Yes ❑ No
       i. If yes, is it listed currently? ❑ Yes ❑ No With whom? ____
       ii. When listed _____ List Price $ _____
       iii. Likely Sale Price $ _____ Proceeds Expected $ _____

10. Are there any restrictions on your home sale? _____

11. Do you have a company buy-out on your home at a certain time? __

12. If yes, how much? _____ And when? _____

13. Number of people who will be living in the home _____

14. Will anyone not listed on the info sheet be occupying the property?
    If so, who and what relationship are they to you? _____

15. Do you have any hobbies or businesses that the house needs to
    accommodate? ❑ Yes ❑ No
    a. If yes, what? _____

16. Are there any absolute requirements that you have for a house?
    Something that, even if everything else were perfect, would keep you
    from purchasing the property? ❑ Yes ❑ No
    a. If yes, what? _____
    b. Why is this important to you? _____

17. Describe the type of neighborhood you want to live in _____
    _____

# of Bedrooms _____ # of Baths _____ Price Range _____

Desired Areas _____

Special Features Required _____

Special Features Desired _____

Other Requirements _____

This form reprinted with permission from *The New Agent's Survival Guide to Real Estate* available through Sparta Success Systems at www.spartasuccess.com.

Exhibit 7-1, Part 2. Additional buyer interview questions.

Describe your perfect house _____
_____

Would you describe your home as being formal, casual, or something in between? _____
_____

What would you like to see happen if everything went perfectly? _____
_____

What would you like to avoid? _____

What will be your biggest frustration with this process? _____
_____

What is your biggest fear about this process? _____
_____

What can I do to make this process easier/less stressful for you? _____
_____

Is there anything else you feel I should know before we get started? _____

This form reprinted with permission from *The New Agent's Survival Guide to Real Estate* available through Sparta Success Systems at www.spartasuccess.com.

Exhibit 7-2. Buyer information sheet.

Buyer #1 Name _____ Birthday _____

Employer Name _____ Work # _____

Buyer #2 Name _____ Birthday _____

(continues)

Exhibit 7-2. (Continued.)

Employer Name _____ Work # _____

Present Address _____ Anniversary _____

_____

Phone # (home) _____ Other # _____

Family Information:

Child #1 _____ Birthday _____

Child #2 _____ Birthday _____

Child #3 _____ Birthday _____

Child #4 _____ Birthday _____

Mortgage Qualification Information

Pre-Qualified by: _____ Bank/Mortgage Co. _____

Pre-Approved? ❏ Yes ❏ No ❏ In process   Qualified to $ _____

Maximum Desired Payment (if less than qualifying amt)
$ _____ For price of $_____

Type of Mortgage: ❏ VA ❏ FHA ❏ CHFA ❏ 203K ❏ Investor
                   ❏ Conventional ❏ Cash ❏ Farmer's Home Loan

Notes

| |
| |
| |
| |

This form reprinted with permission from *The New Agent's Survival Guide to Real Estate* available through Sparta Success Systems at www.spartasuccess.com.

Exhibit 7-3. What to do before you move out of the area.

- Sell your current home. I can refer you to a good agent if you don't have one. You may need to assign someone power of attorney to close for you. Discuss this with your attorney.
- Get copies of your medical records for all members of the family. Don't forget the specialists that you've visited and your dentist. Your new doctors will want this information for reference.
- Move all prescriptions to a national drug store chain, or get new written prescriptions from your current doctor, so you can still get them filled at your new location.

- Get copies of school records for the kids. Inform the school of when you will be leaving.
- Get copies of immunization records for kids.
- Take pictures of all valuables. Preferably video-tape your home prior to the movers showing up. This will help with claims later.
- Pack all items that cannot be replaced and bring them with you. Do not leave anything that you cannot live without in the hands of the movers. Bring all highly valuable items with you as well as the video and pictures of your items.
- If you are packing your items yourself, then make certain you label them with the room and the general contents of each box. This will be really helpful when you are unpacking later.
- Your "Basics Box"—pack one box that contains the basics and label it as such—put big stars on this box so you can find it easily. The box should include:
  - A roll of paper towels
  - A can opener
  - A roll of toilet paper for each bath in your new home
  - One set of silverware for each person in the house
  - Paper plates
  - Plastic cups
  - A sharp knife
  - A small cutting board
  - A screwdriver
  - A hammer
  - A picture hanging kit
  - A pair of pliers
  - An electric drill
  - A box cutter for each adult in the house
  - A dish towel
  - Bath towels for each person in the house
  - A first aid kit.
- Backup your computer and take the backup files with you.
- Have a farewell party to say good-bye to your friends. Provide all your friends with your new contact info.
- Forward your mail to your new location.
- Close bank accounts. Update all automatic deposits and payments with new bank account info.
- File a change of address with the IRS, all investment accounts, insurance agents, and your creditors.
- Inform all groups you volunteer for that you are leaving.
- Give notice to your employer.

Exhibit 7-4. What to do when you arrive at your new destination.

- Apply for a new driver's license (new state) or update your address (same state).
- Get kids set up in new school. Provide school with copies of records.
- Find new doctors and a dentist and give copies of your records to them.
- Meet movers at house. Have them deliver boxes to the rooms they belong in. Put all boxes against the walls so you can still move through the house. Find your basics box and open it immediately—you'll need it.
- Unpack as soon as possible (start with the kitchen—you can live without everything else for a while, you will need to be able to make food immediately). Take pictures of anything that is damaged and file claims in a timely fashion.
- Set up computer and confirm that it is still operational. Restore files if necessary.
- Set up bank accounts.
- Update insurance to include new home, updated files for new address for cars, and adjustments for new personal property. Remember to order additional riders for computers and high-value jewelry and watches.
- Register car(s) in new state.
- Throw a housewarming party. (Call me, I'm happy to help you set this up and invite new people for you to meet.)

Exhibit 7-5. Buyer's pre-closing checklist.

- Apply for mortgage by: _____
- Additional deposit due by: _____. Amount $ _____
- Arrange for inspections to be completed by: _____
- Respond to any issues from the inspections by: _____
- Respond to water/radon tests by (5 days from receipt of report): ___
- Receive commitment from back by: _____
- Purchase a one-year homeowner's insurance policy by: _____
- Order phone hook-up by: _____
- Order electric hook-up by: _____
- Order water/sewer hook-up by: _____
- If desired, order cable hook-up by: _____
- Closing on: _____

Bring to closing:
- Checkbook
- Cashier's check made payable to yourself (you will get amount from your attorney or closing officer)

- Paid receipt for homeowner's insurance
- Testimonial letter about what you liked/didn't like about my service or your completed Performance Evaluation.
- _____
- _____
- _____

This form reprinted with permission from *The New Agent's Survival Guide to Real Estate* available through Sparta Success Systems at www.spartasuccess.com.

Exhibit 7-6. Congratulations letter to buyer.

Congratulations on getting your offer accepted!

Enclosed you'll find some papers you will need to stay on track to close. The Buyer's Pre-Closing Checklist tells you everything you need to do between now and closing and *when* you need to do it. Post this on your refrigerator or bulletin board so that you can check off the items as they are completed. Also enclosed is a utilities list for your area. This should have the phone numbers you will need to get your utilities switched over on your new home.

Also enclosed is a Performance and Service Evaluation so that you can give me feedback on how you liked my services. To make it even easier, I've also enclosed a self-addressed, stamped envelope. I do read these evaluations and take the information to heart, so any comments you have, good or bad, will be appreciated.

I will be in contact with you periodically over the next few weeks, but if you have any questions or concerns in the meantime, please feel free to call me first.

Once again, "Congratulations!"

Sincerely,

Kelle Sparta
Your Real Estate Consultant

P.S. As you know, your referrals are important to me. If your friends or family are thinking of buying or selling, please keep me in mind and pass my name along to them. Or, better yet, call me—I'd love to help them.

This form letter reprinted with permission from *The New Agent's Survival Guide to Real Estate* available through Sparta Success Systems at www.spartasuccess.com.

Exhibit 7-7. Seller interview sheet.

When was property bought? _____ Price paid for property?_____

Why did you buy this property/area? _____

What improvements have you made? _____

_____

Do you have any pictures of your house/gardens/pool, in another season? ❏ Y ❏ N

Why are you moving? ❏ Transfer ❏ Retiring ❏ Moving up
                     ❏ Divorce ❏ Job loss
                     ❏ Other, please specify _____

If moving out of the area, where are you moving to? _____

Do you need to be referred to a buyer's agent in that area? ❏ Y ❏ N

Is your employer helping with costs? ❏ Y ❏ N If yes, what? _____

Ideally, when would you like to be out of the property? _____

Do you have pets? ❏ No ❏ Yes Pet name(s) _____

_____

Would you consider seller financing? ❏ Yes ❏ No

Are you willing to provide the buyers of your property with a home warranty? ❏ Y ❏ N

What are the three most important considerations in hiring your real estate agent? _____

_____

Are there any specific requests you have of me? _____

_____

I will call at least every other week. Are mornings or afternoons better? ❏ AM ❏ PM

Are there any potential buyers you would like me to contact for you? ❏ Yes ❏ No

Name _____ Phone #_____

Name _____ Phone #_____

What is the primary form of contact you prefer?
❏ Phone ❏ E-mail ❏ Letter

This form reprinted with permission from *The New Agent's Survival Guide to Real Estate* available through Sparta Success Systems at www.spartasuccess.com.

Exhibit 7-8, Part 1. Seller information sheet.

Seller #1 Name _____ Birthday _____

Seller #2 Name _____ Birthday _____

Present Address _____ Anniversary _____

City/State/Zip _____

Home Phone _____ Seller #1 (Work) _____ FAX _____

Email Address _____ Seller #2 (Work) _____ FAX_____

Family Information:

Child _____ Birthday _____ Child _____ Birthday _____

Child _____ Birthday _____ Child _____ Birthday _____

Additional or Future Address

Send Mail Care of: _____ Relationship to seller _____

Address: _____ Phone # _____

City/State/Zip _____ When at this address? _____

Utilities and Services

Electric Co. Phone # _____ Water Co. Phone # _____

Phone Co. Phone # _____ Gas Co. Phone # _____

Trash Pick-up Phone # _____ Oil Co. Phone # _____

Schools

Elementary School _____ Bus Pickup _____

Middle School/Jr. High _____ Bus Pickup _____

High School _____ Bus Pickup _____

This form reprinted with permission from *The New Agent's Survival Guide to Real Estate* available through Sparta Success Systems at www.spartasuccess.com.

Exhibit 7-8, Part 2. Additional questions for relocating sellers.

Will the house be vacant or will you be staying until it sells? _____

If the house is vacant, have you arranged for lawn care/snow
removal? _____

(continues)

Exhibit 7-8, Part 2. (Continued.)

If yes, company name _____ Phone _____

Will you be keeping the house heated or winterizing the property? _____

If winterizing, do you need a referral for a plumber? _____

If you're keeping it heated, do you have automatic delivery of heating fuel? _____

If yes, name of company _____

Do you need to set up power of attorney for closing or will you be present? _____

If POA—who will be your POA? _____ Phone _____

Would you like us to handle the utility final readings and shut-off for you? _____

Exhibit 7-9. Congratulations letter to seller.

Congratulations on your accepted offer!

Enclosed you'll find some papers that will help you stay on track to close. The Seller's Pre-Closing Checklist tells you everything you need to do between now and closing and *when* you need to do it. Post this on your refrigerator or bulletin board so that you can check off the items as they are completed.

Also enclosed is a Performance and Service Evaluation so that you can give me feedback on how you liked my services. To make it even easier, I've also enclosed a self-addressed, stamped envelope. I do read these evaluations and take the information to heart, so any comments you have, good or bad, will be appreciated.

I will be in contact with you periodically over the next few weeks, but if you have any questions or concerns in the meantime, please feel free to call me first.

Once again, "Congratulations!"

Sincerely,

Kelle Sparta
Your Real Estate Consultant

P.S. As you know, your referrals are important to me. If your friends or family are thinking of buying or selling, please keep me in mind and pass my name along to them. Or, better yet, call me—I'd love to help them.

This form reprinted with permission from *The New Agent's Survival Guide to Real Estate* available through Sparta Success Systems at www.spartasuccess.com.

Exhibit 7-10. Seller's pre-closing checklist.

- Call moving company, must be moved out by: _____
- Arrange for inspections to be completed by: _____
- Respond to any inspections issues brought up by buyers by: _____
- Complete any required repairs from appraisal by: _____
- Cancel homeowner's insurance policy by: _____
- Cancel phone service by: _____
- Cancel electric service by: _____
- Cancel water/sewer service by: _____
- Cancel gas/oil service by: _____
- Cancel cable service by: _____
- Finish packing by: _____
- Closing on: _____

Bring to closing:

- Checkbook
- Any unrecorded mortgage releases
- All keys and garage door openers (including mailbox keys, shed keys, lawn tractor keys, etc., if applicable)
- Receipt for last oil bill (if applicable)
- Code to security system with written instructions on how to use
- Testimonial letter about what you liked/didn't like about my service or your completed Performance Evaluation.
- _____
- _____
- _____

This form reprinted with permission from *The New Agent's Survival Guide to Real Estate* available through Sparta Success Systems at www.spartasuccess.com.

Exhibit 7-11. Performance and service evaluation.

For: _____
Agent Name

Please answer the following questions openly and honestly. Your valuable input will have a positive impact on our future dealings with our clients, and most importantly, with you, your family, friends, and associates.

1) What part of your real estate experience with your agent did you like the best?

_____
_____
_____

(continues)

Exhibit 7-11. (Continued.)

2) List three specific items that you were particularly pleased with:

_____

_____

_____

3) What part of your real estate experience with your agent did you find the most challenging?

_____

_____

_____

4) List three specific items that you would like to have seen handled differently:

_____

_____

_____

5) Please circle the letter that describes the level of satisfaction you experienced with your agent in the following areas: (A—Very Satisfied   B—Satisfied   C—Dissatisfied)

1. Availability for meeting, appointments	A	B	C
2. Returns call, answers questions	A	B	C
3. Knowledge of real estate, demonstrated	A	B	C
4. Ability to avoid and solve problems	A	B	C
5. Ability to maintain a high level of trust in all dealings	A	B	C
6. Concerned with quality service	A	B	C
7. Concerned with customer satisfaction	A	B	C
8. Overall satisfaction	A	B	C

Additional comments:

_____

_____

6) Why did you choose to work with your agent?

_____

_____

_____

Would you choose to work with your agent again?   ❑ Yes   ❑ No

Why? _____

_____

7) How would you describe your home buying/selling experience with your agent?

_____

_____

_____

_____

8) Was there any point in the process where you felt out of control, anxious, frustrated, or confused? ❑ Yes ❑ No

If yes, when? _____

_____

What could your agent have done to address this problem? _____

_____

_____

9) In your opinion, in what ways can your agent improve his/her service and provide 100 percent customer satisfaction?

_____

_____

_____

10) Who is the next person you know whom you expect to be buying/selling?

Name _____

Address _____

Phone Number _____ ❑ Buying ❑ Selling

It's not what your agent says to potential customers about his/her service that counts—it's what you say!

May your agent share this information you have provided with others? ❑ Yes ❑ No

_____ THANK YOU!

Please print your name(s).

This form reprinted with permission from *The New Agent's Survival Guide to Real Estate* available through Sparta Success Systems at www.spartasuccess.com.

CHAPTER 8

INVESTORS

Investors are a totally different animal from any other real estate
buyer or seller. Investors have a unique way of looking at their real estate.
They are not interested in how pretty the property is or where it is located.
They don't care if it has character. Their only concerns are how they can
make money on the real estate as an investment.

Investment Criteria

Each investor has his own criteria for investment. Some investors prefer
to work fix-and-flip properties. Others are looking for rental properties
that can be purchased and then require nothing more than basic maintenance. Still others like to buy rental properties in poor condition so they
can fix them up and then rent them out. Some of these investors want
houses only in good neighborhoods. Others buy property on the edge of
a bad neighborhood. And still more will do the slum lord thing. Some
investors only buy single families, some buy condos, and others buy multi
families or apartment complexes. Some will buy anything if the numbers
work. Others will turn down a great deal because it doesn't fit their model.
The key with each investor is to understand what they are and are not
interested in and to call them only for appropriate properties that meet
their criteria.

Questions for Investors

What are the criteria you use to decide whether or not to purchase a property? _____

What is your goal when you purchase a property? (fix and flip/rent/etc.) _____

If I find a property that does not fall within that range, but is still a great deal, do you
want to hear about it?   ❏ Yes   ❏ No

Are you working with other agents?   ❏ Yes   ❏ No   If yes, who? _____

How many properties are you capable of purchasing at one time? _____

Are there any financing issues that we need to keep in mind when looking at properties? ❑ Yes ❑ No

---

Are you currently investing in the types of properties you eventually want to be investing in or are these purchases a means to an end? _____

How many properties do you currently own? _____

Are you planning on selling any of these properties in the near future? ❑ Yes ❑ No
If yes, addresses _____

Do you want me to write the offers, or do you prefer to do that yourself? _____

How do you prefer to receive the property information? E-mail FAX Phone Mail

If we keep these criteria in mind when dealing with our investors, then we will keep them happy. Our job is *not* to talk them into investing in other types of properties. Our job is to recommend appropriate properties and strategies to our clients based on their personal criteria. If our client is one of the ones who buys on the edge of a bad neighborhood, then we can suggest that he use a strategy that I learned from one of my investors.

He bought multis in need of rehab. While he was renovating the first and second floors, he offered the third floor to the police to use as a free stakeout location. In this way, he got free security on a vacant building while it was under construction and he got the neighborhood cleaned up for his new tenants. The police got a free space to work from so they liked him and helped him out when he needed it. It was a win-win for everyone.

When we have new investors, we are their sounding board. We can offer them advice on what they should and shouldn't purchase. If they are looking at a property next door to a crack house, we can suggest that this might not be the soundest investment. Perhaps it would be better to buy one property in a nice neighborhood rather than two in bad neighborhoods. We need to look out for them (assuming we are their buyer's agents).

Fix and Flips

Fix and flips are properties that need work and can then be sold at a profit. As with everything else, investors will have their own criteria for what makes a property worth the work. In my experience, most investors in this market are looking for a minimum of a $25,000 profit margin after everything is taken into account. These investors are often contractors who do much of the work on the property themselves. Subsequently, these people tend to invest most often in the winter months since this is the slow time for their contracting businesses and since this is the time when they are most likely to get a good deal on a house.

But these are not the only people who invest in fix and flips. I had a regular investor who would buy properties as an investment for his church. The congregation would get together and work on the property and then they would sell it at a profit. This was how they raised the money they needed to buy their new church building. Anyone can do a fix and flip as long as they are prepared to do the work.

Some fix-and-flip investors are OK with doing major rehabilitation of properties, including plumbing, heating, electrical, etc. Others are looking more for properties that are structurally sound but that need some updating. These people are more interested in doing things like painting, carpeting, refinishing floors, etc. These investors typically will accept a little less in the profit margin than the major rehab people will.

For first-time fix-and-flip investors, we want to connect them with an accountant to explain the tax ramifications of holding a property for less than twelve months. They need to figure the costs of short-term taxes into their model for deciding what properties to purchase. They also need to know that if they owner-occupy and keep the property for two years, then their profits (or most of them) would be tax free. Getting our clients in touch with a good CPA is the first step before they pick a property.

We want to have several investor financing products available for them as well. There are many products on the market that don't make a lot of sense except for the fix-and-flip investor. For instance, a six-month adjustable product is perfect for this type of buyer. If they can accept a higher interest rate in exchange for not having a lot of closing costs, then this is even better since the investor will only be paying a few months' worth of interest. Regardless, we want to make certain that their mortgage product does *not* contain a pre-payment penalty clause since we know they will be paying off the property early.

Rental Property

Rental property is the big item thanks in part to Robert Kiyosaki's *Rich Dad Poor Dad* book series (New York: Warner Business Books). There are many new real estate investors trying to find good rental properties. Experienced investors will be looking for properties in good areas with long-term tenants. They will be looking for returns on their investment, which may be based on total investment or based on cash out-of-pocket.

One of my investors used to look for a 10 percent cash-on-cash return on investment. This meant that he was looking to get back 10 percent per year in profits on the cash that he invested in the deal. For instance, if he put down $18,000 plus $5,000 in closing costs, plus $1,000 in repairs, he was out-of-pocket for a total of $24,000. So he wanted the property to return $2,400 per year in profits, or $200 per month.

Other investors are looking for the tax deduction to reduce their taxable income. So they will look for a property that may be cash neutral—no profits and no losses—but will show a loss on their taxes (the wonders of depreciation). If they spend most of their time doing real estate investing for a living, then they can deduct the losses on this property against the gains on others. These investors will buy properties that other investors would never touch.

With rental properties, we need to be aware of the vacancy rates for properties in the area. We can get this information from the rental agents in the area. If the investor is planning on hiring a rental agent, then they will want that cost figured into their model. Rental agents charge anywhere from 6 percent to 10 percent of a month's rent to manage the property. Most will charge up to one month's rent to rent a property out. This fee may or may not be included in the management fee.

Other items to keep in mind with rentals is that the neighborhood makes a huge difference in determining the quality of tenants that the investor can attract to her property. If she buys in a desirable neighborhood with many amenities, then she will get more reliable tenants than if she buys in a high-crime area. It is easier to get good-quality tenants in a single family or a two-family home than in a three or more family home. The more well maintained the property, the better the level of tenant as well, and the higher rent an investor can charge for the property. So, while an investor may not be interested in the character of a house or how pretty the yard is, a tenant or future buyer will be interested in these factors. When we discuss these factors with the investor we need to do so in terms of how much of a return on an investment she will get on the property because of these features, rather than simply expecting her to be excited because the place is pretty.

Here is a list of desirable amenities that do well in bringing in good-quality tenants and that positively affect resale value:

- Desirable neighborhood (location, location, location)
- Low crime rate

- Off-street parking (garage preferred)
- In-unit laundry facilities
- Updated kitchen and baths
- Dishwasher
- Fireplace
- Hardwood floors
- Well-maintained building

Here are some factors that can negatively affect value and rent-ability:

- Electric heat (not included in rent)
- Cracked plaster or peeling paint—lack of upkeep of property
- Overgrown yard
- Noisy/messy tenants in other units
- Bad smells in unit or on street
- Flimsy outer doors (poor security)
- Paneling
- Lack of counter/cabinet space
- Lack of storage space
- Poor layout

Every investor has her own criteria that she uses to decide which properties to buy. As agents, we are not in a position to create these criteria for her—nor does she expect us to. She will give us some general guidelines to follow in choosing properties for her and then she will do the rest when we pass the properties along. Most investors don't expect us to do the math on whether a property will work for them or not. They only want us to give them the properties that might be close and then they will do the rest.

Connecting with Investors

No matter what criteria an investor is using for purchasing property, he will not be long in investing if he gets emotionally attached to properties. This is a business decision for him. He needs to keep his emotions out of the mix. He can't afford to pay too much for a property just because he fell in love with the fireplace in the second floor unit. You need to respect this requirement of the profession. Do not try to get these investors emotionally attached to the properties we show. Instead, speak their language. Point out the low cost of getting into a property, the repairs that will bring the highest return on investment, and the rental rates that can be expected for the neighborhood.

In this way, you connect emotionally with your investor. This is done on a subtle level that says that you respect his need to maintain an emotional distance from the transaction and, by association, from you personally. This type of client will not let you into his head. He doesn't want you to coach him through the transaction (unless it's his first time out). He wants you to give him what he asks for, do your job, and then get off the phone and move on. He is busy and doesn't have a lot of time to waste chatting with you. By letting him maintain his distance and by not wasting his time, you are honoring his wishes and making the best connection you possibly can with him.

Balancing Act

If an investor is buying very low-priced properties and our commission will be low, then she needs to be prepared to either pay us extra for our work, or do a lot of the work herself in regards to writing up the offers, etc. I've had investors that took both approaches. The key is to make certain that the relationship works both for them and for you. Don't take a lot of time showing properties to investors who low-ball everything only to find that they never actually buy anything. This damages your reputation in the industry with other agents as well as being a tremendous waste of your time and energy. If you have an investor whose approach means that there will be a lot of work for very little commission, then you need to negotiate an hourly rate for your time in order to make this worth your while. Investors are business people, who will respect and appreciate this approach.

Tools

Most investors will have their own tools that they use to identify properties. You don't need to offer them much in terms of paperwork or software. But there are a few forms I have found to be useful in listing multifamily investment properties over the years. Exhibits 8-1 to 8-3 are the forms that I used most often:

Exhibit 8-1. Seller information: multifamily home.

Property _____ Seller _____

When purchased: _____ How much paid _____

What improvements have been made: _____
_____
_____
_____

When they want it sold by: _____

Utilities:

Electricity: ❏ Separate ❏ Single Seller's annual expense $ _____

Heat: ❏ Separate ❏ Single Seller's annual expense $ _____

Water: ❏ Separate ❏ Single Seller's annual expense $ _____

Do you have the option of owner financing? ❏ Yes ❏ No

If yes, would you consider it? ❏ Yes ❏ No

What has your occupancy rate been? _____ percent

How much do you pay for maintenance each year? $ _____

Do you manage the property yourself or hire a
manager? ❏ Myself ❏ Manager $_____/yr

Snow removal/lawn care costs per year: $ _____

Trash pick-up cost per year: $ _____

This form reprinted with permission from *The New Agent's Survival Guide to Real Estate* available through Sparta Success Systems at www.spartasuccess.com.

Exhibit 8-2. Multifamily-home showing instructions.

Number of Units _____

Property _____ Seller _____

Keys: ❏ Lockbox # _____ ❏ At office ❏ Tenant will let in

Unit # _____ Rent $ _____	Unit # _____ Rent $ _____
Tenant Name _____	Tenant Name _____
Home # _____ Work # _____	Home # _____ Work # _____
Work Schedule _____	Work Schedule _____
Notice needed to show _____ ❏ Lease ❏ Month-to-Month	Notice needed to show _____ ❏ Lease ❏ Month-to-Month
Lease began _____ ends _____	Lease began _____ ends _____
Utilities Incl. ❏ water ❏ heat ❏ elec	Utilities Incl. ❏ water ❏ heat ❏ elec
If property vacant winterized? ❏ Y ❏ N	If property vacant winterized? ❏ Y ❏ N
Notes _____ _____	Notes _____ _____
Unit # _____ Rent $ _____	Unit # _____ Rent $ _____
Tenant Name _____	Tenant Name _____
Home # _____ Work # _____	Home # _____ Work # _____
Work Schedule _____	Work Schedule _____
Notice needed to show _____ ❏ Lease ❏ Month-to-Month	Notice needed to show _____ ❏ Lease ❏ Month-to-Month
Lease began _____ ends _____	Lease began _____ ends _____
Utilities Incl. ❏ water ❏ heat ❏ elec	Utilities Incl. ❏ water ❏ heat ❏ elec
If property vacant winterized? ❏ Y ❏ N	If property vacant winterized? ❏ Y ❏ N
Notes _____ _____	Notes _____ _____

This form reprinted with permission from *The New Agent's Survival Guide to Real Estate* available through Sparta Success Systems at www.spartasuccess.com.

Exhibit 8-3. Condominium information sheet.

Property Address _____ Seller _____

Condo Complex _____ Condo Fees _____

Fees Include: Amenities:

❑ Heat   ❑ Pool   ❑ Clubhouse

❑ Hot Water   ❑ Rec Room   ❑ Tennis Courts

❑ Electricity   ❑ Playground   ❑ Basketball Courts

❑ Water/Sewer   ❑ Jacuzzi   ❑ Other _____

❑ Plowing

❑ Mowing

Management Association:_____ Phone #_____

Name of Manager:_____

Approved for what types of financing?

❑ FHA   ❑ Conventional   ❑ FDMC   ❑ Other _____

❑ VA   ❑ FNME   ❑ GNME

Number of assigned parking spaces _____

Pets allowed?   ❑ No   ❑ Yes   If yes, what kind? _____

_____

_____

Type of Heat: ❑ Baseboard ❑ Heat Pump ❑ Forced Hot Air ❑ Radiant

Type of Fuel: ❑ Oil   ❑ Electric   ❑ Gas

Central Air Conditioning?   ❑ Yes   ❑ No

Window A/C Units?   ❑ Yes   ❑ No

Replacement windows?   ❑ Yes   ❑ No

Do window   ❑ All   ❑ None   ❑ Some _____
treatments stay?   _____

This form reprinted with permission from *The New Agent's Survival Guide to Real Estate* available through Sparta Success Systems at www.spartasuccess.com.

P A R T   I I

SETTING UP A

CONSULTATIVE

BUSINESS

CHAPTER 9

CREATING INSTANT RAPPORT

One of the biggest challenges many agents face is how to connect with potential clients quickly and easily. They find that their first meetings can be awkward and uncomfortable. For most people, it takes time to establish rapport and build trust. But the best salespeople know that the ability to accelerate this process is the difference between closing the deal and losing it. They know that fitting in with the prospect is critical. So how do you "fit in" with the prospect right away? Read on.

First Impressions

The first impression we make on someone is usually the most long-lasting. It is hard to overcome a bad first impression, so we need to be certain that we do well at the initial meeting. The first item on the list is the way we dress when we go to an appointment. We should dress the same way the person we are going to see would dress for an interview. If they are a blue-collar worker and their interview would be in khakis and a polo shirt, then that's what we wear. If they're a million dollar buyer, then a high-end suit is in order (unless they're a computer geek who lives in jeans—then corporate casual is more appropriate). The closer we can come in our style of dress to what the prospect is used to, while still being "dressed up," the better we can connect at that first meeting.

Once you have the style of dress chosen, then you need to look at other factors. Obviously, it's a good idea to check in the car mirror before you head into an appointment to make sure that there isn't lipstick on your teeth, your hair isn't sticking up, and that there aren't snoogers hanging out of your nose. A quick fly-check is a good idea too. But then there are other things to think about as well. If you smoke, then an airing-out period is required, especially if you're headed into a nonsmoker's house. And with today's allergies rising rapidly, wearing cologne or perfume or using heavily scented soaps is a big no-no. If the prospect is allergic to you, you'll never close the sale—you may not even make it through the presentation. And, of course, there's always the all-important smile. If you don't smile at the initial meeting, you might as well go home. You've just told the prospect that you're not happy to see them.

All of these items are what can keep you from connecting with a prospect. None of them will make the connection for you. They are simply prerequisites that must be in place before you can even begin to build rapport.

Be Nice to Your Coworkers

In general society we never know what to do when we see someone walking around with his fly down or with lipstick on her teeth. In sales, this is not the case. If you like the person, you will tell him. This is business. You cannot remake a first impression. Tell your coworker if her slip is showing or if he missed a belt loop or if there is spinach in her teeth. And if someone offers you a breath mint—take it. You never know when he is politely telling you that your breath stinks.

Nonverbal Communication

As salespeople, we tend to focus more on *what* we say than on *how* we say it. We practice our scripts for hours, we learn exactly the right things to say to handle objections, we know all the right answers. And yet, that only comprises 10 percent of what we are communicating to our prospective clients. The other 90 percent of our communication is in nonverbal cues. Some of these cues are:

- Tonality (how we say things)
- Languaging (the words we use)
- Body language (what we look like when we say it)

These are the cues that we give to our clients to tell them about ourselves. Often, these cues speak louder than the actual words we are saying.

For example, I once coached a new agent who was just getting into doing buyer agency. He had practiced his script extensively. He had it down cold. And it was a good script. And still, he couldn't close a buyer. I asked him to do his presentation for me. At the crucial moment when he was talking about signing the contract and starting to work together, his voice dropped, his posture slumped, and he trailed off his sentences.

Up until then, his presentation had been powerful and compelling, but suddenly I was uninspired by him. Why? Because he was uninspired.

I asked him why he didn't believe that I should sign up with him as a buyer's agent. He hemmed and hawed and talked around the subject, but what it came down to was that he wasn't sure that it was possible to be a good salesperson and a nice guy at the same time. Since he thought of himself as a nice guy, his desire to be a salesperson (based on his definition of what that was) was out of alignment with who he believed himself to be. Therefore, he sabotaged his presentations. When I explained that the very definition of buyer agency was being a nice guy and looking out for the buyers, he brightened. I asked him to do the presentation again and he nailed it.

In doing his prep work for his presentation, this agent had intended to sign up buyers. But his internal disbelief in what he was doing came through in his demeanor and ruined the sale. All his words pointed toward a successful close, but his nonverbal cues overwhelmingly won the battle—and lost the sale.

This is why groups like Toastmasters suggest that you do your presentations in front of a mirror. You are more apt to catch yourself doing these self-sabotaging movements if you can see yourself. It's hard to notice them if you're not actually watching yourself. Recording your presentation is also a good learning tool. Listen to what your voice sounds like, where you place emphasis, whether you manage to stay on track or if you wander off-topic. These are good tools to use when trying to polish your presentation style.

But what are the presentation skills we want to develop? The answer is: It depends on the prospect. Each person is different and each person will respond to a different approach. How do you know what that approach is? The easy answer is to give back what you get. If the person speaks slowly and deliberately, then do the same. If they are direct and make lots of eye contact, then you do that too. If they speak with a lot of feeling words, then you do the same. If you can entrain with their style, their energy, then you're on the right track.

Tonality

There are different pieces that go into making up a person's communication style. Before we go any further with this, we need to define our terms. Let's start with tonality. Your *tonality* is the way in which you speak the words. You may whine, or speak through your nose, or speak clearly in round tones. You may be short and clipped or long and rambling. You may be glib or deadly serious or any combination thereof. However you approach your presentation that is your tonality.

Languaging

Then there's languaging. Our *languaging* is the words we use and the ways in which we put them together. Everyone has favorite words and phrases that they use often. They also have certain ways of stringing together words and phrases that form a unique speech pattern. If you can reflect pieces of that speech pattern back to a prospect, then you will build rapport with them more quickly and easily. Want an example of differences in languaging? Read a Stephen King novel and a James Mitchner novel back-to-back. You'll notice huge differences. Have you ever seen a movie where the actor or actress did a perfectly lovely British accent and yet still managed to sound wrong? It's usually the script that failed in creating the proper choice of words for the accent. The languaging was wrong.

Some of our language choices are cultural, as is the case with people from the Midwest referring to Coca Cola as "pop" and those on the East Coast referring to it as "soda." Some are personal, such as favorite words or phrases. And some are based in the rules of the language itself—in America you wouldn't expect to say, "Would you be wanting some water?" Instead you'd ask, "Do you want some water?" Regardless of where the languaging comes from, it is up to you to pull out pieces of it and reflect them back to your prospect.

Body Language

Then there's *body language*. For years we've heard about body language and the rules associated with it. I won't go into all of them here, since there are entire tomes on the subject. Suffice it to say that your posture, your demeanor, and your carriage are all factors in your ability to connect with your prospect. If you are self-conscious and distracted, your prospect will be uncomfortable and unimpressed with you. If you are confident—strong in your movements, making good eye contact, and smiling, then your prospect is more likely to be swayed in a positive direction.

Touch

One final item that shouldn't be overlooked is the issue of touch. This is a sensitive subject since it can be so easily misconstrued, but an appropriate form of touch, surgically applied, can make all the difference in establishing rapport. People going through the process of buying or selling a home are stressed out. A warm touch, a shoulder to lean on, a friendly scratch on the back can be very soothing to people in the midst of all this stress. It is important that we are careful when employing this technique since it can backfire on us if we apply it inappropriately.

I find it easiest to identify a person's openness to touch by trying a nonthreatening touch to their lower arm first. I say something like, "I know just what you mean" (touching lower arm), and then I see what their response is. If they are open to it, then I am likely to make a more significant touch (like upper arm or a quick scratch of their back) a little later in the time we spend together. I offer hugs to my clients who seem open to them as well. I do this because I am comfortable with touch and it is part of my life. Obviously, we need to keep this touch to socially acceptable levels, and invading someone else's space is never OK. But studies have shown that most American adults do not receive enough good touches in their day, and this is one other way in which we can connect with our clients.

Once again, I'll reiterate, that if this is not something you feel comfortable with, then you should avoid it. If it's uncomfortable for you, it will be uncomfortable for your client as well. Obviously this is a sensitive subject. If you have any concerns at all about your ability to pull this off, then you should avoid it.

Applying the Rules

All of these examples are good general rules of thumb. But every rule of thumb has its exception; and when it comes to people, the exceptions are sometimes more prevalent than the rules. It's all well and fine to tell us as salespeople that we should be firm in our handshake, look the prospect in the eye, and smile as we pump their hand 2.3 times. That's a rule. The reality of the situation is often quite different. Connecting with someone requires that we take into account the prospect's wants and needs. If she is easily intimidated, then looking her in the eye can be overwhelming for her. If she is delicate, a firm handshake from the salesperson might mean pain for the prospect (especially if she's wearing any rings). If the prospect is uncomfortable with touching people, then gripping his hand firmly can be a problem. This will be doubly true if he is dealing with cultural issues associated with touch. For instance, it is taboo for a male Hassidic Jew to touch a woman who is not his wife. If you break that barrier, you have just lost the sale. So how do we know what to do?

Let the prospect take the lead. If he has a firm grip, then we respond in kind. If he wants to hold our hand as he lets us in the door, then we let him lead us in. If she avoids direct eye contact, then we reduce the amount of direct eye contact we make and shorten its duration. If she looks like she is intimidated, then we soften our tone, reduce the volume, and leave more spaces in between phrases to give her time to think. We are in control of the presentation; the prospect is in control of the style.

Now that we know what the terms are, how do we put them all together? Watch and listen to your prospect. If he is loud and boisterous, then you reflect that back to him. If he is soft and mousey, then tone down your personality too. Let me be clear here. I am *not* saying that you should become someone different for each person you deal with. I am simply saying that you should reflect back to that person a part of your personality that is most in alignment with who he is. If you try to be something you're not, then you run the risk of falling flat because you sound phony. What do I mean by showing a piece of your personality?

If I am in a room filled with people my grandparents' age, then I will speak of my love for Gene Kelly and Jimmy Stewart movies, and I will do so slowly in a quiet tone with smooth, round sounds because this is the way in which I am most likely to connect with them. If I am in a room filled with teenage boys, I'm going to sit back casually in a chair, speak in short words and clipped phrases, and leave long silences in between. I won't ask for details of their lives or dig into their feelings because that's not how they communicate. I will let them tell me things as they see fit and be OK with sitting in silence in the meantime. Why? Because *they* are running the show. *I'm* the one trying to fit in.

A classic example of this premise is the story of a woman I worked with who liked to play at being "The Bickersons." She would whine and complain and curse at me, saying she was mad when she was really playing. I picked up on her game almost immediately from the twinkle in her eye as she threw the first volley. I responded back with a softly worded but smart-ass response and the game was afoot.

The client and I proceeded to pound on each other back and forth through the whole transaction, much to the amusement of her partner who sat back and watched the show. At one point, I was in the conference room at my office writing up an offer for them to purchase a house. We were having our normal tête-à-tête and really getting into it. She was whining about the amount of paperwork I was requiring her to sign and I was calling her a whiny so-and-so (not my actual choice of words). Finally, she said, "Is there anything else you want from me? As though you haven't asked for enough already." I responded with "Yes, write me a check for $1,000 and do it NOW!" She pulled out her checkbook, saying,

"Pushy b****." I responded with "You're damn right." We were having a great time.

Unfortunately for me, my broker walked by at exactly that moment and was horrified to hear this exchange. She pulled me out of the room and started to berate me for my actions. I asked her to calm down and then brought her into the room with the client. I told the client that she had gotten me in trouble with my broker and she needed to tell her that she wasn't angry with me. After making me sweat for a minute as she said that she was incensed, she finally relented. A broad smile washed across her face and she said, "Nah, she's the best agent I've ever met. The only one who could ever take what I threw at her. She's awesome."

You would never think that by cursing and whining at a client you could win their undying affection. And normally you can't. But this is my point. My presentation is about the client, not about me. I can't get anyone to the place I want them to go unless I first walk over to where they are standing. Once I am with them, then I can lead them where I will. Simply put, I cannot even begin to sell my prospect until I watch them to learn how they would like to be sold.

Profiling the Prospect

In the FBI, they have people called profilers whose job it is to deduce the personality, age, and habits of a person based on the crime they've committed. We do something similar in our business. We take our cues from the person's dress, tonality, body language, and speech patterns as well as the price range, style, and condition of their home. We make a thousand little judgments about who they are and what they want out of life by what we see around us. But how accurate are our assumptions? How closely are we paying attention?

We might see a dirty home and assume that we are dealing with a bad housekeeper when in fact it is simply someone who has been injured and hasn't been physically able to clean. We may see someone who is withdrawn and surly and assume it's a character flaw, when actually she's just lost her job and is facing losing her home and is unhappy and embarrassed about having to call us. There are all kinds of reasons that people act the way they do. It is our job to understand those reasons. We've talked already about how to determine what some of those reasons are. Now let's work with what we can observe and assume.

The people who are best at these techniques are ones who are students of human nature. Those of us who watch people and work to understand why they do what they do are terrific at putting together these composites of our prospects as we walk in the door. If what I am about to say to you doesn't sink in the first time or seems too hard, then try some practice. Go out and sit in the park and watch the people. Try to make up a story about each person based on his posture and demeanor. Find two people who are having a conversation and guess what they are saying. Watch them. Notice the little movements they make, the expressions on their faces, the glints in their eyes. Get in the habit of picking up on these clues. Once you make this a habit for yourself, you'll make the process of profiling your prospects that much easier.

So let's start with the assumptions. We can assume that they want us to be there because they made the appointment. We can also assume that they believe that we probably know more than they do about the market. And, unless they were referred to us, we can assume that they don't trust us. (Remember, most people think of real estate agents as one very small step up from used-car salesmen.)

Now for the observations. Who answers the door? How old are they? What gender are they? How are they dressed? Are they happy we're here? Do they have kids? Are the kids going to be an issue while we're giving the presentation? If it's a couple, watch how they interact. Are they getting along well? What are their facial expressions? Are they open or guarded? Who does the talking? Do they want to run the show or are they waiting for us to take the reins? Are they awkward showing us around their home or does it feel like they've given this tour many times before? Are there family pictures on the walls? Who is in them?

All of these questions give us clues to the prospect's personality. They are hints at what is beneath the surface. But how do we translate those hints into a useful profile?

Let's assume that I walk up to a home where the person who answers the door is a woman in her late forties wearing a business suit and looking a little tired. She greets me with a smile and ushers me into the house where she introduces me to her partner, a woman in her early fifties wearing jeans and a T-shirt. During an obviously well-rehearsed tour of the premises, I see a few pictures on the walls of a boy in his late teens/early twenties. I ask and find out that he is the older woman's son who has recently gone to college. The younger woman does the talking while the older one offers me a drink and a snack (which I gratefully accept). The younger woman speaks in soothing tones with larger vocabulary words. The older woman is harsher in her tone and speaks in shorter, simpler words. They smile at each other and often finish each other's sentences. What do I know about this couple?

I know that they entertain often from the fact that the tour of the home was well rehearsed. It's been said before to a lot of other people. I know that one woman probably works in the corporate world. The other one may be a homemaker or she may run her own business or work in a job where she doesn't have to dress up. She probably works with men (based on the harsher tones and shorter words) in a typically male workplace. I know that there is one child who has gone to college recently, so they are probably empty-nesters looking to move down.

I know that they are lesbian and I know that they get along well and are happy as a couple. Based on the fact that they finish each other's sentences, I can assume that they've been together for some time. I can also assume that they can handle adversity since they live together as an openly gay couple. The languaging of the older woman implies a less educated background (although not necessarily true, it may be a function of her work environment) and a more to-the-point conversational style. The younger woman likely has a higher education level and has smoothed off the rough edges (probably to be able to deal with the corporate world). Given that they are together, it is reasonable to assume that the younger woman also appreciates a straightforward, no-nonsense communication style. It is likely that the two will share in the decision-making process, with the older woman chiming in on the emotional side and the younger on the logical end.

This is an extremely simplified version of what actually happens when we meet. There are many more nuances that I could pick up on were I actually sitting in front of these two people. I could tell you how they felt about different things based on how their tonality and facial expressions changed. I could tell you what items were important to them based on repeated words or themes in their conversations. The more I study people, the more they silently tell me about themselves. The more I learn about them, the better able I am to connect with them and build instant rapport.

Observation vs. Judgment

When we engage in these types of observations, we are actually making educated guesses, which we will then need to follow up on by determining if they are true. We can do this through trial and error or by asking (for example, "Oh, is that your son in the picture?"). The one thing, however, that is critical throughout this process of observation is that we hold this information lightly. What I mean by that is that we hold it as *information*, making no judgments about it. The minute we begin to judge another person, we separate ourselves from him. We place ourselves in a superior position and look down on him. No matter how much we try to

hide this mindset, we will not be able to fully eliminate it from our demeanor. It will come across in our body language, facial expressions, tonality—something. And that is when we destroy our ability to develop
rapport.

If I find myself standing in judgment over someone else, the quickest
way to get out of that mindset is to put myself into the other person's
shoes. It is important that I truly embrace being that person and not just
being me in that person's situation. Everyone deals with situations in their
own fashion and I cannot truly understand the situation from that person's perspective until I understand that person's way of dealing with the
world around him. Even if I can't understand why he is making the
choices he is I still need to respect those choices. It's his life and he can
do with it as he chooses. It is not up to me to pass judgment on that. I
am simply there to help him get from where he is now to where he is
going.

Open Houses

Major retailers have studied the buying practices of their customers for
years. They know all of the nuances that go into the buying decision and
they take advantage of them as often as possible. Real estate agents haven't
done this type of research. In fact, we have very little definitive knowledge
about what pieces of the puzzle influence a buying decision. Since this
information is not available to us, I suggest we take a page from the retail
industry and combine it with the information that most agents can tell
you from experience.

Let's start with the retail industry information. It has been shown that
women tend to buy more often when the scent of French Vanilla is in the
air. Women also respond better to more warmly lit spaces. And the type
of music being played in the space will affect the buying decision as well.

What do most agents know from experience? We know that a clean
house sells faster. We know that bad smells in a home (cigarette smoke,
dog odors, strong cooking odors) will keep a house from selling. We
know that a dark home is harder to sell than a light one. We know that
neutral colors are better than stronger tones. And, most of all, we know
that most buyers have no imagination when it comes to places that need
work.

So how do we apply this information to setting the stage properly for
an open house? The first thing we need to remember is the purpose that
the open house serves. That purpose is almost always two-fold: We want
to sell the house, and we want to capture the buyer. So when we stage the

home, we need to keep in mind that we're selling not only the house, but ourselves and our services as well.

Selling the House

When we are staging the open house, we want to make sure that we take advantage of all of the nonverbal cues we can to tell the buyers that this is a great house:

1. Before you even think of having the open house, you want to make sure that the sellers have cleaned the house thoroughly and removed all clutter that might make the home feel unkempt, disorganized, and small.

2. Put on soft, soothing music. Buyers want to feel that their home is a place to relax, so make it feel relaxing.

3. Open all the window shades to bring in as much natural light as possible. Then turn on all of the lights in the house too. A light home is a happy home in the mind of the buyers.

4. Burn a French Vanilla scented candle (since women are the decision makers for most real estate sales) or baked cookies made with vanilla to drag the scent through the house.

5. Offer food to the buyers. The offer of food and drink is a well-established ritual of hospitality recognized all over the world as a way of welcoming a stranger into your home. It makes them feel welcomed and wanted.

6. Offer them a place to sit and relax. Buyers want to feel relaxed in their home. Standing up is not a position that we use to relax. We relax when seated or lying down. Offer a chair (a comfortable one) to make them feel more at home.

7. Don't talk too much. Answer questions and ask a few of your own, but don't talk to hear yourself speak. You should never say, "and this is the dining room"—duh, anyone who sees the table and chairs could tell you that. If it's self-explanatory, then don't say it. The spaces you leave in the conversation are the times that the buyer has to consider how this house fits in his life. If you leave no space, then he can't consider it.

8. Keep the temperature set at a comfortable level. This is important both for you and for the buyers. You need to be physically comfortable for you to be able to be at your best when speaking to the buyers. They need to be comfortable in order for them to consider

lingering to learn more about the house and you. In general, if the house is not heated in the winter nor air-conditioned in the middle of a heat wave, don't have the open house there.

9. Have something soft and fuzzy on the counter for the buyers to play with, like a stuffed animal or a fuzzy ball. Those buyers who are very touch-oriented (kinesthetic) will associate the pleasant sensations with the home and with you.

Exhibit 9-1 is another form that will help you prepare for your open house as well.

Exhibit 9-1. Preparing for an open house.

- Write open house ad.
- Place open house ad in the paper for the day before and day of the open house.
- Make ten copies of MLS printout for property.
- Make ten copies of brochure for property.
- Make ten copies of financing sheet for property.
- Staple all copies together with a business card.
- Make five copies of the Open House Sign-in Sheet—fill in property address on the first one.
- Bring copies of any special buyer or seller reports you may have.
- Bring Agency Disclosure Forms and Agency Disclosure Sign to post.
- Bring a pen (for the sign-in sheet).
- Bring "thank you" notes so that you can write them during lulls.
- Put open-house signs in car—remember to save one for the house itself.
- Bring clipboard with Prospect Sheets.

If the property is vacant:
- Bring toilet paper.
- Bring folding chair(s) to sit on.
- Bring a portable heater if it's winter and the heat is off.
- Bring bottled water to keep your mouth moist when you're talking to buyers.

This form reprinted with permission from *The New Agent's Survival Guide to Real Estate* available through Sparta Success Systems at www.spartasuccess.com.

Selling Our Services

The second thing we are selling when we hold an open house is our services. We know that most of the people walking through the door are interesting in buying a home. We also know that most of them will not buy this one (only 1 to 2 percent of houses sell from an open house). So our goal is to connect with these buyers while they are in front of us. We want them to get to know us and like us so that they will let us find them a house that they will buy. This is when those rapport-building muscles really count.

We are in a setting that is by its very nature a distant and disconnected contact with the prospect. They are there to see the house. We have to respect that. We are there to get the buyers to work with us. Most of them don't know this, but they've probably been hassled by a few other real estate agents along the way as they've looked at other places earlier that day. If it's the fourth home they've seen they're probably getting tired. Once again, stand in their shoes and think about what it is like to be them. They're tired of dodging agents' questions. The houses are starting to run together in their brains. They're probably a little disappointed that they can't afford more house for what they have to spend. They're feeling disheartened, besieged, and grumpy, and we want to connect with them? Are we nuts?

Yes, actually we are. That's why we're real estate agents. I haven't yet met an agent who wasn't cracked even a little. That's what makes us special. We live for the challenge. We want to make them happy again— preferably happy with us.

So what do we do? Given our understanding of how these buyers are feeling, we offer them a seat and a beverage. We ask them to talk for a while about the houses that they've seen today. Did they like what they saw? We get them to tell us stories about the other agents if they even hint that they have something to say about the subject. We don't pry. We don't dig. We let them relax and get comfortable. Would they like a refill on their drinks? Fabulous, we'll be happy to get it. How about a cookie? They're fresh from the oven. Yes? Lovely. If they seem interested, perhaps we'll share about how many people have been through the house today and what our week has been like (good things only please, we're trying to reduce their stress, not drag them into ours). Finally, when they seem like they've calmed down, we might ask what they are looking for. At this point, it's part of the casual conversation that we've established, not a prying question asked by another pushy real estate agent. They begin to open up and we're on our way to signing them on with us. Why? Because we treated them like friends who had come over rather than prospects (a.k.a. fresh meat). People will respond to us the same way we act toward them. If we treat them as friends, then that's how they will react, and they'll love us for it. (For the rules on clients attending other open houses, see Chapter 11.)

Presenting Financial Information

Our tonality and demeanor are never more important than when we are presenting information that relates to someone's finances. This means that when we are discussing an offer with a buyer or a seller, or we are telling the seller what he will get for his house, we need to be keenly aware of not only *what* we say, but *how* we say it.

I didn't realize how much I changed my tonality and demeanor when doing these types of presentations until I was training to be certified to teach ERA's AccelERAtion course. We were practicing on how to present the pricing piece of the CMA and I was playing the agent while another person was playing the seller. When I presented the information, I spoke in softer tones, speaking more slowly than usual, and being very soft in my demeanor as well. I didn't push on anything I said, in fact quite the opposite. I was soft and cuddly in the way that I dealt with the discussion. I didn't say "no" to anything, instead I went back to educating and asked for a decision from the seller based on the new information. My shift in approach was so noticeable, in fact, that the instructor looked at me, laughed, and said, "Well aren't you just my little buttered biscuit." (She was from the South originally—can you tell?)

Now anyone who has met me before will tell you that this is *not* my normal way of being. I am normally loud and boisterous. Honestly, I have often been called intimidating and overwhelming. But not when I talk finances to a client or prospect. Then, I pull back on the reins of the powerhouse side of me and I sit in a "no pressure" space with them. They will never be comfortable making a decision if they feel that I am pushing them in any way.

Most people need space to think and to see whether they feel comfortable with a decision. Few are comfortable making an on-the-spot decision without any time to reflect, especially when it comes to money. Being willing to sit in silence as they ponder their options is one of the best gifts we can offer to the prospect/client and to ourselves. If we can be patient and wait for them, then they are more likely to decide in our favor.

Office Space

Our office is the place where we make our business's first impression. Periodically we need to take a hard look around our office space, to see it from the client's perspective. Is it welcoming? Is it warm? Does it make our clients want to come back again and again? Is there privacy to discuss financial and personal matters? Would our clients feel safe there?

These are all questions that we need to ask ourselves if we are going to create a physical space that inspires referral and repeat business. When designing our work space, we need to keep in mind the psychological effect it will have on our clients. If it doesn't feel welcoming and warm, why would they want to be there? For that matter, why would we?

One of the ways to make our clients feel welcome is to incorporate them into our office space. When I was actively selling real estate, I made a regular practice of taking pictures of my clients in front of their houses or at the closing table. I kept those pictures on my wall in several of those big picture collage hangers. People would ask me when they came into my space if they were pictures of my family. I said yes, in a way they were. They were pictures of my real estate family. All of them were people that I had helped to move forward in their lives by buying or selling a home with them. This always caused my clients' faces to light up, knowing that their picture would soon be on the wall too. They felt as though their faces belonged on my wall, so they felt as though they belonged in my office. It was a simple statement that I cared, and sometimes the simplest statements are the most profound.

Being Professional

One final thought before we move on. I often hear students, especially new agents, talk about the importance of appearing "professional." It seems that they feel that if they give off a professional air, that they will get more business as a result. In response to this statement by them, I ask one question. Do you feel a loyalty to your doctor, dentist, attorney, banker, or anyone else you would consider to be a professional? The answer is almost always "no." If they do feel a loyalty, it is usually as a result of that doctor, attorney, etc., stepping out of their professional role and into a personal relationship with the agent. We don't form loyalty and advocate relationships with professionals. We form them with people. If we don't see the person behind the role, then we will not be driven to help them build their business. This is the way it is with our clients too.

Yes, it is important to be professional in our practice. What I mean by professional in this context is returning calls, cultivating good relationships with other agents, meeting deadlines, properly advising our clients of their rights and responsibilities, completing paperwork in a timely and neat fashion, etc. In short—being a professional in real estate means doing our jobs. It does not mean maintaining a disdainful, superior distance from our clients. It doesn't mean taking a "you need me" approach. These last two items are the things that will destroy any rapport you have built with your prospects. We need to be professional by doing our jobs. Then we need to be personal to build rapport, trust, loyalty, and eventually referral advocates.

CHAPTER 10

MANAGING YOUR CLIENTS' EXPECTATIONS

We all want our clients to love us. We want them to love us so much that they refer all of their friends and family to us. But this is not always the response we get. In fact, sometimes our clients are less than happy with us. They have high hopes about what we will deliver and if we fail to live up to those hopes, then we can say goodbye to those happy feelings and all the referrals we were hoping to get. Sad, but true.

None of us want unhappy clients. None of us set out to disappoint. But disappoint we do when we fail to meet our clients' expectations. The key to creating a good relationship with our client is in the way that we manage their expectations. At the outset, it is important for us to define what they can and cannot expect from us. We need to lay out a clear set of goals, services, and promises. If we don't set our standards of service in the very beginning, then our clients will do it for us. And then we're stuck with it. Better to do it ourselves and stay in control of the relationship than leave our fate up to chance.

Setting the Bar

So how do we set our clients' expectations? How do we lay out our ground rules? It's very simple. We tell them what to expect. We educate them about how a transaction generally flows. We tell them what day we take off each week. We tell them what days and times we are available to them. We tell them when they can expect to hear from us next. Every time we speak to a client, it is likely that we will, at some point in that conversation, set a new expectation for them. So the key to setting our clients' expectations where we want them is to be careful about what we tell them to expect.

119

Systems for Setting Clients' Expectations

We should have a Client Expectations list. This is a written list of every-thing a buyer or a seller can expect of us. Obviously, we will need a different list for buyers and for sellers. This list should detail all of the services that we offer, the times we will make contact, our response rate on phone calls, the fact that we will be taking time off each week to rest and rejuvenate, etc. Exhibits 10-1 and 10-2 are samples of the type of information I would give to my clients.

Exhibit 10-1. What you can expect when you list your home with me.

- I will return your calls promptly. The best number to use to reach me is 555-555-5555. You will hear from me within two hours if you call between 9:00 A.M. and 5:00 P.M. on one of my work days. You will hear from me by noon the following work day if you call after 5:00 P.M. or on my day off.
- You will receive a copy of my typical schedule so that you will know the best times to reach me.
- I will consult with you on your home sale. I will educate you about the market so that you will make an informed decision that is right for you. I will never try to make that decision for you.
- I will help you to properly stage your home to sell. I will do this by offering you tips on how to rearrange furniture, what repairs to make, and what to pack away before we begin showing the house.
- You will receive weekly updates on the progress of your listing. These may come as phone calls, letters, or e-mails.
- You will receive a copy of each ad I place for your home within a week of when it was run.
- I will keep all of your personal information confidential except what you expressly tell me to share with buyers and their agents.
- We will review the market and how your house is positioned in relation to the market on a monthly basis. I will make recommendations based on these reviews.
- I will be honest and fair in all my dealings with you and the buyers of your home.
- I place all offers received at the top of my priority list, everything else comes second.
- I will negotiate on your behalf to get you the best deal while still maintaining a positive relationship between us and the people on the buyer's side of the deal.
- When you accept an offer on your house, you will receive a list from me of all the things you need to do before closing.
- I want to know how you are feeling throughout the process. I deal

with a lot of people in transition and I can often offer you tools that will help you to better handle the stresses involved in your move.

- I will take at least one full day off per week to rest and rejuvenate myself, so I can be at the top of my game for you. I am not available on my days off. I will arrange for another agent to cover for me on those days.
- I will participate in ongoing education so that I can learn about the latest developments in the industry and create more value for you, my client. This will occasionally mean that I am not available on the day of a class, except at breaks.

Exhibit 10-2. What you can expect when you hire me as your buyer's agent.

- I will return your calls promptly. The best number to use to reach me is 555-555-5555. You will hear from me within two hours if you call between 9:00 A.M. and 5:00 P.M. on one of my work days. You will hear from me by noon the following work day if you call after 5:00 P.M. or on my day off.
- You will receive a copy of my typical schedule so that you will know the best times to reach me.
- You will receive daily updates on the properties available in your area and price range that meet your stated needs.
- I will never show you more than six houses in a day. This is for your benefit so that you can accurately remember the houses you have seen and be able to reflect appropriately on their ability to meet your needs.
- I will consult with you on your home purchase. I will educate you about the market so that you will make an informed decision that is right for you. I will never try to make that decision for you.
- I will keep all of your personal information confidential except what you expressly tell me to share with the sellers and their agent.
- We will review the market and how your needs fit in relation to the market on a monthly basis. I will make recommendations based on these reviews.
- I place all offers written at the top of my priority list, everything else comes second.
- I will negotiate on your behalf to get you the best deal while still maintaining a positive relationship between us and the people on the seller's side of the deal.
- When your offer on a house is accepted, you will receive a list from me of all the things you need to do before closing.
- I will be honest and fair in all my dealings with you and the sellers of your home.

- I want to know how you are feeling throughout the process. I deal with a lot of people in transition and I can often offer you tools that will help you to better handle the stresses involved in your move.
- I will take at least one full day off per week to rest and rejuvenate myself, so I can be at the top of my game for you. I am not available on my days off. I will arrange for another agent to cover for me on those days.
- I will participate in ongoing education so that I can learn about the latest developments in the industry and create more value for you, my client. This will occasionally mean that I am not available on the day of a class, except at breaks.

By setting our clients' expectations of us up front, we limit their ability to set them in a way we would rather not have to meet. It also gives us the opportunity to keep the clients reasonable, honest, and on track.

Here's an example of setting good expectations. When I met with a buyer for the first time, I told them: "Great! OK, be prepared. I know the market so well that I should be able to find your house for you in six showings or less. If we get to the sixth house and we haven't found your home yet, then I didn't understand something about what you wanted. If this happens, we will have to go back to the office and go over what you want again so I can make sure I understand it. OK?"

In offering up these comments, I told the buyers several things. First, they needed to be ready to buy immediately. Second, they didn't need to see the entire market before making a decision because I knew the market for them. And third, that if they didn't find a house in the first six houses, there would be a consequence (going back to the drawing board). At no point in the conversation did I say that they *had* to pick one of the first six houses—in fact I told them it would be my fault if we didn't find the house for them. But I also set up the expectation in their minds that they would *want* to buy one of those first six houses.

Obviously if I use this approach, I need to be very careful about the houses that I choose to show them. I will want to only show them properties that meet their criteria. Otherwise I lose face based on this comment. If I do happen to show someone something by accident that doesn't work for them, I always apologize saying "Wow, I'm sorry. I thought this house would be close to what you wanted, but this is not at all what I expected to see when we got inside." This way I let the buyers know that I didn't think the house was appropriate, it just didn't meet my expectations.

It's also important to set expectations when negotiating. I once had a listing that was being purchased by relocation buyers with a local company. From what I had discovered from the other agents in the area, I expected that these buyers would negotiate until the very last instant, taking every opportunity to reduce the price. So I set my sellers' expectations for this. I told them to make sure they only negotiated down to $1,000 more than what they would actually be willing to take on the property. The last $1,000 was left for negotiations on the home inspection. The sellers agreed to this plan. So when the buyers came back at the home inspection and asked for $500 toward repairs, the sellers happily agreed. Now in the sellers' minds, they had gotten $500 more than they expected, rather than feeling that they were out $500. They also thought that I was the most amazing agent they had seen—all because I set their expectations in advance.

Discovering Hidden Expectations

Sometimes our clients harbor hidden expectations. There are things that they expect to happen (or not to happen) that they have not told us about. After telling them what they can expect from us, we should ask our clients what they would like to be able to expect from us. This way, we get a chance to address those issues up front. If they are reasonable, we can tell them that we will be happy to accommodate them. If they are unreasonable, then we have the opportunity to address that as well. It is important to reset expectations that are unreasonable. We can't let them fester or we will ensure that we will have problems in the future.

We shouldn't worry about telling a client up front that he is not going to get some service that he wants. Instead, we should explain to him *why* it is that we can't reasonably offer this service to him—let him in behind the scenes of our business, explain how our business works and what our lives are like. We should tell him the reasoning behind our refusal. If the reason is valid, then he will see that. If he doesn't accept it, then this is a good indicator that we don't want him as a client. If he won't see reason now, then he certainly won't do so later either. Better to get out now before you're too invested in him.

Sometimes clients have expectations they haven't voiced, even though we specifically asked. These unvoiced expectations will fester if we're not meeting them. It is not hard to determine when this is happening. Usually the client will get surly with us. She will give us curt answers and be cold toward us. The first thing we have to do is to identify what it is that she is expecting that we are not delivering. At this point, we shouldn't be afraid to jump out of whatever conversation we are having and simply ask her what the problem is. The question could be posed in this way: "Sally,

I'm sensing that you are not happy. Is there something that you were expecting of me that I haven't come through on?"

We can't be afraid to open that door. We *want* Sally to express her complaints. Only when she complains do we have the opportunity to fix the problem. And how we handle the complaint is more important than anything we have done to date. If we argue with her about what she feels to be a valid position on her part, we will do more damage than has already been done. We need to try to step into her shoes—try to understand why it is that Sally is unhappy. We should start off our response with an acknowledgment that she is upset.

"Wow, I'm really sorry you're upset, Sally."

Notice we haven't admitted fault with this comment, only that we are sorry she's upset. And we *are* sorry she's upset. If she wasn't upset, then we wouldn't have to be having this uncomfortable conversation.

Next, we're going to more clearly identify the problem while showing her that we've heard and understood her complaint.

"So, if I understand you correctly, you're upset that I'm not responding to your messages fast enough. Is that right?" This gives her the opportunity to correct us if we didn't understand what her real concern was.

"What was your expectation about how quickly I should be getting back to you?"

We need to identify her expectation, so that we know where she is coming from. We must be careful here. We can't ask, "Well, what did you expect?" This can come off as aggressive and rude. *Phrasing is everything when we are dealing with someone who is upset.*

"And why is that timing so important to you?"

The tone that we use to say this phrase (or one like it) is critical. We need to be smooth and calm in our tone. We must convey that we really want to understand why she needs to hear back from us so quickly. If she starts to bristle, then we explain to her that we are not questioning her need, only trying to understand it better.

"Is there anything else you feel I need to understand about this issue that we haven't discussed?"

This gives her the opportunity to expand on the problem if she has something to add that wasn't covered by one of our previous questions. It is also her final chance to vent. We have made it clear that we are willing to listen if she will express herself.

"OK, so let me make sure I heard you right. You are concerned that I don't return your calls within half an hour. You're worried about this because you're afraid that you might lose a house if you don't move fast enough. Is that right?"

This is one final chance for her to change her mind. It's also us proving to her that we listened. Now it's our chance to respond. We have been reasonable in listening to her concerns, now she owes us the same in return.

"I can see how that would be a concern for you, Sally. I want to make this work for you. But I have a problem on my end. I go into appointments with clients periodically. Those appointments last for up to two hours at times. Just like when I had my appointment with you, remember? I turn off my cell phone when I meet with other people so that I can give them my undivided attention. I can't retrieve my messages until I am done with that appointment. I don't want to short-change my other clients from getting the same level of service you got, and I'm sure you don't want that either. So how can we solve this problem? Is there some way that I can meet your needs without short-changing my other clients?"

We've validated Sally's concern. We've expressed a desire to make it right. We've let her in behind the scenes of our business so that she understands where we are coming from as well. We've gotten her to acknowledge that expecting us to call within half an hour would be damaging to the service that other people get and unfair to them. And finally, we've enlisted Sally as part of the solution. She may not have an answer when we ask that question, but at least she will understand that coming up with an answer is a challenge, and that will make her appreciate the effort all the more.

"So let me ask you this, Sally. If I were to arrange for you to immediately get the address of the property you are interested in so you could drive by and see if the neighborhood works for you, would that be a good solution? Obviously, I would call you immediately when I got out of my appointment so that we could schedule a showing if you liked what you saw on the drive-by. How does that sound?" Although we can't reasonably meet Sally's expectations, we can address her underlying concern, which is losing out on the house.

We are proposing a solution, which is fairly simple to implement. When we send Sally listings, she gets the addresses. There is nothing more for us to do. If she likes the drive-by then she calls for an appointment.

"I do need one thing from you to make this work though. I need you to be clear when you leave your message for me. You need to tell me the address, the MLS number, the agent's name, and their phone number when you call. You also need to tell me what times you have available to see the property. You need to give me three times that will work for you so that I have options when I call to schedule. If you can do this, you won't have to wait for me to return to the office and be able to look up the listing before I can call to schedule the appointment. Does this work for you?"

Now, we've placed the burden of a quick response back on Sally. If she fails to give us the information we've requested, then we have the right to take longer to make the call.

"Also, there's one more rule here. I don't normally give out the information including the agent's name and contact info. I'm doing this especially for you to meet your needs. You need to promise me that, no matter how desperate you are to get into a property, you will NOT call the listing agent directly. That would create a major problem for both of us if you decide to buy the property and it will get me yelled at by the other agent. I'm breaking my rules for you here and I'm trusting you to keep up your end of the bargain. Can you live with that?"

We have told Sally that we are doing something special for her, changing our way of doing business, to make sure she is happy. She will feel honored that we are taking such efforts. She will agree not to call the agent directly.

"OK, so in the future, I'll send you complete listings including the agent's name and number. You can drive by anything that looks good to you. When you find something you like you're going to call me with the following information." We should write this list down so she doesn't forget anything. "I need the agent's name, phone number, the address of the house, and the MLS number. I also need you to list at least three times when you are available for showings. And you need to leave me your phone numbers where you'll be for the next few hours so that I can reach you if I need to change anything. OK? Good. Is this an acceptable solution to the problem?"

We should get one final approval from Sally before we let this particular issue drop. And then we make sure she takes the list we wrote down with her so that she remembers what her commitment is in the deal.

"Great! I'm really glad you talked to me about this. I want you to be happy with the service you receive from me. If you have any other concerns, now or in the future, please let me know as soon as they come up. I don't want you to be unhappy for any longer than absolutely necessary. Give me the chance to fix it. I'm great at coming up with equitable solutions. OK?"

This tells Sally that we are open to hearing other problems she may have. It also tells her that we have no hard feelings over her expressing this one.

Now obviously, this is not a script that we can use with everyone. It's simply an example of the type of conversation we might have with a client. The idea is for us to take this example and use it to understand the underlying structure of the discussion.

Understand the Possible Pitfalls

- *Don't get stuck in a blaming discussion.* When someone is upset, it is her show. She is the one who gets to be emotional. We need to be rational and reasonable and above all compassionate about her feelings. The last thing we want to do is point fingers and say that she has unreasonable expectations. We need to bring her to a point of understanding of our situation, but we can only do this by first seeking to understand hers. Until she feels heard, she is not going to listen to us.

- *Don't argue over something that isn't relevant.* Many times people get stuck in conversations that go nowhere because the issue they are arguing about isn't the actual problem. They are fighting over a symptom, not the core issue. When we speak with a client who is upset, our first goal is to find out what the core issue is. We need to keep asking questions until we feel relatively sure (we can never actually be certain) that we are talking about the real problem.

- *Don't get defensive.* The minute we get defensive, we have lost control of the conversation. This is not about us—it's about the client. We can't give her back a sense of equanimity if we have lost our own.

Problem-Solving Tools

- *Use the word "we."* The key in any dispute is to get both parties to feel as though they are on the same side working together to find a solution. Using the word "we" assumes that you and the client are on the same side.

- *Get the client to invest finding a solution.* When she calls, Sally assumes that this is our problem and therefore our job to fix it—she has abdicated any responsibility in the situation. You need to get her to take some of that responsibility back by having her help you find a good solution to her problem.

- *Solve the underlying problem, not the symptom.* When seeking to resolve the issue, it is important that you look to solve the core issue with the client. This may not always be obvious. You may need to do a little digging to find out what the actual issue is.

A Quick Review

The minute we realize there is a problem, we need to:

- Address the client's concern directly—don't beat around the bush.
- Ask for details to identify the problem.
- Rephrase those concerns back to the client to be certain that we understand what she is upset about.
- Ask for the underlying reasons why this is a concern for the client.
- Ask for more information if we feel we may not have the whole story.
- Explain our situation to the client.
- Ask for the client's help in creating a workable solution.
- Agree upon a solution for the current moment.
- If necessary, put in place a plan for solving or avoiding the problem in the future as well.

This is a hard conversation to have, but it's a worthwhile one. If we don't address the issue, then it will fester. And issues that fester only get worse over time. No matter how afraid of confrontation we are, we need to get over it. The sooner we deal with a problem, the sooner it goes away. We only make it worse when we worry and fret over things. We add more energy into the situation than it deserves and we blow it all out of proportion. We can't let our fear of our client's reaction keep us from talking to her.

When It's Not About Us

Occasionally, we will find that people are upset and distant for a completely unrelated reason. We may think that they are upset with us, but instead we find that they are simply stressed about some other aspect of the deal or their life. We should be careful when managing our clients' expectations that we also manage our own.

We as agents tend to take on responsibility for everything we touch. We assume that if someone is angry, then it is our fault. This is not always the case and should not be our automatic assumption. Sometimes people are just overwhelmed. It's not our fault. We should be patient and willing to listen. A friendly shoulder to lean on in tough times is often worth its weight in gold to the person doing the leaning.

Underpromise and Overdeliver

As agents, most of us are people-pleasers. We want to be able to give a client everything he wants. We want to say "yes" to every request, no matter how outrageous. We want the client to think we walk on water. So we tend to overpromise. And this can be disastrous to our relationship with that client when we fail to deliver on those promises.

No matter where we set our clients' expectations, it had better be someplace where we can meet them. If we promise the moon and the stars, we will get no credit for just delivering the moon—no matter how amazing that feat may be. So we must be careful what we promise. Even if we think we can have it to our client by the end of the day, we should tell him that he will have it tomorrow by noon. Then, if we deliver it early, we're a hero. And if we're running late by our schedule, we're still on-time by his.

If we are not good at keeping our promises, then we need to take a hard look at a couple of things. Are we being unreasonable with our promises or are we just failing to follow up? If we are failing to follow up, then we need to do one of two things. Either we need to hire someone to be our promise-keeper, or we need to set aside some time each day to focus on keeping our promises. We'll talk more about this in the chapter on time management (Chapter 20).

However, if we find that we are making unrealistic promises to our clients, then we need to really look at why we are doing this. Are we trying to glean short-term admiration from our clients? Or are we just promising them something to avoid conflict? Habitual, unrealistic, over-promising is often the result of a self-esteem problem in the agent. We need to figure out why we do it and address that issue. When we do, we will find it much easier to be honest with our clients about what we can and can't do for them in the future.

We can't avoid this issue. It is a terrible downward spiral. When we overpromise to make someone happy, then we fail to deliver, we make him angry. His anger causes him to yell at us and this degrades our self-esteem even further, making it even more likely that we will overpromise again. We can't fall into this trap. We need to deal with our self-esteem problems first.

Beating Out the Competition

Sometimes we overpromise in the hopes of getting the business. We think that another agent has been able to promise something, so we should promise it too. This is a fallacy. Just as that agent didn't arrange his business around our promises, neither should we build our business around his.

Perhaps that agent can promise a faster response time because he has very little business to pull him away from the few clients he has. Perhaps he has five agents on staff who can return the call, but none of them are fully familiar with the listing to be able to speak intelligently about it. For every positive that any agent offers, there is a drawback that comes with it. This is the nature of the business. Agents choose what is important to them to offer in their businesses and then they build their practices around those services.

We cannot hope to compete with another agent on his own turf. And we shouldn't try. We need to know what our value proposition is and why the client should care. If we do a good job of selling the client on that value proposition, she will not expect us to keep the other agent's promises. If we believe that what we are offering has value and we can convey that value to the potential client, then we don't have to make unreasonable promises to get the business.

CHAPTER 11

SALES
PRESENTATIONS

There are some logistical issues that need to be addressed before we sit down with a potential client to begin the presentation. The majority of these issues focus around the environment in which we are presenting. We want to arrange the physical environment in such a way as to create the most comfortable, least distracting environment for the client. We want the client to be relaxed and in a position to be able to make a decision by the end of the presentation.

No Distractions

The first issue we want to address is one of distractions. If the potential client has children with them, then we need to find a way to occupy the children while we are doing our presentation. Whether this is by putting them in a room with a television and playing a DVD or giving them a coloring book, we need to keep them occupied so that they are not continually vying for their parents' attention.

Speaking of televisions, we need to be out of earshot of any TVs that are on. The noise in the background makes it difficult both for us and for the potential clients to focus on the issue at hand. This is also true for radios (unless it is a CD with soothing music playing in the background). If there is a nosy animal in the place (like a dog that is pushy for attention), we may also ask whether the dog can be put in another room for the duration of the presentation. (We need to be careful when we do this not to insult the sellers or indicate that we don't like the animal.)

For ourselves, we need to make a point of turning off our cell phone. We can do this in front of the potential clients so that they are clear that we are setting this time aside especially for them. It also gives us the opportunity to ask them to turn off their cell phones as well.

Seating

Finally, we want to be in control of where people sit at the table. If we are in the office, then we will be in the conference room. If we are at the client's house, then we'll be at the dining room table. In either instance, we want to be in one of two configurations. Either we want to be at the head of the table with both clients either to our right or left—this is the preferred position since it puts us in the power seat. Alternatively, we want to be on one side of the table with one client at the head of the table and the other sitting across from us. We do not want to be at the head of the table with a client on either side since this creates a problem with showing our presentation to the clients (it's always upside down to one of them) and it makes us go back and forth "ping-ponging" our presentation from one person to another. The absolutely worst way for us to be sitting is with us on one side and the clients on the other. This puts us psychologically at odds with them (see Exhibit 11-1).

Exhibit 11-1. Layout of presentation table. (White box represents the agent, the black boxes represent the clients.)

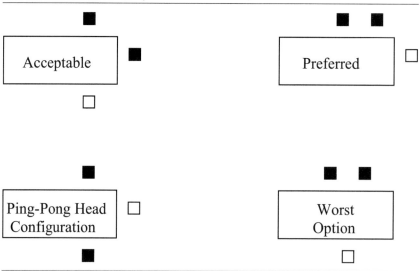

Buyer Presentations

Now that we have the basics of presentations down, we can move on to the issue of the buyer agency presentation in particular. Depending on where we are in the country, buyer agency may be brand new or commonplace. Make no mistake, buyer agency is the wave of the future. And with the advent of buyer agency, it becomes even more important to be able to connect with the buyers in the initial consultation phase. When we connect with the buyers, it is easier to get them to sign on with us as their buyer's agent. It's also easier to work throughout the process, since connection often translates quickly to trust.

The key to this process is that it is an extremely soft sell. We approach it as educators. We teach the buyers what they need to know about the process, no matter who they decide to work with. We repeat phrases such as, "No matter whom you hire, what you'll need to know is . . ." and "Whether you're working with me or someone else, here's the important thing to remember . . ." over and over again throughout a presentation. This backs us off from the salesperson mode and puts us into a consultant mode. It gives the buyers space to make their decision without pressure from us. And it builds trust.

Setting the Stage

The first thing we want to do in our presentation is to tell the buyer what our presentation will be about and the order that we will go through it. It gives the buyer a sense of safety that they will know what comes next. It puts them as ease and lets them know, up front, what is expected of them. We should be clear with them that we are intending to educate them throughout the process and give them permission to stop us along the way if they have any questions.

Assessing the Buyer's History with Real Estate Agents

Next, we want to find out whether the buyers have had a bad experience with a real estate agent. If they have, then we want them to tell the story. Whatever issues they found to be that agent's faults are the same issues we need to address to sell them on hiring us. If they had a great experience, then we need to find out why they enjoyed it and then sell them on the fact that we can offer them a similar experience. If the buyer had a good experience with their last agent and they aren't using them this time around, then ask why that is. The answers to these questions are always enlightening.

What we find most often is that the buyer has lost track of their agent over the years (actually we all know it's the other way around—the agent lost track of the buyer). They would have used that agent again, but they don't because the agent failed to keep in touch or got out of the business.

We'll want to remember this tidbit when we talk about past client contact programs a little later in the conversation. If the buyers have never worked with an agent before, then we want to give them an idea of what our role is in the transaction. They currently have no context for what our job is and now is the time for us to explain that to them.

Setting Up the Consultant Role

No matter whether these buyers have worked with an agent before or not, we will want to explain to them what we see our role as being. We should explain that we see ourselves as a consultant. It allows us to set ourselves up in buyers' minds as a helper rather than a salesperson. We also want to explain to the buyers that our job is to educate them, not to make decisions for them. This will provide the buyers with a sense of security and safety in dealing with us. People are always on the defensive around salespeople because they're afraid of being talked into buying something they don't want.

Explaining the Process

When we asked whether the buyers had worked with an agent before, we probably got a good idea of how experienced they are in buying homes. Regardless of their experience level, we should at the very least quickly run through the process with them. It's usually been several years since their last purchase and they probably don't remember everything. And even if they do, there are always law changes and varying customs for different areas that can affect the transaction's flow along the way.

If these are first-time homebuyers, then this will be a much longer conversation. We will want to go into detail about how the transaction works. They will need definitions of terms as well as an understanding of the role each person in the transaction plays. Remember that this is all new to them. Try to make it friendly by using simple, non-jargon-like terms. Expect to have to repeat yourself too. They will ask a lot of questions. Questions are good. They let us know that the buyers are listening.

Lead Paint and Fair Housing

As a matter of law, we need to give our buyers a copy of the lead paint booklet. I like to cover fair housing with them at the same time. We want to educate them about lead paint, answering any immediate questions that they may have and telling them how important it is that they read the booklet before they have to make an offer on a house. This way they will be educated enough to know whether they want a lead paint test done.

This is also our opportunity to tell the buyers about how we will not discriminate. Since this is a sensitive subject for some people, I often throw in a little humor. I say, "I don't discriminate when selling you a home. If your money is green—I'll take it." This usually gets a little giggle and lowers the tension levels all around.

Negotiations

Not all agents are created equal. Some have good negotiating skills and some do not. If this is a particular skill we possess, then we should brag about it. We should also take this time to set our buyers' expectations around the negotiating we will do for them.

Buyers need to understand that we will *not* be trying to rake the sellers over the coals in this transaction. It is rarely in a client's best interests for us to try to steal the house from the sellers. There are so many things that a seller can do in a transaction—good and bad—to affect the outcome. I have seen sellers put in brand-new carpeting for buyers they liked (without being asked). I have also seen sellers purposely throw away thousands of dollars' worth of lawn equipment, fail to maintain the yard, and avoid doing maintenance on a house because they didn't like the buyers. There are a hundred little things that sellers can do to help or hinder buyers in the transaction. It pays (literally) to make the sellers like the buyers.

The other reason not to work on raking the sellers over the coals is the other agent in the transaction. Agents are sensitive people—and we have long memories. Many of us adopt our clients as family and we take it very personally when someone makes it their business to try to steal our clients' money from them. If we do manage to get the steal of the century on this house, our next client will pay the price for this client's good fortune. The agent whose seller got the short end of the stick will start talking it up in the real estate community. All the listing agents will be on the lookout for us. They will make it more difficult to get into properties so that they have less chance of having to co-broke with us. They will coach their sellers not to negotiate down so quickly because they will assume that we will ask for more than what is reasonable. In short, we will be paying for the "good deal" we got for years to come.

Buyers need to realize that one of the best things they have going for them is our good name in the industry. An agent's reputation is what gets her in the door to listings. If she is known as being difficult to work with, then listing agents will be slower to return her calls. They will make it more difficult for her to schedule a showing at a convenient time for her. And, in the event that there are multiple offers on a house, they will take the other offers over hers if they can at all arrange for it. When an agent has a good reputation in the industry, the opposite is true. It is in the buyer's best interests for us to maintain those strong relationships with other agents.

Interviewing the Buyer

This process is a significant one. We are looking to find out how the buyers use their home. We need to get into their head, ask if they have any hobbies that the home needs to accommodate, or if anyone else is living with them who needs to be accounted for in the plans. Do they have pets? Why are they looking where they are? Are they comfortable purchasing in the price range the mortgage officer gave them or would their budget be happier if they looked a little lower? How long do they plan to be in the home? What sort of neighborhood (if any) do they want to be in and why?

When we interview the buyer, we will want to get both the physical requirements of the home (3 bedrooms, 2 baths, garage, etc.) and the reasons for those requirements (one of the bedrooms will be a den; the garage will be used for storage, not for parking cars). In this way we can modify the physical details if needed without damaging the client's ability to make full use of the home in the ways they intend. For instance, if the garage is used for storage, then a walk-up attic, a barn, or a large storage shed would likely serve the same purpose.

The buyer will be ready with the answers about number of bedrooms and baths as well as location and price. But she will be surprised when we start asking about how she will use the home. These are the critical factor questions though. These are the ones that if we don't ask them, we could think that the old "buyers are liars" adage is true. It's not. The truth is that agents don't ask the right questions.

When interviewing the buyer, we want to listen for repeated words, concepts, phrases, and feelings. These are the indicators of what is truly important to this client. It is those factors that we will repeat back to the buyers at the end of this interview process.

When the interview is complete, we need to rephrase the items off of our list and repeat them back to the buyers with the understanding that we are making sure we have it right. The comments we make should include the emotional content of the reasons that they want certain items. For instance, we might say:

> OK, Sally, I'm going to repeat this back to you to make sure that I understand you and we have everything down that is important. We're looking for a house with a master bedroom, a guest room, and an office space. There needs to be at least one and a half baths so that you don't have to let your guests into your personal bathroom. We want the house to be on a quiet street in a nice neighborhood within a close commuting distance to your work. There should be a small yard that you can sit in to relax but that doesn't require huge amounts of maintenance. It should have a pool so that you can get your exercise in the morning without having to deal with all those kids at your fitness center. It will be a place for you to have a few moments of peace and quiet before you begin your hectic day at work. Plus, it will add another facet to your entertaining options when you have friends over. In short, we're looking for a retreat for you—someplace where you can go to hide away from the cares of the world. It should be a place where you can relax, have your friends over, and not have to worry about anything. Do I have that right?

By telling the client not only the physical factors that they requested, but also putting them into the emotional context, we are proving to the client that we understand her needs. She feels heard and she knows that we not only have her best interests at heart, but we also understand those interests very well. If we do this process well, then we will be in a position to sign the buyer on immediately after this conversation.

Discussing Agency

At this point, it's time to bring out the buyer agency contract. We will need to inform the buyer of his options in regards to hiring or not hiring an agent to represent him. Again, we want to stay in consultant mode during this discussion, reminding the client that "whether you choose to hire me or someone else, I definitely believe that it's in your best interests to have a buyer's agent working for you."

Many buyers don't understand how a buyer's agent gets paid. This is doubly true for first-time buyers. Before we ask them to sign the contract, we will want to make it clear how we get paid. Oftentimes, the only objection a buyer has to signing on with a buyer's agent is that they think that they will have to pay the commission. If we can show them how they can avoid that, then they will sign on with us without another question.

Being Able to Explain the Contract

Whether we are talking about buyer agency contracts, listing contracts, or offers to purchase, we should always be able to explain to our client or prospect exactly what it is that they are signing. We need to be able to translate the legalese on the contract into simple language that the average eighth-grader could understand. If you are not so good at this, then practice. Nothing is better for reducing barriers to signing than being able to make the contract more friendly by explaining it.

Guarantee

It takes so little to offer a guarantee. We know we're going to give great service. We know our clients will love us. What risk is there in offering a guarantee? Almost none. A guarantee offers buyers peace of mind. This is especially true if they have ever had a bad experience with an agent before. They want to know that they are not stuck with us. Let's be honest, if they're not happy with us, we're not going to keep them anyway. So it doesn't hurt us to offer them a guarantee, and it builds trust and credibility in the minds of our buyers.

Rules for Open House and Finding Properties

These rules are designed to train the buyers not to do anything that would jeopardize our ability to represent them in a transaction. We present these rules to them as a service to help them understand the industry and to prevent them from making a costly mistake. (We also do it to avoid having procuring cause complaints with other agents; and to avoid getting angry phone calls from other agents because our buyers are going around us.) We need to not mince words when we have this discussion with the buyers. We want them to be scared. We'd prefer that they never go to an open house, then we would never have a problem, but—if they insist—they need to be clear that if they don't follow the rules exactly, it could cost them thousands of dollars. Exhibit 11-2 is the page I hand out to my buyers.

Exhibit 11-2. Rules for open houses and seeing properties.

Open House Rules

1. Before you go into a home, let the listing agent know that you are working with me as your buyer's agent. Ask if it is OK to see the house without me. If they say "no," then leave immediately and we

will schedule another time to get in. Failure to do this may cause you to have to pay my commission.

2. Always sign my name next to yours on the guest register.
3. Do not give the listing agent any personal information about yourself. Remember, he or she works for the seller.
4. Always write any offer on a property with me. Do not allow the listing agent to talk you into writing it there. No matter how hot they may say the property is.

Seeing Properties

1. I'll give you a list of properties in the areas you want at the price range you can afford.
2. Then you can drive by the properties to see if you like the neighborhood and the outside of the home.
3. If you do like them, then call me and we'll schedule an appointment to get in.
4. Please remember not to knock on the seller's door without an appointment. Nor should you stop by to talk if you see the seller outside of their home. If you do, you will damage your negotiating position and limit my ability to help you in the transaction.
5. Remember, you must always see these properties with me to avoid paying my commission. Do NOT call the listing agent.
6. I will keep you updated about new properties that meet your criteria as they become available.

The buyers will not understand why all of these rules apply. It is up to us to explain to them why each rule is necessary. We want to be certain that they grasp the concept of procuring cause and what it means to them (paying our commission) if they put another agent in that role. They need to be clear that we are the ones who schedule the showings. We are the ones who need to show them the house. We are the ones who must write the offer. Anything less than this, and they risk paying our commission. (For a discussion of how to set up an open house, see Chapter 9.)

We also need to explain to them that sellers hire a listing agent for a reason. Most sellers don't want to be in direct contact with the buyers. It makes them uncomfortable. We need to warn them to stay away from the sellers. They risk making the sellers unhappy and unhappy sellers can be difficult to deal with. The only way that buyers will follow these rules is if we make it clear to them that the rules are in their own best interests.

Don't Panic

Before the buyers leave, there is one more issue we need to set their expectations on, and that is their tendency to panic. First-time buyers are especially susceptive to this emotion. We need to tell them this:

> Before you leave, I have one final rule for you. There will be times in this process that are stressful, even harrowing for you. It is my job to make sure this deal goes through, and I am very good at my job. I promise you, if the time comes for you to panic about the situation, I will tell you. But until I do, you're not allowed to panic. Got it? No panicking until I tell you it's time. Deal?

The buyers will laugh. We need to ask them to repeat the rule back to us to cement the rule in their heads. Then, when they begin to panic (and they almost always do at some point), we can ask, "What's the rule?" This question serves two purposes. First, it breaks them out of the panic cycle because they have to figure out what we're talking about. And, second, it makes them repeat the rule about panicking and remember that we said this would happen. Knowing that we anticipated this moment gives the buyer a sense of safety. Even if they are feeling out of control, they know that we are not and this gives them comfort. If they can't remember on the first try, then we say, "Remember the rule about panicking?" We should give them every opportunity to say the words out loud for themselves. It is a moment of empowerment in the process. It's better if they can do it, rather than us doing it for them. If they don't get it after two tries, then we should just give them the rule again—there's no point in making them feel stupid on top of feeling panicked.

Listing Presentations

Now that we understand how to do a buyer presentation, the next step is a listing presentation. There is a slightly different approach when doing a listing presentation than a buyer presentation. Buyers will hire you because they like you. Sellers are a little more demanding. They want more facts. They want more of a track record. Sellers are trusting you with the biggest asset they own—they want to know that you can do the job. So, while it is important for them to like you, they also need to come away from the presentation with a sense of your competence and ability to market their home effectively.

As we structure our presentation to the sellers, we need to keep in mind one salient point: The last thing we say is always the thing the client remembers. For this reason, the presentation goes from the least important information to most important.

Unless you are a new agent, I don't recommend talking a lot about your company. The seller isn't buying your company's services, he's buying yours. Build your company's marketing program into your marketing plan for the seller. Mention your company in passing, but usually there is no need to bring it up. It is you who he's hiring.

Now many of you may be thinking that you want to lean on the fact that your company is the biggest in the area. OK. Fine. But what happens if the seller is concerned about getting lost in the shuffle of a big agency? Haven't you just talked yourself out of a listing? What if the seller is really into the idea that you belong to the biggest agency out there? Fabulous! Play it up! Here's the thing. I don't recommend having a canned approach to talking about your company. You never know what is a selling point and what is a drawback until you get to the presentation. If your company's info helps you, then use it. If it doesn't, then leave it out. You are who they are hiring. The company's credentials are just gravy.

Setting the Stage

Just like we did with the buyer presentation, we want to tell the seller what the presentation is about and what he can expect along the way. It gives the seller a sense of safety that he will know what comes next. When the seller is feeling comfortable, he is in a much better position to make a positive decision about us.

It is important that we take control during this stage. We want the seller to agree to the order of events here. We want to show him that we will be doing the sales pitch first and then talking about pricing—not the other way around. The seller wants the price—that's really the only reason he's allowed us to come over. And most sellers will choose an agent based on the price she gives them unless we teach them not to. Since all the seller wants is to know the price, then the minute we mention the price, the presentation is over. This is why it's important to get him to agree to waiting until the end of the presentation to talk about the price. If he agrees to it now, then we can hold him to his word later if he gets antsy and asks for the price in the middle of the presentation.

The Seller's History with Real Estate Agents

We want to find out whether the seller has had a bad experience with a real estate agent. If he has, then we need to get him to tell the story.

Whatever issues he found to be faults in that agent are the same issues we will need to address to sell him on hiring us. If he had a great experience, then we want to find out why he liked the experience and then sell him on the fact that we can provide similar (or better) service. If he enjoyed working with his agent before, we also need to determine why he isn't working with that agent again. Did the agent fall out of touch? Did she get out of the business? If we understand the reason, then we will know more about the situation at hand.

On rare occasions, we may come across a seller who has never worked with an agent. In this instance, it will be our responsibility to explain to the seller what our job is in the transaction. We may also want to go through the same explanation of the buying process that we take our buyers through so that she will understand the process itself. This is especially important if we are dealing with a seller who inherited the house and has never owned a home before. She will need a lot of context for the decisions she will be asked to make.

Interviewing the Seller

This is the time we want to let the sellers talk. We need to get as much information as possible from them. There are emotional issues involved in this transaction. What are they? Are the sellers getting transferred or divorced? Are they moving up? Is this a happy move for them or an unhappy one? We need to get into the emotional side of the discussion to go deeper with our clients.

Listening is crucial at this juncture. We need to listen not only to what the clients are saying, but also to what is left unsaid. Is there a piece of the puzzle that they left out? If so, then we need to ask about it. We can't be afraid to open the can of worms. It's best to know where we stand rather than let things fester beneath the surface and pop up at inopportune moments.

We also want to ask: "If this process were to go perfectly for you— what would that look like? What would happen and what would *not* happen?" This gives the sellers the opportunity to tell us exactly what they want and to express their fears. We should take good notes when they are answering this question. This answer is the roadmap to a happy client.

Mission Statement

Sellers want to see that we are running our business like a business. And real businesses have mission statements. We need to provide them with ours—a statement about how we choose to do our business, how we treat our clients, and what we get in return. It needs to connect with the sellers on an emotional level, and provide insight into our reasons for being a real estate agent. This is the feel-good section of the presentation designed to cement the emotional connection between us and our clients.

Systems for Success

Sellers have a great affinity for systems. They want to see that we have a system in place to stay on top of their listing. They want to know that we are not going to forget them, or take the listing and then never call again. They want some assurance that we will be actively producing a sale for them. Nothing short of that will make them feel comfortable. So we need to bring them into our back office systems and show them what we do to take care of our clients on a consistent basis. This means that we need to bring the forms, checklists, and procedures that we use to the listing presentation. We should walk them through the processes and show them how we do business. This gives the sellers that sense of security. It also sets us apart from other agents. After all, most agents don't even have systems. And even if they do, they probably don't think to bring them to a listing presentation. (If you need a system for your back office, see *The New Agent's Survival Guide to Real Estate* or *Taking It to the Next Level— Systems for Successful Agents* manuals on our website at www.spartasuc cess.com.) I've actually gotten listings as a result of having systems in place. There have been sellers (mostly engineers) who have told me that my systems were the deciding factor for them.

Marketing Plan

We need to explain to the sellers that there are two target markets for their house. The first market is obviously the buyers themselves. The second market is the other agents in the industry. In most areas, this market represents more than half of the sales. It is likely that the sellers have never considered the fact that they have to target market to other agents in the industry—or even what that means. This is not a topic that most agents cover with their sellers. In explaining this factor to our sellers, we differentiate ourselves from the competition. And if we're competing with another agent for the listing, it's definitely a way to look good in comparison.

Marketing to the Public

Other than price, this is the piece of information that the sellers most wanted to know before we began our presentation. In talking about marketing to the public, we want to explain our marketing plan, including advertising, web presence, direct mail, signage, open houses, etc. The sellers want to know, in writing, exactly what we plan to do to bring buyers in the door and get them to write an offer. We need to be able to give the sellers a single piece of paper that clearly spells out this plan. And then we need to be able to show them that we have a system in place to make certain that the plan gets carried out.

The more statistics we can offer sellers about how buyers make their buying decisions, the better off we are. Sellers don't know about marketing. They still believe that newspaper advertising is critical. They know that the web is a factor now, but the thought of trying to advertise on the web is more than most sellers (and many agents) can face. They have no idea where to begin. If we can show them that we are fluent in the ways of advertising, and that we know how to target buyers effectively based on where they actually come from, we are well on our way to getting the listing.

Marketing to Other Agents

Sellers haven't even thought about this part of the marketing. They are totally at a loss when we begin this discussion with them. The great thing about this approach when speaking with a seller is that this is our opportunity to talk about the commission rate and how it affects the sale of the seller's home. We can point out to the sellers that if we offer a less-than-stellar commission rate, then our listing will get put at the bottom of the showing list. This is especially true when we are dealing with buyer's agents. Buyer's agents have a contract in place to get a certain amount of commission. If the seller isn't offering it, then they will have to either negotiate it with the seller or with the buyer. They really don't want to have to deal with either situation, so they avoid it by not showing our listing until they have to. When buyers' agents avoid showing the listing, then it sits on the market for longer than normal. Now buyers start wondering what is wrong with the house. Their wondering turns into a longer time on the market and an even lower offer when we eventually get one. Not the ideal scenario. To avoid this problem, we will need to offer a good commission rate to the buyer's agent. "Can you see how this is important to the marketing of your home, Mr. Seller?"

Brilliant isn't it? We've just removed all of the discussion about reducing the commission because we've shown that by paying less than what we are asking for, the seller is shooting himself in the foot. And the best part is—it's true! We're not even pulling a fast one. We're simply explaining it to the seller up front, before it becomes an issue.

This is also our opportunity to train the seller to be flexible about showing times and to have a lockbox on the door. After all it's easier to get an agent to show the property if it's available to be shown when *they* want to see it and they don't have to schedule around the listing agent's timetable to show it. Pointing out the fact that the availability of showings is the seller's responsibility in marketing their property is a way of empowering our sellers to be actively involved in their home sale.

One final thing we can discuss in this section is the importance of a well-written MLS description and a completed MLS information sheet. Many listings in the MLS are put in without room sizes or other vital information. Most are put in without a carefully crafted description section. We've all seen it—"Nice house, big LR, DR, KT combo. Sliders to deck. Large yard."—totally unimaginative and lacking all emotional content. When buyers see this, all they can think is that this was the best thing the agent could think of to say about the property. It doesn't bode well for getting many showings. Listing agents are in a rush to get the information into the computer and so they throw whatever they can think of on the sheet at the moment. Most think they will go back later and refine it, but most never do. And even if they did, they would have missed the gaggle of buyers who looked at the property listing in the first few days.

When we are careful to word our listing descriptions well and attractively, using emotionally triggering words, we give our sellers the best chance of selling their home quickly. Pointing out the number of listings that had inadequate descriptions—especially if they are the listings of the agent we're competing with for this house—is a helpful tool for coming out on top.

Defining Our Services

At this point, we will want to tell the sellers what services they can expect for their money. This is our value proposition. Why should a seller list with us? What is it about us that is better than/different from our competition? What are the benefits we offer to a client?

We can either simply list those services, or—if we want to get premium commissions—we can offer three levels of service to choose from. Now we know when we're presenting this information that the three levels of service equate to three different commission structures:

Basic = x
Extended = x + 1
Pinnacle = x + 2

But we DON'T MENTION THE COMMISSION STRUCTURES HERE! We just talk about the levels of service. We'll cover the commission later, when we are doing the listing contract. Once they have agreed that they want to hire us, we then revisit the conversation about the level of service. We ask whether they want the Basic, Extended, or Pinnacle level. We may discuss the price with them or not depending on their answer. Then we fill in the commission amount on the listing sheet.

Basic Services/Extended Services/Pinnacle Services

If we are offering levels of service, then we need to do a single page for each service level to describe what the client gets at each level. We want the different service levels to include enough that they are attractive to the client, but not so much that they cost us more to offer than we get extra in the commission. Be creative when planning these services. Think about what your target market would want—perhaps a housecleaning service, or a personal organizer to help them pack, or a massage to reduce their stress levels. Do they need a handyman to come out and spruce the place up? Or perhaps they want a professional decorator to stage their home for sale. Whatever you can think of, within reason, is fair game. If you think your sellers will like it, then put it on the list and see how they react. Not everyone will opt for this higher level of service, but some will. And the people willing to pay for these benefits are the ones most likely to become great referral sources in the future.

Guarantee

Once again I say—offer a guarantee!!!! Guarantees give sellers in particular peace of mind. This is especially true if they have ever had a bad experience with an agent before. They want to know that they are not stuck with us. If they're not happy with us, we're not going to keep them anyway. So it doesn't hurt us to offer them a guarantee, and it builds trust and credibility in the minds of our sellers.

Negotiations

Just like with our buyers, we need to educate our sellers that not all agents are created equal. Some have good negotiation skills and some do not. Sellers will appreciate this section. They are nervous about how the sale of their largest asset is handled. They need every dime of equity out of their property. Our ability to negotiate effectively is a great comfort for them and will ultimately figure into their decision to list with us.

Trial Close

At this point the bulk of our presentation is done. It's time to see how we did. We need to take a deep breath and ask: "So, Mr. Seller, assuming that we can come to terms on the price, is there any other reason you wouldn't want to hire me as your agent tonight?" This question gives the seller the opportunity to raise any objections that he might have at this point. It also makes him commit to hiring us based on our services and abilities, rather than on the price we present. We want the seller to realize that an agent is chosen based on her ability to market a property, not based on the price she brings to the table.

Pricing

We want to educate the seller about the market. She needs to understand that the market determines the price, not the agent. Once the market is evaluated (via the Competitive Market Analysis, or CMA), then we will ask the seller to set a price for the property. Once the seller has set the price, it is then our turn to determine whether it is a good business decision for us to take the listing. The seller needs to realize that we will not take the listing if it is overpriced.

From here, we transition into the presentation of the Competitive Market Analysis. Now I will assume that we all know how to present a CMA. What I will mention though is that I have a slightly different approach when it comes to bringing active comparables to the seller. When I bring the active listings, I bring ALL the active listings in the price range, not just the supposed "comps." The reason I do this is that the seller needs to see what the buyers will be seeing. The buyers will not be looking only at four-bedroom colonials, so we can't just be pricing against other four-bedroom colonials. We need to see the entire market. We need to know what the buyer is comparing us to. So I bring everything. This is just one more way I set myself apart from the competition.

Ask for the Listing

Once we have covered all of our bases, it is time to ask for the listing. This is the place where many agents (especially new agents) fall down on the job. We need to be willing to make eye contact with the seller when we ask for her listing. We need to be willing to sit in silence after we ask and wait for her reply. The last thing we want to do is start to try to sell again after we have asked this question and before we have received an answer. This is the kiss of death. Be patient. If you've given a good presentation, it will show, and the seller will say "yes."

Training Your Clients to Give You Referrals

Clients do not know that we need their referrals unless we ask for them. Some of them even think that we are way to busy and they don't want to bother us with more business. Can you imagine? But it's true. We spend much of the time we are working with a client apologizing for being hassled and harried and talking about how busy we are. To our clients, this sounds like we are overwhelmed with business. Since they too are feeling overwhelmed at the moment, they really feel for us. They want to help reduce our stress levels. They will do this by ignoring business that they could be referring to us. By doing this, they think they are helping. We need to disabuse them of this notion.

The first thing we need to remember when we are thinking about this is that we should make an effort not to complain about being busy. Being busy is good. We want our clients to think that we can always take on more business.

The second thing we need to remember is that we are not likely to get what we don't ask for. Therefore, it is important that we ask our clients for referrals. But when do we do that? We should do it up front, in the very beginning. Because it is during their transaction that they are most likely to hear about other real estate purchases and sales, since they are paying attention to the market at this time. We don't want to miss out on the opportunity to get these leads from them.

But how do we ask for referrals when we haven't done anything to deserve them yet? The script goes something like this "My goal is to work 100 percent by referral. You see, right now I spend a lot of my time looking for new business when what I'd rather be doing is working for my clients. I'm sure you'd prefer that too. So what I'm going to ask you is this: if you're happy with my service as we go along in this process, would you be comfortable giving me referrals as you hear about people looking to buy or sell?" (They'll say sure.) You say "Great! And after we close, it would really help me if you could try to send me a couple people a year. This way you'll know that I'm spending as much time working for the people you refer to me as I am for you right now. Would that work for you?" They'll say "sure" again and we're done!

I know this may sound pushy to you—and it is a little pushy. But clients understand it. They know that this is how we make our living. If we tell them that the reason we approach our business this way is because this is the way we can give them the best service, how are they going to argue with that? They won't—they can't! It makes too much sense. Don't be afraid to try this approach, it works like magic. You will increase your referral rate dramatically when you put this practice into place.

Humor as a Sales Tool

One of the biggest challenges we face when we are doing presentations is the defensiveness that comes when potential clients sit down to a sales presentation. They don't want to be sold. They are there only because they feel that they have no choice. They are guarded because they are afraid that we will push them into something they don't want.

The best way I have found to defuse this defensiveness is to make them laugh. Laughter is a great sales tool. When we laugh, we breathe deeper, causing our bodies to relax more. Laughter releases chemicals in the brain, which reduce stress levels as well. Laughter reduces the tension in the room and provides a much-needed break from the sales pitch.

Shakespeare understood the value of laughter. In all of his plays, he uses small little scenes with bit-part characters to act as the comic relief in the story line. When the tension gets too high, we can break it by inserting some humor into the situation.

I do have one warning about using humor though. It is never appropriate to use humor when a client is angry. It makes the client feel as though we are taking his concerns lightly. Otherwise though, laughter is indeed the best technique to reduce the stress in a sales presentation.

Presentation Skills

It is worth noting here, before we move on to other topics, that our skills at giving the presentations and our willingness to ask for the sale are crucial to the success of this process. If we don't know our book, don't know what we will say on each page, or even worse, if we are uncomfortable asking for the sale, then we will fail. We will also fail if we program our clients to say "no" to us.

I have heard many agents over the years say things like, "If you don't want to sign today, that's OK," or "I'm sure you probably want to think about it," or even, "You probably don't want to sign up with me today, right?" These are all self-sabotaging moves by agents. We need to *know* that we are the right person for the job. We need to believe that we will do the best job for the client. If we don't believe these things, then we shouldn't bother going to the appointment.

One of the best things we can do as agents to improve our presentation skills is to record our presentation and review it later to see how we did. Did we ask any questions that presupposed a negative response from the client? Did we lead the client to say "no"? Did we ever ask them to sign the listing or buyer agency contract? Did we let them talk? Did we listen and reflect back to the clients what we heard? If we were to receive a grade for our presentation, what would that grade be?

The only way to improve is to acknowledge our weaknesses and make efforts to compensate for them. Then we identify our strengths and work to build upon them. We create systems to keep us out of dangerous waters and we learn how to navigate back to safer shores when we're blown out to sea by accident. Practice makes perfect, but we want to be certain that we are practicing a presentation that actually gets us the signed contract or it won't matter how good we are at it.

CHAPTER 12

RELATIONSHIP MANAGEMENT AFTER THE SALE

According to a recent NAR survey, when asked at the closing table, 80 percent of all buyers and sellers would use their agent again, and yet, only 11 percent do. Why? Usually it's because their agent failed to keep in touch with them.

We all want more referrals. Referrals are free business, and they are business where we don't have to spend a lot of time building trust with our new client. They come to us with a level of trust already established, so it makes our jobs significantly easier. The funny thing is, no matter how much we as agents admit that referral business is the best, cheapest, and easiest business to close, we spend the majority of our time chasing new business instead. Many of us have never even asked our clients to send us referrals. We think that if we give them good service then they will send us business, it's understood, right? Not!

Our clients don't know that we need their help in finding business unless we ask them for it. They see us running like chickens with our heads cut off talking about how busy we are and they think that we don't have time to take on anyone new. So, subsequently, we end up doing all this hard work, which they appreciate at the time, but then we don't get referrals from them because they don't want to bother us. And, if we don't keep in touch with them after the sale, they think we've forgotten them or gotten out of the business, so they don't even come back to us when they buy or sell again. It's a vicious cycle.

There are many ways we can keep in touch with our clients after the sale. Here are a few ideas:

- Drop-bys
- Mailings
- Personal notes

- Calls
- Cards
- E-mails
- Relationship-based follow-up
- Parties/events

Drop-Bys

The Drop-by is the easiest form of follow-up. Whenever you happen to be driving in the neighborhood of one of your past clients, stop by and ring the bell. You're just there to say "hi" and see how they're doing with the house. If they answer, then you have a few minutes to chat and catch up. If they're not home, then leave a note on the door that says you're sorry you missed them. Keep a pad of notepaper in the car for just such an event. Some agents like to keep personalized notepads or other promotional items in their car for this purpose. No matter what you leave, the whole point is that the client knows that you cared enough to actually stop by.

Mailings

Mailings are the obvious answer to a busy agent's need to keep in touch with clients. Mailings can be automated. You never have to touch them personally. You can hire a company to mail out something for you every month and never have to deal with it again. It's a great first start to keeping in touch with your clients. Don't rely on this as your sole form of communication though since it is so impersonal. Remember, we're building relationships here and relationships need to be maintained.

Personal Notes and Calls

Personal notes are one way of maintaining those relationships. We discussed this in Chapter 11. They are an easy way to create a personal connection with little investment of time on our part.

We can also place calls to our clients when we have a spare moment. Most of our clients will probably not be home, but we don't actually need to speak to them. All we need to do is check in and let them know that we haven't forgotten them (which also keeps them from forgetting us). A quick message on the answering machine and we've made contact.

Cards

If you set up your systems so that you capture your clients' birthdays and anniversaries, you have the opportunity to keep in touch by acknowledging dates that are important to them. You can send holiday cards, birthday cards, anniversary cards, a card for the anniversary of their home purchase, and more. Almost every month there is some sort of holiday that will be relevant to one of your clients. Send cards to the mothers on Mother's Day and to the fathers on Father's Day. Take every opportunity to send out cards. They are different and unexpected and personalized.

One of my favorite things to do is to send out Valentine's Day cards. I don't send cards in December since they will only get lost in the crush of cards from everyone else. Instead, I send Valentine's Day cards. The cards are humorous looking and say "I love my clients! Be My Valentine!" For some people, this is the only Valentine's Day card they will receive. It will be a bright point in an otherwise depressing day.

E-Mails

Also consider the efficiency of e-mail. A quick e-mail can be a great way to connect quickly with your clients and get instant response. And to do it you never have to leave your office, never have to buy a stamp, and didn't have to risk getting stuck on the phone for longer than you had for free time. You can send these notes in the middle of the night without fear of waking your clients. E-mail is a great way to do an instant connection. And, to top it off, if you join one of the online e-mail card companies, you can send out e-cards "just because" to your clients. It's a low-cost, high emotional-touch way of connecting.

Relationship-Based Follow-Up

Also keep your eyes and ears open. If you read in the paper that one of your clients got a promotion or had a baby, then follow up with a card. If their son is due to graduate this year, then send a card for that. If you sold them a fixer upper, then letting them know about sales at home improvement stores is a great way to make contact. Following up on these types of issues maintains the connection between you and your clients.

Parties and Events

One other way we can keep in touch with our clients is to host events or parties for past clients. Especially when we sell to a lot of people who are new to the area, these events are seen in a very positive way by our clients. They get a chance to meet other people in the area whom they might not have otherwise met. We don't have to do anything really fancy for this if we don't want to. We can do something as simple as holding a party in our back yard. I've done this very successfully. I've also rented out a skating rink for just my clients. The bonus to these types of events is that we can take lots of pictures of them and include them in our next newsletter to our clients talking about the event. That way even those people who didn't come to the event feel as though they have managed to be part of the festivities.

I have found these events to be a great way to connect with my clients on a more relaxed level. We had plenty of time to hang out and catch up on each others' lives. And, as my clients got to know each other, they would exchange stories about how their transactions went and just how wonderful I was to them throughout the transaction. This is a great way to expand our clients' knowledge of what we can handle and how to refer business to us. The more stories our clients hear (from us or from other clients), the better able they are to tell someone they know how we can help them.

CHAPTER 13

CREATING A UNIQUE SELLING PROPOSITION

Can you say what you do and make it sound interesting enough that the person you are talking to will ask you to tell her more? Can you do it in thirty seconds or less? If you had just a few moments in an elevator with a prospective client, could you impress her enough to give you an appointment? If not, then you need to work on developing a Unique Selling Proposition. ("Unique Selling Proposition" is a term coined by Jay Conrad Levinson in his book *Guerilla Marketing* [Boston: Aspatore, 2001].)

A Unique Selling Proposition is your tag line, the single sentence that describes your business to your target audience. For Nike, it's "Just Do It." Wendy's had "Where's the Beef?" And Avis says "We Try Harder." Each one tells a story to the target market of the company. Nike sells shoes to active people. "Just Do It" appeals to their target market on a visceral level. Wendy's ran a campaign in the 1980s that had an elderly woman shouting "Where's the Beef?" to point out the difference in the size of the hamburger patties that they used versus their competition. It was a smash hit. Avis, in an effort to compete against Hertz (the number one car rental company), pointed out "We Try Harder," implying that the customer gets better service when they rent from Avis.

All of these tag lines are relevant to the target market of the company. They don't necessarily mean anything to people who aren't in the target market. For instance, if we've never eaten at Burger King or McDonald's, we might not know that the burger patties are very thin, making the "Where's the Beef" campaign pointless to us. And "Just Do It" doesn't really appeal to the sedentary people of the world. But it doesn't matter. These people will never buy from Nike. And if we've never bought fast food before, we're probably not going to buy it from Wendy's now. We are not their target market, so they don't care if we don't understand their tag line.

The key is to make an emotional connection with our clients. The tag line needs to say what we do and why our target market should care all at once. It needs to differentiate us from our competition. And it needs to do all of this in just a few words—the shorter the better—ideally less than eight syllables.

Wow—that's a tall order for a short sentence. How in the world are you supposed to come up with something like that? More importantly, how do you not sound like every other agent out there?

Who Is Your Target Market?

There are several steps you can take to get to your Unique Selling Proposition. The first step is to identify your target market. You need to be able to say not only who these people are, but also what the personality profile is of your average client. If profiling your clients seems like a daunting task, just remember one truism: You are most likely to work with people who are just like you. So if you describe yourself, you are probably also describing your target market.

For instance, when I was selling real estate in Connecticut, I was married to a Navy Submariner. He was stationed at the Groton/New London Navy Base. We were a military family with a military background. So who was my largest target market? Other military families. Seventy percent of the houses I sold were purchased with a veteran's loan. The vast majority of the families I sold to were all roughly in my age range and with similar needs and goals to what I had when I moved to the area.

All of us have this same sort of market happening around us. By the very nature of who we are, we attract a certain clientele. We do this because we go to events that these people attend. We participate in the same social circles as these people. We word our ads in ways that appeal to people who are like us. There are all sorts of subtle and obvious ways in which we attract these clients.

So if we know how to attract them, do we know who they are? In aggregate, yes, we do. It's like creating a stereotype of ourselves. We can describe the average person based on our own description. For instance, when I pitched this book to my publisher, my editor asked me for input about the name of the book. She had suggested using something with "boot camp" in the title. I told her that this was a bad idea since my target market would not be interested in something like that. I proceeded to give her an idea of what my target market looked like. Here's some of what I told her. See if this description sounds familiar.

My target market is comprised of people who are very relationship-based in their approach to the world. They are people-pleasers and problem solvers. They like to grease the wheels of the world around them. They hate conflict. They want to be liked (preferably loved) by everyone. They need to be needed. They look for external validation. They are independent people by nature, but they have a longing for community. They have a strong connection to their spiritual nature, although they are not necessarily religious. They believe in good karma, even if they don't call it that. They are highly intuitive people, and they are sensitive to other people's feelings—many are empathic. They have a strong sense of right and wrong and high ethical and moral standards. They believe in giving back to their community either through volunteer work, donations, or other support. They recycle. They don't like to waste anything—connections with people or natural resources. They are fascinated by the inner workings of the mind and want to know what makes people tick. They do real estate more for the joy of helping people than for the money. They are gracious and generous with friends and strangers alike. They make people around them feel welcome. They give of their time and energy. They are team players. They play by the rules, but think outside of the box. Their greatest joy is appreciation from their friends, family, and clients.

How much of that profile applied to you? I'll wager that much of it did. You are my target market. I wrote this book with you in mind. The marketing was created with you in mind. And, based on the fact that you're reading this book—it was successful. If I were to go back into selling real estate full time again today, the personality profile I've written above would still apply. Why? Because much of it describes me. And I will tend to end up working with other people who are just like me—just like you will end up working with people just like you.

This is the type of personality profile you need to do in order to get into the heads of your target market. You need to know what makes them tick, why they make the decisions that they do. You want to know why they choose to work with you and why they would choose to do so again. When you know what is important to your clients, then you know what emotions your tag line needs to evoke.

When you work on our personality profile, one thing you need to keep in mind is that when you are describing your target market, you are also describing yourself. You will find that the people who most want to work with you and the people you are most comfortable working with are people just like you. So if you have trouble describing your target market's personality profile, all you need to do is to look at your closest friends and yourself. If you can describe your friends' personalities, then you know what personalities your clients will likely have too.

Before you get started on your target market's personality profile let me just point out one thing. The profile will not completely describe any one person. There will be variations between people. After all, we are not made from cookie-cutters. When I noted the personality profile of my market, I said that I'd bet that much of the profile applied to you. I don't by any means expect it all to apply to you. We are each individual, unique beings. I am not saying that we should lump people into a single category. What I am saying is that we can make some universal assumptions about groups of people. We can assume that engineers will want facts and figures because—as a whole—they do. That doesn't mean that every engineer will want facts and figures, only that the group does. Our goal is to connect with the group as a whole. We can't market to individuals—it's too expensive and too difficult. We must make some aggregate assumptions to get our point across. So don't worry if not everyone will fit this profile exactly. It only has to be close.

Exercise

Write the personality profile of your target market:

_____

_____

_____

(Note: Use a separate notebook to write your responses to the exercises in this chapter.)

Core Values

Next, you need to know what core values your business is built upon. How do you run your business? What values do you use to make day-to-day decisions? Do you make certain to do your business with integrity? Are you honest to a fault? Are you careful to get the details right all the time? What are the rules you live by and apply to your business practices? These are your core values.

When I sold real estate, I was known for being highly ethical in my practices. I was also known for telling my clients what they needed to know—even if I knew it was *not* what they wanted to hear. I was committed to educating my clients so that they always made fully informed decisions. I was focused much more intently on preserving the relationship with the client than I was on making that particular sale. I was reasonable to negotiate with but unmerciful in my pursuit of justice if my client was wronged. With these thoughts in mind, my core values would have read something like this:

- Integrity first—always.
- Informed decisions are the best decisions—even if the information isn't always what you want to hear.
- The client is more important than the sale.
- Win-win is always the goal.

Exercise

Write your core values:

_____

_____

_____

Once you have your core values and the personality profile of your target market, you're on the way to creating a stellar Unique Selling Proposition. Keep in mind that your statement needs to be short, sweet, and to the point. The words should not have many syllables. It must flow off the tongue easily. It must evoke an emotion. Here are a few words that you should avoid at all costs because they are overdone in the industry and will come off sounding trite: dream home, integrity, honesty, trust, key, and door.

Focus on the Message—Not the Industry

I have faith that we can do some thinking outside of the box on this issue. (After all, that was part of your personality profile as my average reader.) We don't have to use the words "house" or "home" or "property." Our target market knows we're in real estate, they know what we are talking about. "Just Do It" says nothing about shoes. So we need to let go of the attachment to the words "real estate" in our tag lines. Instead, we should focus on what we want to say to the client. We want to say it in a way that speaks from the client's perspective. Nike wanted to say "you should buy from us because we understand you." To do this, they got into the head of their target market and they found what they felt boiled down to the core value that all of these people shared: "Just Do It." By using that as their tag line, they *showed* people that they understood, rather than just *saying* it.

Why Clients Work with You

If you have past clients who will share with you why they chose to work with you, then this is a good piece to put into the puzzle as well. The reasons that they chose to work with you will often be the same reasons that other people will make that decision too. Add these concepts to your list.

Exercise

Write a list of why your past clients worked with you:

_____

_____

Now you have a list of concepts, descriptive words, reasons people have worked with you, etc. The goal is to identify the unifying concept of all the ideas—an emotion or sense of being that brings it all together. Then, when you have that concept, look for ways to express it in simple terms using archetypal imagery or emotional phrasing.

For instance, when I was working on coming up with my Unique Selling Proposition for my business, I went through a variety of concepts. What the information ultimately came down to was that my students and coaching clients felt that they were better prepared, more educated, more confident about themselves, and more balanced in their lives and businesses after working with me. When I thought about what I enjoyed about the work I do, it was watching people get a concept, watching their faces light up with sudden excitement as a concept suddenly made sense to them. I really enjoyed helping people figure out how to get out of problems they were having and how to get from where they were in their lives to where they wanted to be. When I thought about what word or phrase would address these concepts, I realized that what I was doing was empowering people to create the lives they wanted. Then I needed to bring the concept back to my target market. Hence "Empowerment for Realtors®" was born as my tag line.

If I were to go back to selling real estate today, I might use something like "Competence and Compassion." I'd use this because the people in my target market want to know that I can get the job done, but they also want to know that I care about them too. I can't use "caring" because it's trite and overused, so I'd use "compassion" since that is still alliterative and is an even better word to describe how I approach my business. It's short, sweet, and to the point. Could I come up with something even better? Probably—I haven't thought about it for long and I find that these things are much like a fine wine. The ideas meld and come to a full body over time.

The tag line I created for one of my coaching clients is "No Fears, No Worries, Just Nina!" This was a great reflection of her personality as well as how her clients looked at her. She is a motherly-type figure and her focus is on taking the fear out of the transaction for her clients.

Another client got "Straight Talk—Straight Up" because she is a no-nonsense kind of person and that's who her target market is as well. She has decided to focus on working with tradesmen and this tag line will serve her well in that target market. The personality profile we did together was part of the reason she decided on this market. When I looked at the profile, it was the same profile as tradesmen have, and so it was an obvious fit.

Each tag line will be different. Each person has something that evokes a completely different set of emotions and that appeals to a completely different target market. And this is exactly as it should be. Not every tag line will appeal to every person either. If you don't have at least one person say that they hate your tag line, then it's probably too general and won't have the impact you're looking for.

This is a complex process and it is often difficult to do for yourself. I went through several iterations of tag lines before finally deciding on my current one, *and I help people create tag lines all the time*. Bounce ideas off of friends and family in your target market. (Remember that your tag line may not be relevant to people outside that market, so don't pay a lot of attention to those people's opinion of it.)

Here's a quick test to determine if your tag line is a good one:

- Does your tag line evoke an emotion?
- Is it short, sweet, and to the point?
- Does it have less than eight syllables?
- Do you read it and instantly think "Yes! That's it! That's me!"

If all of these aren't true for you, then go back to the drawing board and try again. Hang in there. It's hard work, but it's worth it.

A Creative Answer to the Question, "What Do You Do?"

Now that you have your tag line, the next step is to find a Creative Answer to the question "What do you do for a living?" *Don't* answer that question with a simple "I'm a real estate agent" or "I sell houses." Yawn! It's boring! You need an answer that makes people sit up and take notice. Something that makes them say, "Really, how do you do that? Tell me more!"

On page 205 of her book *The Wealthy Spirit—Daily Affirmations for Financial Stress Reduction* (Naperville, Ill.: Sourcebooks, 2002), Chellie Campbell says that she used to tell people that she was a bookkeeper and she'd watch them as they closed off from her or turned and ran away:

> [When she changed her answer to] "I do financial stress reduction," the difference in reactions was truly amazing. People laughed, leaned forward and asked me, "How do you do that? Do you give away money?" One woman threw her arms around me in a giant hug! I could tell by a person's reaction to that one statement if they were interested in my services."

For my part, when someone asks me what I do for a living, I tell them that I help people create lives and businesses they can love. This always gets a positive response. People want to know more about what I do and how I do it. It opens the door for me to give them my "Elevator Pitch."

Exercise

Write what you can say when people ask you what you do for a living. How creative can you get with your answer? Look at the words and phrases you've put down on paper already. Think about what experience your clients have when they work with you. Back up your concept of what you do to include everything that is going on in the client's life. Is there a larger perspective you can place on this concept?

Here's a thought for an answer: As a real estate agent, you work with people who are in major life transitions. Could you perhaps say, "I help people through major life transitions"? Or maybe, "When people's lives are up in the air, I take care of what's on the ground"? Think outside of the box. Try not to use the words house, home, property, or real estate. And for heaven's sake, avoid the phrase "dream home." See what you can come up with.

Your Creative Answer:

_____

_____

The Elevator Pitch

Now that we have an answer when people ask us what we do for a living, we need to come up with a follow-up response for when they ask us to tell them more. This is our *Elevator Pitch*. It is the thirty-to-sixty-second response that sums up our business in a neat package. It presents not only *what* we do, but *how* and *why* we do it, as well as identifying what makes us different from our competition in the marketplace. For instance, here's my elevator pitch:

> When I work with you, I step into your shoes. You give me a feel for your life and your business. You tell me your dreams and goals. And then together we look at what's in place in your life already and how we can get you from where you are now to where you want to be. Whether the blocks to your progress are practical, mental, or emotional, I can help move them out of the way. I'm your partner on the path to success. I know that change can be an intimidating proposition. Don't worry; I'll lend you my courage until you can find your own.

This Elevator Pitch puts my comments in terms of what I could do for the person I am speaking to. It uses emotional hooks to bring the person into the vision I am creating with the pitch. And it makes people stop and think about what they would tell me and what advice I might offer them in return. In short, it makes them think about doing business with me.

Exercise

Write your Elevator Pitch. Keep in mind that the words and sentences need to be easy to speak, not just to read. You will be using this as a verbal brochure on your business, so you also need to be able to memorize it. Don't make it too long or too complicated or people won't understand it. Use emotional hooks to bring them in and phrases reflecting your values to drive your message home.

CHAPTER 14

BUILDING A BROCHURE

A brochure is a great way to introduce yourself to your clients. It can be included with a prelisting package. It can be handed out at promotional events. It can be given to buyers at open houses. A brochure is a calling card that says so much more about you than your business cards could ever hope to say. A brochure is a critical marketing piece that is designed to set an emotional tone with the prospect that makes him want to work with you.

The problem with brochures is that they take time and money to create. Generally only the top agents nationwide have brochures. Most of us never get around to designing one for ourselves because we are not sure what to put in it, or how to make it say what we want. And we all know how unlikely it is that we will ever spend the money to hire a professional to do it. But we do know that if we had a brochure, it would offer us credibility and improve our chances of getting clients. So what do we do?

Conveniently, we have already done most of the work behind a good brochure by creating our Unique Selling Proposition and Elevator Pitch. The importance of these elements cannot be understated. They set the tone for the entire marketing piece. When we can connect with the emotional pieces associated with these elements, then we create something that is compelling to the prospect.

There are several factors we need to consider when we decide to design our own brochure. The first is that we want to keep it simple. It is a marketing piece, not a sales piece. We will not sell the client on our services by giving them the brochure. All the brochure is designed to do is to create interest on the part of the prospect and provide credibility that we are professionals.

Elements of a Good Marketing Brochure

For the purposes of this discussion, we will assume that we are planning a tri-fold brochure. Here are six elements for a good marketing piece. Let's explore each of these in turn.

- Tag line
- Theme
- Design
- White space
- Page layout
- Content

Tag Line

Our tag line (also known as our Unique Selling Proposition) should be prominently displayed on the front cover of the brochure. This is the phrase that will catch our target prospect's eye and incite them to read further. Everything in the brochure should work with the theme of the tag line. If there is room to put the tag line at the end of the message on the interior of the piece, we should put it there as well.

Theme

The theme is what the piece looks and feels like. Are we trying to evoke joy? Then we will want soft colors and a font that is bright and open in its styling. Are we evoking laughter? Then perhaps a cartoon-like font is more appropriate with primary colors and visuals of balloons. What is the emotion that we are working to bring out of our prospects? What are the images and colors that reflect those emotions? These will be our theme for the piece.

Design

The design is the actual layout of the piece. Where do we put the pictures? Do we have backgrounds that have color? Are we printing on colored paper? Are we using clip art or pictures? How are we setting the titles off from the text?

As for fonts, we should never use more than two fonts for the main text of the document—one font for the titles and another for the text. The tag line and/or our logo may be done in a third font, but that's it. Nothing else should vary from that theme. Our text font should be an easy-to-read font. We should avoid using fonts that look like handwriting or that have bizarrely-shaped letters because they will discourage the prospect from reading the piece. We can use the fancier fonts in our titles. But we shouldn't get too attached to a particular font. If we find that we can't tell what a title says because of the font, we need to throw the font out—not the title.

White Space

Prospects don't like to read a lot of information. If we don't make it simple, clear, and easy to read, they won't read it. So we need to keep a fair amount of white space on the page. White space is the empty area around the message. Remember, this piece is only designed to get the prospect excited—not to sell them. All we have to do is tickle their curiosity and get them to ask us for more. The more white space and graphical elements we use, the easier it is to get our message across to the prospect. The key to remember here: Less is more.

Page Layout

The front of the brochure needs to say what is inside and it needs to have a simple message that tells the prospect why they should care. This page should also include our name, company name, contact number, and website.

As we open the first page of the brochure, the next page should be a series of bullet points that explain what make us different from the competition. These points should be phrased as value propositions identifying the benefits to the client, not the features that we offer. For instance, if we guarantee our service, then our bullet point would say something like:

Never Get Stuck with a Bad Agent Again: We guarantee that you'll be happy, or we'll let you out of your listing, no questions asked.

Or if we take care of all the details, then we could say something like:

No Stress, No Fuss: We take care of the details, so you don't have to.

The shorter we can make these bullet points, the better. Remember, our prospects don't like to read. If they want more information, they'll go to the website; this is just a teaser.

Inside the brochure can be treated in a variety of fashions. We can treat the entire page as a single page, or we can split it into two or three columns, or we can split the page horizontally. Be creative. The more exciting we can make the inside, the better off we are. Remember that we're trying to create the majority of the feel of the piece with the visuals, not the text. So start with the layout and then move to content. The purpose of the interior is to flesh out the concepts presented on the bulleted page and to make the emotional connection with the prospect.

The back of the brochure is our chance to talk about ourselves. We can give our resume, background, production, testimonials, etc. It is the area in which we build credibility. We also need to put our contact information on this page as well since we want the prospect to be able to contact us easily no matter whether they are looking at the front or the back of the piece.

Content

I left this discussion to last because it is important to consider all of the other elements first. If we know that we can convey one particular concept through the pictures we have, then we don't need to address that in the text of the piece. If we have done a good job with creating an emotional context for the piece through the fonts and colors we use, then we don't have to work so hard at creating that in the content. The purpose of the content is to fill in the blanks—to express those feelings and concepts that we were not able to convey through other means.

We should keep anything we say in these sections to a minimum. Bullet points are the best option. Remember though that we need to keep the language choice consistent with the emotions we are working to evoke from the prospect. If we are trying to be funny, then using high-level vocabulary words is probably not our best choice. The same is true if our target market is the average American. We need to be certain that we are not talking above their comprehension level. If we shoot for roughly an eighth-grade vocabulary, then we should be safe in that instance. If, however, we are marketing to an industry-specific niche, then we should include the jargon that fits that industry, but not so much as to be detrimental to the emotional thrust of the piece.

Testing

Once we have been working on this piece extensively, we will lose our perspective on it. We need to go out and get other people to look at the brochure for us. We want their feedback on how it makes them feel about us in our business. Does it make us look credible? Does it evoke the emotions we wanted? Is it compelling? Would they call us? This type of testing is important as we determine whether we have hit the mark with our brochure. One word of caution, however: We want to be certain that the people we are using as our focus group are people who are part of our target market. If they aren't, then the feedback is useless to us. It doesn't matter whether our message gets across well to retirees if first-time buyers are our target market. In fact, it's likely that a well-targeted marketing piece will *not* appeal to both of these groups. We don't care if it doesn't appeal to everyone since we are targeting a particular group. As long as it appeals to that group, then our job is done.

The other benefit of testing is that our testers become our proofreaders as well. There have been many times I've seen agents (including myself) leave out critical pieces of information (like phone numbers, websites, etc.). When we are entrenched in the creative process, practical items often escape our attention. By testing the piece before we send it out to the printers, we can catch the vast majority of these types of errors.

CHAPTER 15

EFFECTIVE ADVERTISING IN TODAY'S MARKET

Big companies brand their products so that consumers know how to think of them. They use consistent colors, fonts, tag lines, and images that trigger the consumers' minds so that they know that they have seen this before. In this age of mass marketing, when we have to see something more and more often before it registers, it's important that we know how to compete.

The first rule of thumb in marketing is: If we're not going to repeat our message consistently over time, then we shouldn't waste our time and money sending it the *first* time. A one-shot marketing piece will rarely yield results. It is the story of the tortoise and the hare all over again. Slow and steady wins the race. If we mail, then we need to plan to do so, at least once per month, for the next year or more. Preferably, we will start our marketing with a once-per-week-for-eight-weeks plan, which transitions into once per month thereafter.

Depending on what source we reference, marketing experts say that we need to touch someone with a piece of marketing anywhere from six to twenty-one times before they begin to recognize us and our message. Regardless of the number we choose in this range, it is a lot of contacts that need to be made before we begin to see a return on our investment. And if we fail to give a consistent message or brand through those contacts, we run the risk of expanding that number out further.

Key Elements of Marketing

Before we put our money into the marketing field, we need to make certain that the message we are conveying has a few, simple, key elements. Those elements are as follows:

- A simple core message
- A consistent emotional trigger
- An obvious brand image
- Congruency of the message with the delivery of that message
- Languaging that is appropriate to the target market
- Consistent delivery of the message

Without these items, a marketing piece can fail to make any impression at all or, worse yet, make a bad impression.

A Simple Core Message

When we look at our tag line/Unique Selling Proposition, we get a feel for what we are saying to the consumer. That is the simple core message we are trying to convey. For instance, Sparta Success Systems' tag line is "Empowerment for Realtors."® I am telling my target market that I provide tools, emotional support, coaching, and education to help my target market become more empowered in their lives and businesses. Therefore, every time I send out a piece of marketing material, newsletter, e-mail, etc, it needs to support that message. If I send out a piece based in fear that undermined my audience's confidence in themselves, then I would be in violation of my core message. I need to stay on message by sending out communications that empower my clients. The same is true for us when we send out communications to our prospects and clients. We need to stay on message—stay consistent with our Unique Selling Proposition.

Consistent Emotional Trigger

While we stay on message, we also want to stick with a consistent emotional message. In communicating with our market, we can get faster brand recognition when each piece is designed to evoke the same emotion. This emotion becomes attached to the message and establishes its own familiarity with the consumer, so that, if we trigger that emotion over and over again, eventually, the consumer will associate that emotion with us. Using Sparta Success Systems as an example again, we can see that the emotion that we are triggering is empowerment. This emotion is made up of a variety of other emotions such as confidence, safety, security, strength, support, and comfort. Each time I communicate with my target market, I tap into one of those emotions. Eventually, over time, those emotions (and the one they all build into, which is a sense of empowerment) become associated with my company and my products and services. People who want to feel this way are drawn toward me. Those who do not are not. It is a simple way for me to attract the clientele that I most want to work with.

An Obvious Brand Image

A logo, a picture, a color scheme, a set of fonts: all of these comprise our brand image. They need to be prominent within the piece. Simply placing a picture or a logo on the piece is not sufficient to "brand" it. There can be no doubt who sent it when I pick up the piece. If there is, then the branding isn't done right. If the piece we are planning on sending out doesn't look distinctive, then we shouldn't bother sending it. We are not adding to our brand awareness. But if we can make it distinctive, then we will get that brand recognition in fewer touches.

Congruency of the Message with the Delivery of That Message

I cannot say how many times I have seen agents send out letters purporting to give personalized service, but touting that service in a form letter. Shortly after his closing, my friend (who was recently divorced and lived with a roommate and no children), received a letter from his real estate agent welcoming him to the neighborhood. In this letter (which was barely branded at all), she said that she was happy to help him get oriented by directing him to service providers in the area. It was one more way she provided personalized service to her clients. She concluded the letter by saying that she hoped he and his family would be happy in their new home. Was the message on target? Yes. She was offering personalized service and going above and beyond the call of duty. Was the emotion on target? Yes, she was offering support and help. Was the message effective? No. She sent it in a form letter that made it clear that this letter was most certainly *not* personalized. The way in which she conveyed the message was out of congruency with the message itself.

Another example of this sort of faux pas would be for an environmental action group to hand out fliers to people on the street. The fliers use up natural resources and quickly become garbage, many becoming litter as people drop them on the street. They fill the landfills and add to the problem. This is in direct opposition to the message of the group, which is to find renewable resources and reduce waste.

When we offer our message, we need to be certain that we are doing so in a fashion that is most congruent with our message. If we pick a medium that is contrary to our message, then we run the risk of killing the message as well.

Languaging That Is Appropriate to Your Target Market

When we write the content of our messages, we want that content to speak to our target market. We will not use big words and fancy, flowery vocabulary for communicating with blue-collar workers. We'll use common language and wording for our target market. If we're targeting a specific industry, then we will use the jargon of that industry. If we're talking to geeks, we will make geek references and jokes. If we are talking to investors, we'll talk in terms of dollars and cents rather than emotions. Our languaging will reflect the same languaging our target market would use in a similar conversation. It should also reflect the emotional content of the message. If we are trying to be straightforward in our message, then we should be straightforward in how we phrase it, using short, simple sentences with one- and two-syllable words. If we are trying to appeal to a sense of comfort and security, then we will use softer words and phrasings. We want the language to have a "feel" to it, much like the message does.

Consistent Delivery of the Message

Once more, we need to remember that the message is only as good as our ability to remember it. We don't even notice something until we've seen it several times. In today's age of mass advertising at every turn, we are fast becoming experts at ignoring the vast majority of what we see and read. This is why we include the emotional triggers. Those get us past most people's screening mechanisms. But it is the consistency of the message that imbeds us in their brains. Most of us can recite multiple different company slogans from our childhoods because of the sheer number of times we heard them.

For instance:

Timex: Takes a Licking and _____[1]
Wendy's: Where's the _____[2]
Coca Cola: It's The Real _____[3]
AMEX: Membership Has Its _____[4]
Calgon: Calgon! Take _____[5]
Enjolie: I can bring home the bacon, _____[6]

Charmin: Please don't _____[7]
Ford: Built Ford _____[8]

1. Keeps on ticking. 2. Beef? 3. thing. 4. privileges. 5. me away. 6. fry it up in a pan, and never let you forget you're a man. cause I'm a woman. Enjolie. 7. squeeze the Charmin. 8. Tough.

The reason we remember these is because they were embedded through repetition. Some of them come back to us with music attached as well. Who can't remember the Chili's baby back ribs ad? (I want my baby back baby back baby back ribs. I want my baby back baby back baby back ribs. Barbeque Sauce!) It was fun and different and stuck in our minds. It was the perfect jingle. But it wouldn't matter how perfect that jingle was if we didn't hear it more than once.

This is why we need to put systems in place to be certain that we stay in contact with our market consistently. No amount of branding can make up for a lack of repetition. The problem with us as agents is that we have this terrible habit of marketing like mad when we're slow and then stopping altogether when we're busy. We turn the faucet on and off and then we wonder why, three months after we turned the faucet off, we have no business.

Planning Ahead

We know that we will not have the time to send out mailers mid-summer when we're slammed with business. We know this in January when we are bored and business is slow. And yet, most of us do nothing about it. Most of us just lament in January that we are bored. Instead, what we should be doing is prepping a year's worth of mailings to our sphere of influence and prospects. We should be printing all the letters/postcards/newsletters, addressing them (including addressing a bunch of blanks for each mailing so that we can add people to the list as we go along), and stamping them. This way, all we have to do at the beginning of each month is drop these items in the mail. Even when we're slammed with business, we can manage to put something in the mail. This way we get consistency to our message and we don't end up with unpleasant dry spells because we fell down on our marketing when we were busy.

Value-Added Proposition

When we market ourselves to people outside of our sphere of influence, we need to have a way to differentiate ourselves from the competition. This means that we need to have a value proposition that is better than the next guy. A value-added proposition is a way of telling someone what value we can add to the process if they work with us. In this case, we are telling buyers and sellers what we can do for them that no one else can.

By reading this book, we are learning the tools of coaching clients through major life transitions. This is a value-added proposition. This is a service that no one else offers—even if they do it intuitively, I guarantee that they are not advertising it. I know this because that is what I did for years. I coached every client I had through the process of whatever transition they were facing, but I never used it as a marketing tool. Why? Because I didn't know what to call it, or how to describe it.

Even now, I am at a loss for how to describe this process to others. It's really Holistic Realty—Real Estate for the Whole Person. But you can't sell that (well maybe you could in California). You could call yourself a Real Estate Coach. With the current trend toward coaching in the general workforce, you have a little more chance of people knowing what it is, but it's still vague. Transition Facilitator? Perhaps. The point is, whatever you call it, you should use your knowledge of this information as a way to add value to your clients. Many agents out there are only looking for a way to get the deal done faster with less exposure to the client. You are actively engaged in walking the client through the process. You *want* to be close to them. You *want* them to share their problems and concerns. You *want* to take care of them. That alone is sufficient to get you most people's business.

So as you're thinking about how to create your marketing pieces, your sales presentations, and your elevator pitches, you need to keep the value-added proposition in mind. It should be integrated into everything you say and do. The client will not know how awesome you are until you tell them. And your ability to articulate how great you are compared to the competition is the difference between getting the business and not.

Websites

In today's market, you cannot hope to survive without a website. There are many ways to get a website in our business. There are multiple companies who will build a site for you in the blink of an eye for a very reasonable price. They have various templates so that the site looks different from other real estate agents in your area. Some of them can brand the site to your company. Some of your companies actually provide you with a ready-made site from the company. And if you have nothing up on the web right now, you should definitely do one of these things to at least have *something* out there.

Once you have your presence established though, you should really start to take a look at how you are marketing your business through that site. There is one and only one purpose to your website: to get prospects to call you. All of the other functions of the site are spiffy and pretty, but if they don't get the prospect to pick up the phone, then they are not doing their jobs effectively.

Every real estate agent wants to have a market-search option on his site. Let's look at Bob's website. Bob wants buyers to be able to log onto his site so that they can get regular updates on properties that work for them. They sign in telling Bob what they are looking for, how often they are looking, and what towns they are interested in. Bob gets a wealth of information about the types of properties the buyers are looking for. This is great. This is wonderful. The question is: Will all this information do Bob any good? If he isn't collecting contact information from the buyers then all he is doing is effectively providing a service for free. Since the buyers don't have to speak to him or meet with him, he isn't even developing any loyalty from these buyers. When they go to buy, they are much more likely to call the listing agent than they are to call Bob.

This is not effective marketing. Sure it brings people to Bob's site, but it's what they do when they're there that matters. Instead of giving the buyers what they think they want, Bob should be thinking about how he can give them what they actually need—an interview with him to be their buyer's agent. This way they both win. The buyers end up working with someone on their side for the negotiations, and Bob gets a sale.

Pre-Sales Presentation Format

Think of your website as your pre-sales presentation—the goal of *this* presentation being to get an appointment. If you design your website so that buyers take one particular route through your site, sellers take another, and any other specific target market (like the agent marketing to tradesmen) takes a different, more specialized route, then you can offer a targeted marketing pitch speaking directly to the people going through the site. Otherwise, prospects are just wandering around your site at random. And we all know how effective a sales pitch is when given out of order (not very).

Buyers

Your format should be directed toward removing the barriers that buyers and sellers have to contacting you.

Objection: Buyers think they don't need you.

Answer: Counter that assumption by including a page about buyer agency and the benefits of working with a buyer's agent.

Objection: Buyers think they will get a better deal if they buy direct from the listing agent.

Answer: Counter that argument by again mentioning buyer agency and the benefits of having someone working for them.

Objection: Buyers think that they can find the house and *then* get an agent.

Answer: Correct this misconception. Explain to them that the person with whom they see the house is the person they are stuck with unless they want to pay their agent's commission.

Objection: Buyers don't realize that agents can show them properties from any company—they think you can only show your own listings.

Answer: Educate them about the function of the MLS system and cooperation between brokers.

Objection: Buyers think that they have to pay a commission to get a buyer's agent.

Answer: Not true! Explain to them how you get paid.

Objection: Buyers think that an agent will force them to buy a house they hate.

Answer: Put in a page of testimonials from past clients and friends talking about how easy you are to work with and what a joy it was to deal with you.

Sellers

Sellers are looking for someone who knows what she's doing and is professional. Include pages in your presentation to them that have information on:

- Sales history for your towns
- Your personal production levels (if they are good)
- Testimonials from past clients
- Your company's production stats
- Informational links to town government sites (have them open in a new page—you don't want them to lose your site)

- Your personal mission statement and core values
- A list of the systems you use to run your business effectively and guarantee superior service to your clients
- Links to any (good) publicity about you or your company

Regardless of what you put onto your website, it should speak to the needs of the prospect. Whether you are alleviating their fears, building on their dreams, or helping them with their plans, it should all be focused on achieving the end result of getting the prospect to contact you for an appointment.

Offer Something of Value

Finally, after you've talked about everything that you can think of that buyers and sellers could use as objections to keep them from calling you—offer them something of value. A free report targeted to their specific needs that will cause them to sit up and take notice. If they want this free report, then they need to fill in the required information on the web page to get it. The report gets e-mailed to them, so they have to give a good e-mail address. In addition to the free reports offered, your final page of your presentation should also include your phone number and a button to allow them to send you e-mail. (Don't put your actual e-mail on your web page or you'll get added to TONS of e-mail spam lists.)

By providing a call to action, you will increase your response rate significantly. If you are offering a free seminar for buyers or sellers, then you can add that information to your website too in the hopes of getting them to attend. The goal is to meet the person face to face and eventually to get an appointment to discuss their specific needs.

Bringing Visitors to Your Website

There are many ways to bring visitors to your website. The most obvious one is to put your web address on *everything*. Your signs, your car (assuming you don't drive like a maniac), your business cards, your advertising, your fliers, your mailers, your newsletters—absolutely everything should contain your web address.

Pay Per Click

There are other ways to drive business to your site as well. You can bid for space on Yahoo words (formerly Overture), Google, or other per-click providers. These sites charge you each time a person clicks on the link to your site. The clicks cost anywhere from $0.10 and up depending on how much you bid to be at or near the top of the list. However, I wouldn't get into this type of advertising until you have your pre-sales presentation in place, because they can get to be quite expensive. And without your presentation in place, you're not going to get much in the way of actual results, so it won't pay for itself.

Link Trades

Another form of advertising is web links. You can trade links with your mortgage officer in the hopes of getting more cross-over business. You can also ask other business people in related fields in your area to trade links with you: accountants, bookkeepers, financial planners, real estate attorneys, handymen, contractors, etc. Trading links increases traffic to your site, but it also has one other benefit. When you have many links to and from your website, you actually get ranked higher in the search engines for relevancy-based searches. So it's a double-benefit.

The whole point is to drive business to your website. You want people to reach your site and then you want them to stay. Hopefully, you want them to come back again and again. But no amount of traffic, no amount of interesting materials, and no amount of return business will be of any use to you unless you offer your prospects a call to action that causes them to set an appointment with you. So get your pre-sales presentation in place ASAP!

Advertise Your Buyers!

I have one final note before we get off the subject of marketing. I've avoided talking about marketing to the general population because I truly believe that we are better off focusing on our target markets. But if we absolutely must advertise to the populace at large, let's consider how we do that.

It's long been said in our industry that "you have to list to last." And in the days of sub agency, where the only side of the deal that was guaranteed was the listing side, this was true. But today, with the advent of buyer agency, there is more to real estate than listings.

One of the challenges our industry faces is that, even in the markets where buyer agency is established, we're still thinking with listing agents' brains. We want listings because they give us something to advertise to bring in buyers and more listings. But here's a new thought.

What if we advertised our buyers instead? Wouldn't sellers want to list their home more with an agency that had a lot buyers rather than a lot of listings? Sellers want results. If we can show them that we have the resources to come up with buyers for them, then why wouldn't they want to list with us? So, rather than going out and cold calling for that next listing today, why don't we try something different? Let's send out a mailing or place an ad that lists the current buyer clients we are working with and what they are looking for. Any seller who is thinking about putting their house on the market will be interested to know what buyers are looking for and call us. And, if we word the ad with the rules of our target marketing in mind, who knows? Maybe we'll actually get someone in who fits in and is a joy to work with.

CHAPTER 16

SYSTEMS FOR SUPERIOR CUSTOMER SERVICE

In Chapter 10 we discussed the fact that we needed to set our clients' expectations if we were to have any chance at all of exceeding them. If we are looking to develop repeat and referral business, then we need to do this by "wowing" our clients. We need to provide them with a level of service that causes them to sit up and think, "Wow! That was awesome! I never expected that!" In order to accomplish this task we need two pieces in place. First, we need realistic expectations on the part of the client, and this is what we covered in Chapter 1. Second, we need systems in place to make certain that we exceed those expectations on a regular, repeatable basis.

When we put systems in place in our businesses, we do two things at once. First, we give ourselves a break. We offer ourselves a fail-safe, something that we can rely on in the event our brains mutiny (and who among us hasn't had that happen every now and then). The second thing we accomplish is to provide us with a plan to create that "wow" moment for the client. We don't have to find a way to make it up as we go along, it's already built into the system for us. No thinking is required after we have it in place.

The downside to putting systems in place is that creating those systems can be a very time-consuming process. It took me over two years to write up the systems in my *New Agent's Survival Guide to Real Estate*. It took that long because I was writing them nights, weekends, and anytime I could squeeze in a few hours at the office. I wrote my systems because I hired an assistant and I needed to teach her how to run my business. In the process, I added in services and contacts to my clients that they had never had before. With just a little time spent on the side, I made continual progress until I had a fully integrated system in place that let me wow my clients every time.

Now we don't have to spend two years writing systems if we don't want to. There are many systems available in the industry that we can purchase and put into place in our business. It will, however, take time to re-typeset those systems if we are buying a paper copy. It will also take time to add them into our office. We need to create files, or file boxes, or make copies or something to add the system in. Then we need to remember to use it. Systemizing our businesses is no small task. But for each system we put in place, we give ourselves the gift of some extra free time. So with each one we implement, we have a little more time to implement the next. Each system also allows us to free up a little brain space, which reduces our overall stress levels and increases our efficiency.

Procedures

By creating procedures and checklists, we create systems that can be implemented quickly and easily. Having these systems in place in our businesses also make it significantly easier to hire an assistant down the road. Procedures and checklists are internal steps that we take to complete the process of implementing our systems. They are the regular steps we take to accomplish a task. Exhibits 16-1 to 16-7 are samples of some of the procedures and checklists from *The New Agent Survival Guide to Real Estate*.

Integrating Systems into Our Business

Now we have an idea of how we can create systems in our businesses. It's only a matter of time to get them in place. If we commit to getting one system in place each week, we will find by the end of the first month that we have more time to put even more systems in place. Once we have a total system in place for our businesses, then we will have time to do another ten to fifteen deals per year in the same amount of time it used to take us before. Plus, when we get to the point where we are doing even more deals extra per year than that, we will find it easy to bring in and train an assistant.

The "Wow" Factor

To create a "wow" factor for our clients, we need to put systems in place in our business that cost us little in terms of time or money, but still provide that something extra that makes the client realize that we were paying attention to them. One of the easiest ways to wow a client that I have found is my card box.

I used to go out to Hallmark and other card stores during their super sales. I would buy a little of everything: condolence, congratulations, happy birthday, happy anniversary, thank you, graduation cards, etc. I bought different styles of each type of card, some funny, some sappy, some flowery, some simple. I even bought a few blank cards just in case I needed something out of the ordinary. By keeping cards on hand for all occasions, I could respond immediately when someone mentioned a special event. While I was on the phone with them, I would pull out an appropriate card and start writing it out. By the time I hung up the phone, the card was in the mail. Because these cards were the ones you buy individually in a store and not standardized cards, people thought I had gone out and purchased those cards specifically for them after having the conversation. It created a sense of personal attention without costing me a lot of time or money. And, since I always bought the cards in bulk and on sale, it was cheaper than if I had gone out and bought them individually.

Another way to create a sense of personalization without having to take a lot of time is to hand-write an extra comment on a form letter. Our clients know that we use form letters. They know that much of what we have to say to people is the same and therefore it makes little sense to rewrite it each time. But they also want to know that we care about them. We can print out our form letter addressed to them and then add a quick note at the bottom just for them. For instance, we might send a seller a letter with copies of his ads for that week. At the bottom we might write a note saying something like, "Hang in there—it's looking good!" or "I'll call you Friday to catch you up on what's happening in the market." It doesn't have to be complex, it just has to be especially for them. Just that one line makes the difference between an impersonal communication and a personal one.

And speaking of personal notes, one of the best ways to get on the good side of a client or prospect is to write them a personal note. This is where the blank note cards and thank-you cards come in most handy. I always kept a stack of them in my car. Whenever I had a few moments when I had to wait for someone to show up at a house or for an appointment, I'd pull out a card and write a quick note to one of my past clients. It wasn't much, just a little something to let them know I was thinking of them. I got more calls from the people who received these notes than from any other marketing I did. Personal contact is always the best contact.

A "wow" factor doesn't have to be something incredible, it just has to be something more than what the client expected. Perhaps we have a contact at a warehouse receiving company that gets tons of boxes in each day. We can help the company by taking some of the boxes off their hands and help our clients by providing boxes for free. No cost to us, just a little effort to transport the boxes. Perhaps we put together a loaner moving prep box for our clients, which consists of a packing tape dispenser with tape, a magic marker, and a clip board with a bunch of inventory sheets. Our cost is only the original supplies plus replacement tape, markers, and copies for the inventory sheets. Or we could give our buyers a move-in box that has a picture hanging kit, a hammer, a contractor's knife, and a roll of toilet paper. Or we can have pizza and soda delivered to the buyers on their first night in their new home. Or we can offer to come over with our digital camera and take pictures of their valuables for insurance purposes.

Much of what we can offer our clients costs us very little in time or money. But each one is a way in which we can "wow" them into coming back to us time and time again and bringing their friends.

Exhibit 16-1. Fax feedback filing system.

This is a system that allows you or your assistant to reach to one spot to send out a fax when an agent is showing your property. The fax will contain the following information:

- Agent Fax Feedback Form (Exhibit 16-2)
- Property description sheet (MLS printout)
- Seller's Property Condition Report (Seller's Disclosure)
- Lead Paint Disclosure
- Property Map (Plot Plan)—Optional

These sheets are single-sided copies ready to feed through the fax machine to the agent showing the property. They are stored paper-clipped together by listing address in an accordion file, alphabetically by property address.

Supplies List

To set up this system you will need:

- Accordion file with alphabetic dividers
- Fax post-it notes
- Paper clips (to keep copies for each listing together)

This form reprinted with permission from *The New Agent's Survival Guide to Real Estate* available through Sparta Success Systems at www.spartasuccess.com.

Exhibit 16-2. Agent's fax feedback form.

DATE: _____
TO: _____
FROM: _____

Property Address _____

Agent Feedback

How is property priced? ❏ On Target ❏ Too High ❏ Too Low

Check all that apply

❏ Good Curb Appeal ❏ Poor Curb Appeal, suggest change _____

❏ Shows well ❏ Shows poorly, why _____

❏ Needs work _____

❏ Dirty ❏ Clean

❏ Dark ❏ Bright

Other Comments: _____

_____

Buyer Feedback

Is this property still on your list of possibles? ❏ yes ❏ no

If no, why not? _____

If yes, what would make you want to buy it? _____

_____

Other Comments _____

_____

This form reprinted with permission from *The New Agent's Survival Guide to Real Estate* available through Sparta Success Systems at www.spartasuccess.com.

Exhibit 16-3. Listing file set-up checklist.

Owner Name _____ Phone _____

Property Location _____ Date Listed _____

❑ Make file (type label)
❑ Order sign installation/install sign—note signs installed on Sign Log

Schedule Open House	__/__/__
Schedule MLS Caravan	__/__/__
Schedule Office Caravan	__/__/__

❑ Deliver brochure box

❑ Give info to front desk for entry into MLS system

❑ Take pictures

❑ Download pictures—send to the MLS

❑ Check file for:
    ❑ Seller's Disclosure
    ❑ Field/Street Card
    ❑ Legal Description
    ❑ Map of property
    ❑ Copy of keys to property
    ❑ Seller Info & Interview Sheets
    ❑ Signed letter to neighbors for seller
    ❑ Copy of listing & MLS input sheets—signed and initialed as required
    ❑ Copy of MLS printout for file—MLS# _____

❑ Make Copies:
    ❑ 10 copies of printout & Seller's Disclosure, put in showing folder
    ❑ Copy of Seller's Disclosure for fax file

❑ Put copy of MLS printout with seller/tenant's phone # and showing instructions in a sheet protector. File with other copies in showing folder.

❑ Enter listing into computer; input all information on property, including showing info for property. Print out fax feedback sheet on property for fax file. Attach to copy of Seller's Disclosure and file by address in fax file.

❑ Enter Seller as a new client contact (make sure to include info on where lead came from, add to newsletter, and status).

❑ Fill out a Listing Tracking Sheet and a Listing Contact Record for this listing—put in Office Info Binder.

(continues)

Exhibit 16-3. (Continued.)

❑ Send out 60 "Just Listed" letters to neighbors (copies of letter that seller signed).

❑ Launch new seller plan.

❑ Write ads on Advertising Prep Sheet—file in Office Info Binder.

❑ Create brochure for property, make 30 copies, set appointment to deliver (or mail).

❑ Deliver lockbox by: _____ Lockbox combination: _____ (or add Key Log to Office Info Binder) (Note on Sign Log & Lockbox Log)

❑ Fill out request for Hotline Script

This form reprinted with permission from *The New Agent's Survival Guide to Real Estate* available through Sparta Success Systems at www.spartasuccess.com.

Exhibit 16-4. Buyer file set-up checklist.

Buyer Name:	**Buyer Broker Client? ❑ Y ❑ N**

❑ Make File (type label).

❑ Confirm that buyer received a copy of the "Protect Your Family from Lead in the Home" booklet.

❑ Input client into computer (check to make sure they are not there already). Make certain to include info on how lead came in and status info, as well as putting them on the newsletter list.

❑ Set up "Our Goal" Letters to be sent out at 1 month, 2 months, 4 months, and 6 months.

❑ Input buyer as a prospect in the MLS system for regular searches.

❑ Pull listings for buyer—arrange for pick-up or mail out.

❑ File in buyer section.

❑ Note expiration of Buyer Agency Agreement in calendar so that we can extend.

Other activities:

❑ Schedule appts. for buyer for _____ (date) starting at _____ (time). Client will meet Agent at ❑ _____ or ❑ the office at _____(time).

Other notes/items to be completed:

_____

_____

_____

_____

This form reprinted with permission from *The New Agent's Survival Guide to Real Estate* available through Sparta Success Systems at www.spartasuccess.com.

Exhibit 16-5. Accepted contract checklist.

- ❏ Check Contract—make sure everything is signed and initialed as required.
- ❏ Set up new file in contact manager.
- ❏ Set up appointments for contingencies.
- ❏ Note all due dates on the Files in Progress Checklist.
- ❏ Note commitment, closing, and home inspection dates on the erasable wall calendar.
- ❏ If our buyer, fax a copy of the signed contract to mortgage officer, mail original to them.
- ❏ If our seller, fax a copy of the legal description to the mortgage officer.
- ❏ Call the other agent to find out who the closing attorney will be for the other side.
  Attorney Name _____ Phone # _____
- ❏ Fax copy of the contract to our client's attorney along with the Attorney Closing Sheet.
- ❏ File copy of contract in the file folder on the left-hand side, pages in order, most recent copy on top.
- ❏ Schedule reminder about appraisal for about 14 days from today.
- ❏ Schedule reminder for Pre-Closing Checklist to be completed ten (10) days prior to scheduled closing.
- ❏ Fill out Closing Sheet for office, and provide a copy of contract, all addenda, deposit check, agency disclosure, lead disclosure, and seller's disclosure. If our listing, turn in the deposit check as well.
- ❏ Update commission schedule with sale info and print a new copy.
- ❏ Send a letter within two (2) days with a Buyer's or Seller's Pre-Closing Checklist, a Performance Evaluation, and a self-addressed stamped envelope. If our buyer, also send a utilities sheet for the area.

(continues)

Exhibit 16-5. (Continued.)

❏ If our buyer, start first 10-day process for this client.

❏ If our listing, put "pending" rider on sign.

❏ Put file in the red "pending" section of file drawer.

This form reprinted with permission from *The New Agent's Survival Guide to Real Estate* available through Sparta Success Systems at www.spartasuccess.com.

Exhibit 16-6. Closed contract checklist.

❏ Make two copies of HUD Statement:
Original—to file (left hand side on top of contract)
Copy 1—to "HUD Statements to be sent out next year" file
Copy 2—to office file—submit with commission check (see below)

❏ Make copy of the closing check, put in our file on top of HUD Statement.

❏ Submit sales report, copy 2 of HUD from above, office closing sheet and the closing check to office.

❏ Close file in contact manager.

In client contact manager:

❏ Change Status to "Past Client" and Priority to "Low."

❏ Update address section with new address of client either from "Seller Moving Sheet" or update address to that of the property purchased if buyer is purchasing own residence.

❏ Update phone number.

❏ In "Notes" section, indicate that client closed on property and the date. Also, add any additional information that was noted on the "At Closing Checklist" re: move-in date, etc.

❏ Schedule appointment with this client for date and time set at closing on the "At Closing Checklist" to meet re: mortgage buy-down lesson and pictures.

❏ Print out Contact Summary Report and file in Date/Contact Book in "Past Client" section. Remove old printout from "Current Client" section and discard.

❏ Launch Buyer or Seller Follow-Up plan.

❏ Send out a "Congratulations" note on the day after the buyers move in or sellers reach their new destination.

❏ Put sale info in newsletter file.

If this was our listing:

❑ Order sign removal/remove sign—note on Sign Log.

❑ Remove lockbox—note on Lockbox Log.

❑ Send out "Just Sold" letters/postcards to neighbors.

❑ Remove fax feedback form and seller's disclosure from Fax file.

❑ Throw away listing copies and showing instructions from listing box.

❑ Take pictures out of file box and put in file folder.

❑ Move Listing Tracker, Listing Contact Record(s), Ad Prep Sheets, and Listing/Showing Instructions from Office Info Binder. File on right side of listing file folder.

❑ When complete, file this checklist on the right hand side of the file folder and put entire file in the "Closed Listing" or the "Closed Buyer" box for storage.

This form reprinted with permission from *The New Agent's Survival Guide to Real Estate* available through Sparta Success Systems at www.spartasuccess.com.

Exhibit 16-7. HUD statement letter. (Send in January.)

Dear (Client Name),

Enclosed is a copy of your HUD1 Settlement Statement on your home (purchase/sale) last year. As you get ready to do your taxes this year, you will want to make sure you put this in with your tax information. There are items on this form that you can deduct on your taxes that appear nowhere else in your records, most notably any pre-paid interest and points you paid on the loan. There may be additional items as well, so make sure you bring this to your accountant's attention.

Hopefully, your tax year will be treating you well this time around. If I can be of any assistance, now or in the future, just give me a call. I'd love to help.

Sincerely,

Your Real Estate Consultant

P.S. As always, if you know of anyone who is looking to buy or sell property, either locally or long distance, please call me. Your referrals are the lifeblood of my business.

This form reprinted with permission from *The New Agent's Survival Guide to Real Estate* available through Sparta Success Systems at www.spartasuccess.com.

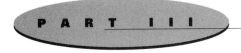

PART III

DEVELOPING

SKILLS FOR

SUCCESS

CHAPTER 17

DEEPER LISTENING

In today's society, we rarely listen. We are so busy, that we have diffi-culty slowing down enough to truly hear what the other person is saying. We graze the surface of what the other person is saying, picking up only the bits that we believe are important and letting the rest roll away with-out so much as a notice. We skim our conversations much like we would skim books in college: looking only for what we needed to know rather than investing in the content as a whole. Rather than hearing what the other person has to say on all levels, we find ourselves waiting for our turn to talk. In the stress of our everyday lives, we are too hurried, too stressed, too overwhelmed with our own existence to make room for any-one else's. Subsequently, we are a society of people silently begging to be noticed—to be heard.

It is when we are at our most stressed that we most need that kind ear, someone who will listen without judgment, sometimes even without comment. The simple act of being able to fully express ourselves is liberat-ing, even if what we have expressed cannot be fixed. The fact that some-one would take time from his busy day to sit and listen to us is a statement about our importance, our worthiness. It improves our self-worth and makes us feel wanted and accepted. All of us want to feel this way.

Exercise

Think for a moment about the last time you felt completely heard.

Who was doing the listening? Was it someone you loved? Or was it a therapist who was paid to listen? Where were you? What was the person doing? Were they involved in doing something else while they listened? Were they in a hurry to get somewhere else? Did they have a deadline for when they had to leave by? Did this person judge you for your comments? Did they try to solve whatever problem you were having? Did you want them to? Take a moment and cement that memory in your head. Think about what that person did that made you feel heard. These are the things you need to do with your client.

What Makes Someone a Good Listener?

A good listener gives the person she is sitting with the impression that she is happy to be listening to what the person has to say. She is fully present in the conversation, meaning she is not distracted by other things she is doing or by other thoughts running through her head. She has nowhere else she has to be and nothing else she'd rather be doing in that moment. She is invested in the conversation and its outcome. She is truly interested in what the other person is saying—so much so that she is listening not only to the text of the discussion, but also to the subtext. She is NOT trying to share information about herself. She is not judging the speaker based on what is being said. She does not try to solve a problem unless the speaker requests it. She is simply listening.

Whew! That's a lot to think about. I call this process of listening "holding space" for the person who is speaking. I think of it as being completely *his* time. He is the one who is speaking. It is not my place to say anything except what is necessary for me to indicate that I am still present in the moment ("uh huh," "tell me more," "really," etc.). If I am to speak, then it is only to ask a question to get what I need to understand what he is saying.

This deeper listening process is liberating not only for the speaker, but also for the listener. It allows me, as the listener, to slow down. Because I need to be completely present in the moment to hear all of the nuances of the conversation, there is no space in that moment for me to mentally be elsewhere. I can clear my mind of all extraneous concerns. I know that they will be there again when we finish, but for now they can wait. This is a space in which I can relax and simply be.

OK, this is all great, but why, as agents, do we care? We all know that to build rapport with someone we need to find a point of commonality with the person, a place where we have common experiences. We should listen only so long as to find that commonality and then be able to point it out to the other person so that we click, right? Wrong. Common wisdom would tell us that this is true, that we like other people who are just like us. I would say that the truth of this thought is more along the lines of: *We like people who like us*. And people who like us are people who take the time to listen—without interrupting with stories about themselves.

So how do we listen effectively other than not talking about ourselves? The key here is to listen not only to what is said, but also to what goes unspoken. If someone mentions that the best vacation he ever had was one that he took alone, we have to wonder if there is a reason that this story doesn't include his wife. If he hangs his head as he says that he guesses he'll look for a house in a particular town, we need to identify why he said it that way. Is he embarrassed to say he wants to live there? Does he wish that he could live somewhere else but is certain that he can't afford it? Why the negative body language and the qualifying statement ("I guess")? We talked about tonality before. What does the tonality of this man say to us? Is he happy to be talking about this? Is he uncomfortable? Is he guarded? What's going on in his head?

Listen for the "Push"

The next piece is to listen for the "push." The push is the place in which the energy of the conversation shifts. We can feel that there is something more behind the statement as it comes out of the person's mouth. Sometimes, the push comes in the form of repeated words or concepts in a conversation.

For example, I did a buyer interview with an agent in one of my classes. During our dialogue about what she wanted in a house, she used the words "belong," "feels right," "comfortable," and "fit in." She repeated some of these words more than once. In listening to not only the text of her responses, but the subtext of the repeated words and concepts, it became clear to me that as a buyer she would purchase any house in which she felt like she belonged. It was more a quality of being than a physical reality that she was seeking. I said this to her and she agreed that this was true. A house could be completely different from what she had just described and if it "felt" right, she'd buy it anyway.

It is important that we pick up on these clues. If I were to look for a house for this person, I would need to know what "felt" good to her in order to find the right home. It would be pursuing this concept rather than the typical criteria of number of bedrooms and baths that would be the determining factor for her.

In interviewing this agent, I did not go further into the conversation about what would make her feel like she belonged, since that was not the purpose of the exercise at the time. But if I had, I would have asked her to tell me about the feelings of belonging that she wanted. When had she felt them before? What physical factors in a house made her feel most comfortable? I'd ask her to describe places she had been before where she felt as though she fit in. In this way I would find the keys to what would make a house her home.

Finding the Subtext

When we listen carefully, we can pick up on the subtext, the subtle clues that tell us what is really important to this person. These clues come out as patterns in people's language, repeated words, concepts, or feelings, or we may even get our information from what thoughts or comments people avoid. Once we identify these triggers, we then ask the client to expound upon them so we can get more clarity around the issue. For instance, if a seller says that he "wants to know what's going on," and asks about the systems we have in place to keep track of the details, and wants all the written material we have available on real estate sales, and asks us if we're sure of everything we're saying, then we know that this person is looking for a sense of control. We can confirm this assumption by asking him if our comments have made him feel like he has a grip on the issues. We can even say something like, "So I'm hearing that it's important to you to have a sense of control over this process—is that right?"

We shouldn't be afraid to state the obvious. If we can tell that someone is uncomfortable, we should feel empowered to say, "I can tell you're uncomfortable. Can you tell me what is making you feel that way or let me know how I can make you feel better?" I am known to my friends as "Captain Obvious" because I have the habit of stating the obvious. It is a way of clearing the air. It puts it on the table that everyone is aware of the issue, so we can stop avoiding it now. It says, "Hey! There's a white elephant in the middle of the room! How'd that get there?" Once the white elephant is identified, we are in a position to escort it from the room together.

Converting Ad Callers by Stating the Obvious

This is a particularly good technique for talking to ad callers. They don't want to be talking to us. We know it and they know it. They just want the address and to get on to the next call to another agent they don't want to talk to. If we can commiserate with them by acknowledging this fact, then we are halfway home to getting them into the office. While we are looking up the property, we say something like, "Wow, how many of these calls have you made today? It's got to be exhausting playing chicken with so many agents." They will likely open up and admit that it has been a hassle. Then you are free to offer to solve this problem for them by having them come into the office and get a complete listing of everything that's on the MLS that meets their needs. No one likes to be in conflict—it's unpleasant and it wears us down. The verbal sparring that buyers do with duty agents to get addresses is more work than most buyers want to do. We can be their hero by having them work with us.

Nonverbal Cues

Most of the content of any conversation is nonverbal. Being able to read someone's body language and discern other nonverbal cues are advantages when we are trying to listen effectively. Here are a few items of nonverbal communication that every agent should know:

- Mumbling: The person is apologizing for what she is saying or is afraid she will be judged for the comment.
- He is talking with a hand over the mouth—see *Mumbling*.
- The person who had seemed wide awake before is now yawning and his eyes are glazing over. We've given him too much information. His brain is shutting down and he will be unable to hear anything else we say until he has had time to integrate what he's already heard. We need to make another appointment to finish the conversation later.
- She's speaking in short, clipped phrases—she's feeling defensive. She wants to give up no more information than absolutely required.
- The person won't quite face us and keeps talking slightly off to the side—she doesn't trust us. When we fully face someone we are open to attack, in profile we present a smaller target and are more prepared to get away.
- She is leaning back in the chair with arms crossed—a defensive stance. The person either doesn't trust us or is feeling defensive.
- He is leaning forward, arms open—the person is engaged, interested, and open. Add a smile to this mix and we're in like Flynn.
- She is refusing to make eye contact—this could have several meanings and must be considered in context. If it is consistent throughout the conversation and accompanied by nonconfident language, then it is likely a reflection of poor self-esteem. If it is associated with the short, clipped language, then it is likely the person is lying to us about something. If it is accompanied by mumbling, then it could be a shame-based reaction to what the person is saying. In some Asian cultures, not making eye contact is a sign of respect.

We need to consider everything in context to understand what the actual meaning is. If in doubt, it's always better to ask than to risk assuming incorrectly.

Judgment

No matter what else we may do or say in the process of listening deeply to the person in front of us, we must remember one thing—we cannot judge. The minute we begin to judge the speaker for what he is saying, we lose. The judgment will show on our face, the speaker will sense it, and the conversation will shut down. We need to sit in a place of acceptance for whatever comes out of the person's mouth. We don't need to agree with it, we simply need to accept that it is true for him and that this fact makes it relevant to us.

Silencing the Inner Commentary

One of the biggest challenges for agents learning these techniques is how to silence the inner commentary. We are, by nature, such talkative creatures. We love the sound of our own voices. We have so many good stories to tell, so many pearls of wisdom to share. How could we possibly let go of all of these thoughts and simply listen?

The key is to remove ourselves from the conversation. I don't mean that we should leave the room. What I mean is that we need to be clear that the conversation we are having has nothing to do with us. Therefore, anything we say must be about the other person, not about us. So no matter how many cute stories we have that go along with the stories the other person is telling, we don't get to share them. This is not our conversation—it is his. At first, this will be difficult.

As a culture, we are desperately in need of being heard, and agents are no exception to this rule. It is so hard for us to simply listen to someone else. We feel as though we should get our time in the sun, and in social conversation, this would be true. But this is business. It is our job to listen. We are getting paid to listen. This is not about us, it is about the client. Every time our thoughts stray to one of our stories or to our wants and needs, we need to simply remind ourselves of the fact that this is the client's conversation, not ours.

Digging Deeper

Once we have learned how to be present with the person in front of us rather than being continually distracted by the thoughts in our head, we will recognize when and how we can take the conversation deeper. Our own thoughts are the things that most often get in the way of our being able to recognize an opening. And make no mistake, we are looking for openings.

An *opening* is an opportunity to take the conversation to the next level. It is a chance for us to ask a question that will bring us to a greater understanding of the client and his needs. Here are a few examples of openings we may encounter:

- Moments when the client seems to get lost in his thoughts. The conversation trails off. This is when we ask for clarification of what he had just been speaking about.
- When the "push" comes. Ask more questions and dig deeper around the "push" issue.
- Repeated words, thoughts, or feelings—ask questions that get into why these things are important to the client.
- Moments when the client asks for our opinion. This is when he is not certain. Explore the uncertainty and ask for his opinion. Support him by saying it is a good question, one that many people don't know the right answer to if his answer was wrong. Or let your face light up as you tell him he is exactly right. Bolster his feelings of competency.
- "I don't know . . ." or "I guess . . ." are statements of a lack of confidence. Offer supportive statements to reinforce his confidence.

Letting the Conversation Run Its Course

It is important that we not stick our noses into the conversation too soon. All of the techniques I listed above are good techniques, but if they are applied too soon or too often, they can shut the conversation down. We need to apply them sparingly and only after we have listened for a while. We want to wait for the client's monologue to slow down of its own accord before we interrupt. Let him get everything out onto the table before we start to pick it apart.

Often we will find that when we do this, there are several issues that show up along the way. It is more important for us to sit and listen than it is for us to address each issue as it comes up. If we know that we will need to address something eventually, then we should write it down—just a quick, short note to remind us of what we want to discuss.

Try not to write too much or too often, since it makes the person who is talking stop in their thoughts and instead wonder what you have written. And don't let them see what you have written or else you'll be off talking about that subject rather than getting to the issues that would have come up had you finished the initial conversation.

Good Questions to Ask

- Tell me more about (insert repeated thought, phrase, or feeling).
- I noticed you specifically avoided talking about (subject/person/ etc.). Why is that?
- I noticed you left out X. Was that on purpose?
- You seem to be very focused on X. Can you tell me what about X is important to you?
- What does (emotion/thought/concept) mean to you?
- How would you like to translate (emotion/thought/concept) into your new home?
- Hmmm, that's very interesting—tell me more about that.

Each of these questions is open-ended. Even the one question that offers the opportunity to simply say "yes" or "no" (I noticed you left out X, was that on purpose?) implies that we are asking for a reason to go with the answer. We want the client to talk to us some more. The more they talk, the more information we gather.

This is not a hard-target search. It is more like wading through murky waters and watching for the flash of the fish's scales as it darts past our legs. We can't find the fish without wading a little, but the more we move, the more we muddy the waters with our own comments. So we try to move only enough to make the fish swim and show itself to us. Think of your conversations in this way. Move enough to make the fish swim, but not so much that you stir up the silt and can't see through the water anymore.

Tonality is key in these conversations. The calmer we are, the more quiet our voices are, the smoother we are in our questions, the better. Using the fish analogy again, we want to move softly. The softer we go, the less jerky our movements, the slower we move, the less the silt is disturbed. We don't want the client to really notice us. It is better if they think of us as a reflection of themselves. We are less threatening this way and that makes it easier for them to open up.

CHAPTER 18

EFFECTIVE

COMMUNICATION

No matter how well we learn to understand our clients, it does us no good unless we can communicate that understanding back to them. In this chapter, we will explore the different aspects of good communication.

Different people communicate in different ways. There are three distinct ways in which people learn and these are the best ways to approach these people when you are trying to communicate with them. The three learning formats are: visual, auditory, and kinesthetic.

Visual learners are people who learn by seeing. They can read something and learn from it. They can watch something and learn from it. But if you explain something to them verbally, they are less likely to understand what you are saying and to retain that information.

Auditory learners are people who learn by hearing. They do best in environments where a teacher explains a concept to them verbally. These are the people who like to purchase programs on tape or CD. Audio books were a great boon to this group.

Kinesthetic learners are people who learn by doing. You can talk until you're blue in the face, you can draw pictures on the board, and still they aren't interested. They want to touch it and feel it and get a grip on the subject, literally.

Very few people learn in only one fashion. Most of us have aspects of all three types within our learning structure, so this is not a hard and fast rule. But, it is a general indicator. How we communicate effectively with each group is determined by their approach to learning.

When we listen carefully, we can pick up on the cues that tell us what kind of a learner someone is. For instance, a visual learner will use language like "I see where you're coming from," and "can you see what I mean," or even "looks good to me." Whereas an auditory learner will say things like "I hear you," or "how does that sound to you," or "that's music to my ears." Kinesthetic learners, on the other hand, will use phrases such as "That feels good to me," or "I just can't seem to get a grip on what you're saying," or "I'm touched by your sentiment."

By picking up on these phrases, we can then use those same types of phrases back to our clients to put our language into a mode most comfortable to the client. In this way, we can make our communications more accessible and we can build a stronger sense of rapport. These factors go a long way toward creating a strong communication bond. This technique works not only for these types of phrases, but also for all of the clients' languaging. Each of us has words and phrases that we like to use most often. If we can find out what those words and phrases are for our clients and then use those back to them in our communication, we can connect with them more easily and more deeply.

How We Say Things Matters—a Lot!

When I started in real estate, I was twenty-three years old and I just couldn't understand why my phraseology mattered. If someone was an idiot, I felt it was my option (neigh, my responsibility!) to point this fact out to them. I pushed my way through deals leaving enemies in my wake, never understanding the long-term damage I would have to eventually go back and repair if my career were to continue. I didn't see why I needed to couch my language in niceties or even sometimes take the blame for things that we both knew were the other person's fault. I was then what I now affectionately refer to as "the tactless wonder."

Oddly enough, I knew the appropriate ways to say things. I had done a lot of study on relationships and communication. I had read all the books on the subject, but I didn't see that I needed to use them in business. It was only over time that I learned the importance of this skill. As I watched the successful agents in my office and saw the reactions they got to their comments and compared them to the reactions that I got, I realized that they were on to something. Over time, I developed a much more reserved style of communication. I still told people the same things, I just did it in better ways than before—and lo and behold I got better reactions!

This continued until one day, about five years into my business, I was applying to become a certified trainer for Mind Empowerment International, a company that offered personal empowerment training. As part of the application process I had to interview a friend and have them describe me. I picked a fairly new friend, someone I had met while selling her a house. When I asked her to describe me, the first word out of her mouth was "diplomatic." I almost fell out of my chair. "Could you repeat that?" I asked. She said it again. Sure enough, I wasn't imagining it. Somehow, over the time I had spent in the business, the tactless wonder had become a diplomat. Who knew? Certainly not I.

The point of this story is that in order to flourish in this business, we need to learn to be effective diplomats. We serve in the same capacity as any ambassador. Our job is to represent the interests of our client, while maintaining diplomatic relations with the other side. If we fail, the result is a shutting-down of communication and, possibly, war.

Obviously, the first person we need to learn to communicate effectively with is our client. She is the person to whom we are bound. We must represent her best interests. In order to accomplish this task, we must understand what those interests are. This involves both listening well and communicating the information back in such a way as to be understood by the client.

Once we have a good understanding of the situation with the client, then we need to communicate the client's need to the other agent in the deal. He is our adversary, but he is also our partner in the transaction. It is a fine line to walk. We need to be friendly, but not give ground in the negotiations—and we need to be careful not to break confidentiality with our client.

Once we have the deal hammered out with the agent, then we have to communicate the client's desires to the attorney. He will need to know the same things we needed to know about the client, since he will be the one working on the remainder of the transaction on the client's behalf. We can save the client a lot of time and frustration by conveying that information to the attorney for her.

We also need to communicate with the bank through the mortgage lender to let them know that we've found a property and it's time to get an appraisal done. It's important that the lender is on the same page as we are to eliminate any possible problems. If there are issues, then we must address those as quickly as possible.

Of course, there's also the home inspector. We need to be able to get the information that we need from the home inspector—preferably while avoiding spinning the buyer out of control in the process. This means being able to keep calm and identify which issues are major and which aren't and what costs are associated with them.

And finally, there's the appraiser. Talking to an appraiser is always a challenging experience when we're trying to influence the outcome of the appraisal without alienating the appraiser. We want to give her the comps. We want her to use them. We want her to not list any items on the CRV that need repair prior to closing. We want her to appraise the property at or above the purchase price. We want, we want, we want. How we communicate that want can mean the difference between getting a positive appraisal or a negative one.

Wow! That's a lot of people with whom we need to be able to communicate effectively. And we can only add to that list when we're dealing with a mobile home park owner or a builder or a condo/coop/homeowners' association. Now that we recognize our role as ambassador to these people, it's time to look at how we can fulfill that role most effectively.

Keep in mind as you're reading that we are dealing with communication under a variety of conditions. When people are happy, it is easy for communication to go well. It is when people are stressed or upset in any way that communications tend to break down. The reason for this is that under these strains, they tend to react in ways that are defensive. They will automatically assume that the other person is on the attack and they will respond out of fear. It is important to note as we explore these communication techniques that many of them are designed to reduce the level of tension in the room. This is not an extraneous step. It is the critical first step to getting back on track with our communications.

Tonality

We've already discussed tonality a little in terms of communication skills in Chapter 9, Creating Instant Rapport. Let's go a little more in-depth at this point. We'll be addressing tonality both in terms of how it applies in times when stress levels are low as well as how to use it when stress levels are ramping up.

In Bad Times

Tonality is the way we say things. Are we positive and confident, or whiny and annoying? Are we friendly or are we confrontational? The tone with which we engage the conversation will create the environment for the exchange. We need to be conscious of the choices we make with this issue. There have been many times in my career when I wanted nothing more than to walk up to someone and explain to them in no uncertain terms exactly how stupid they had been and why the industry would be better if they considered a change of career. We've all had those moments. And, often, our comments would be completely true. The problem is that making those comments probably will not get us what we want out of the conversation. As emotionally satisfying as it would be, we have to remember that the person we ream out today is the person we'll need to help us through a sticky situation tomorrow.

So when we pick up the phone to make the call we've been dreading, we need to decide what our tone will be. That decision needs to be based on what we, upon rational, reasoned consideration, believe will get us the best result. I try *never* to pick up the phone when I am angry. It is almost guaranteed that I will blow the conversation. If I'm upset, I'll take a walk, count to ten, play a computer game, do something to get my mind off of being upset. Once I am calmed down, I'll think about what I want to accomplish with the call. Once I have that, then I pick the tone of voice most likely to accomplish that end. Only then do I finally pick up the phone to make the call.

In Good Times

The tone of voice we use is just as important when things are going well as it is in times of stress. Developing relationships with the people in our industry is crucial to ongoing success. These relationships are best built in good times so that we can depend upon them in bad times. When we get on the phone with our colleagues in the industry, we want to be wearing a smile. We need to chat, engage in personal conversation, commiserate about the trials of the day (without being a whiner—nobody likes a whiner), and generally be friendly. Our tonality should reflect the feeling that we are happy to be speaking with that person, that we value her input, and that we feel friendly toward her. By the end of the conversation, the tonality in our voice should have encouraged her to speak to us again because she enjoyed the conversation so much this time.

Blame-Neutral Wording

When we engage in a problem-related conversation, no matter which of the people we are speaking to in the transaction, we need to choose our words carefully. It is all too easy to get into blaming and name-calling, especially when we are watching our commissions evaporate right before our eyes. Taking the high road is often the most difficult thing we can do, but it's also the best practice.

Blame-neutral wording means that when we speak of the issue, we don't discuss whose fault the problem is. We simply address the issue from the current moment and then move forward. We don't look back at how the problem arose. After all, does it really matter how we got here? What matters is how we're getting out of this pickle and moving on to the next step. When addressing these types of issues, it's often useful to speak in terms that imply that both parties are on the same side. For instance, we might call the other agent and say, "We've got a problem, here's how I'd like to solve it." This is a far better approach than, "You've got a problem and you need to take care of it."

In fact, if we can avoid using the word "you" at all, we are well on our way to staying in blame-free speech patterns. When we use the word "you," we are usually placing assumptions, blame, or expectations on the other person. None of these is a good idea. When striving for blame-free conversations, it is best to use the words "I" or "we." This keeps us focused on positive, forward movement and forces us to address our feelings about the issues rather than using blame to avoid those feelings.

The other benefit to blame-free communication is that it defuses the other party's defensive stance. It is far easier to get solutions agreed to and implemented when both parties are focused on the solution rather than being stuck in defensiveness. And, remember, we are trying to get the deal closed. It is not our job (no matter how much we might like it to be) to police the industry and correct the idiots.

Here's an amusing story on this subject:

It was a new construction house. There was something that the agent was supposed to handle that she didn't. I don't remember the exact details of the problem that was going on, but I clearly remember this agent's response. *I* knew it was her fault. *She* knew it was her fault. But, keeping in mind that I had a deal to salvage and using my blame-free communication skills, I called her up and said:

"We've got a problem and here's what I'd like to do to fix it." Before I got through my sentence, she was saying:

"It's not my fault."

I told her that I wasn't concerned with whose fault it was, my only concern was that we fix the problem. She repeated that it wasn't her fault. I repeated that I didn't care who was to blame, I wanted to fix it. These same words went back and forth a couple more times until it became clear to me that this woman would be unwilling to solve the problem until she was absolved of guilt for its creation. I took a deep breath, thought about what was best for my client, and said:

"If I say it's all my fault, can we solve the problem?" There was a moment of silence as she stumbled mentally on what I'd just said.

"What did you say?" she asked.

"I said it's all my fault. Now can we please solve the problem?"

She said, "Oh, all right." And we proceeded to work out a solution.

In reality what would happen is that I would tell my client that she was to blame and she would tell her builder that it was my fault and each of us would come out smelling like a rose with our respective clients. So what did it matter what we agreed to on the phone with regards to blame? I wanted to solve the problem. I couldn't get it solved until I could get her out of panic and defensive mode. I did what needed to be done to get the issue resolved. It was really quite funny, when I think about it. I felt a little sorry for her. It was obvious from her response that this was not her first time in the hot seat for not getting something accomplished. I had the feeling from the strength of her emotion that she was in danger of being fired by the builder if she made another mistake. My comment taking blame may have just saved her job. And what did it cost me? Nothing.

When we look at our communication patterns with our clients and colleagues in the industry, we find a variety of ways in which we can positively affect our relationships without changing our direct communications. All we need change is the way in which we word our phrases and the tonality we use to deliver them. With these small shifts in approach we can reap huge rewards.

CHAPTER 19

BUILDING GOOD INDUSTRY RELATIONSHIPS

When we build good relationships in the industry, we build good careers as well. The process of creating a bond with other agents, mortgage officers, attorneys, home inspectors, appraisers, and contractors is really very simple. Be nice to them. Be respectful of them. Don't waste their time. It's the golden rule all over again. It takes a little effort to create and maintain these relationships, but it's worth it in the long run.

Don't believe me? Do you think that these people need you and therefore it doesn't matter what you say to them? Well, here's a series of stories that might change your mind.

The Clueless Attorney

One of the agents in my office came to me with a problem one day. He told me that an attorney involved in his transaction was insisting that the refrigerator did not have to be included in the offer to purchase, even though the buyer wanted it. She was insisting that the refrigerator was a fixture and that it had to convey. I asked him who the attorney was (since this was not common practice for our area at all). He told me that the attorney was the buyer's cousin and was not a real estate attorney, but a generalist. This explained a lot to me.

Attorneys from outside the industry, especially those who are representing friends or family, often look for ways to make themselves useful and go about creating problems where none exist. They have no relationships in the industry to maintain to keep their businesses afloat, so they will happily blow up our deals without a thought.

The challenge this agent faced was how to tell an attorney she was wrong about the law. I explained to the agent that he didn't need to tell her this. His only job was to get the refrigerator into the purchase and sale agreement. This was my suggestion: Blame the other agent.

Here's what I told him to say:

> "You know, I'm sure you're absolutely correct about the letter of the law. The problem that I have is that it is not common practice in this area to do it that way. If the buyer wants the refrigerator, then we write it in. If we don't write it in, then the listing agent will direct the seller to either take the refrigerator with him or dispose of it. And then we'll get to the walk-through and there will be no refrigerator and someone at the closing table will have to buy him a new one. Now, I'm certain that you're fully in the right about the law, but for the listing agent's sake, can't we just write it in? It won't hurt anything, will it?"

> The agent used just this approach with the attorney and it worked like a charm. The buyer got his refrigerator. The attorney got to feel like she was superior to the agents in the deal. And the agent got his closing commission—without paying for a refrigerator.

The Master Chief and the Home Inspector

I had a client who was a Master Chief at fifteen years in the service. For those of you who don't know, this is a very big deal. Most enlisted personnel never make it to the Master Chief level—just getting there is an honor. But to make it to that level when he had only been in the Navy for fifteen years, that was a feat I have never personally seen before or since. Basically, the Navy was saying that this man walked on water. He was assigned to a prototype submarine. The Navy trusted him—a lot—which meant that this man was as anal retentive as you can get. He questioned everything.

When the time came for his home inspection, I called in my marker. I had been doing business regularly with Tiger Home Inspections in my area. I had fed them twenty to thirty deals a year for several years. They owed me.

I called the owner of the company and said, "Joe, it's Kelle, I need a favor. I need you to do this home inspection." Now Joe didn't do a lot of home inspections anymore, he had guys on staff to do that for him. But I knew that no one other than the owner of the company, who knew how much my business meant to his company, would have the patience to deal with this client.

He asked me why I wanted him to do it and I said, "He's the Master Chief of the prototype submarine. He's got fifteen years in." I heard a big sigh on the other end of the phone as the situation sunk in and he realized what he was in for.

"Yep, I'm doing this one myself," he said.

"Plan to be there for four hours," I said.

"Why? It's only a 2,000-square-foot raised ranch," he asked.

"Trust me, plan on four hours."

"OK," he said, with another heavy sigh.

The home inspection did indeed take four hours. Every time Joe went to move on to the next area, the buyer would bring him back to a spot he had just left and ask a question about it. They went into the attic together. They went into the basement together. Had there been a crawl space, I have no doubt the buyer would have gone there too. I have never seen Joe's patience tried as hard as it was that day. The only reason he didn't blow up at the buyer was that he knew how important my business was to him. It was our relationship that saved the deal.

Agent's Fax Feedback Form

In Chapter 16, you will find a copy of the "Agent's Fax Feedback Form" I used when I took buyers out to houses (see Exhibit 16-2). I created this form so that I and the buyer could fill out what we thought about the house while we were driving from one house to the next (I had the buyer fill in my responses). Then, when I got back to the office, my assistant could fax the page to the agents and I could save a lot of time in not having to call each agent with feedback. I loved it because it saved me time. The other agents loved it because they never had to track me down for feedback, and because they now had written proof of the feedback for the seller.

One of my coaching clients recently started using this form. She sent it to the agents for one day's showings. Within two hours, she had received phone calls from two of the agents thanking her for the form. One of them had used it to get a $15,000 price reduction on the house. The other was going to use it to get the seller to do some work on improving the showing condition of the house. They both appreciated having the feedback in writing so much that they called to say so. Her relationships with those agents improved while she saved time and effort. What could be better than that?

Preferred Treatment

The Agent's Fax Feedback Form was a win-win all around. Because of this form (and my commitment to giving good feedback to listing agents), I had a great relationship with the listing agents in the industry. I was also known for doing my job. And, I was known for my can-do attitude in getting problems solved. If I put a deal together, it stayed together.

I would get calls from listing agents bringing a property on the market before it hit the MLS asking if I had a buyer for the property and offering me first shot at a showing. In multiple-offer situations, if my deal was close, I usually got the deal. I even did enough business with one agent that I got a referral for a listing in my area because it was out of his marketing area. I got a lot of business from other agents that I wouldn't have gotten if I hadn't had good industry relationships.

Keep Me in the Loop

The other benefit of having these relationships in place is the gossip tree. You'd be amazed what you can find out about on the gossip tree. I heard which home inspector is insolvent so that buyers can't sue if he misses something. I found out what builder was strapped for cash and was the president and treasurer of the condo association that he was building. (I knew to avoid sending buyer clients that way because he was also known for having slightly shady dealings and I didn't trust him not to use condo funds to finish the build-out of his units.) You found out what properties had been foreclosed on, who was getting sued for what, and how the world of real estate was being impacted by all of these issues.

Do you really need to know the gossip? I think so. Imagine bringing in an offer to a typically reliable agent who is in the middle of an ugly divorce. If you didn't know this then you wouldn't know to check all the details to make sure she hasn't missed anything in her distraction. Your buyer might lose the deal because you weren't informed.

Enforced Volunteerism

I volunteered on the board of directors for the local affiliate of Habitat for Humanity in my area. Being the only real estate agent (and being that there were no attorneys on the board), it fell to me to head up the committee on getting properties transferred. The affiliate had several properties that had not been conveyed to the homeowners because of title problems. Either they needed condo documents filed, or they had encroachments or easements on the property. This was several thousand dollars' worth of attorney's fees to get this work done.

I got on the phone to an agent friend of mine and told him the problem. We each contacted the attorneys that we regularly used for closings. We asked them what they were doing for pro bono work these days and neither one had a good answer. We told them that they would each be doing some pro bono work for Habitat. Through the grapevine we also heard of a third attorney who was interested in helping out.

Over the next few months, we cleared up the majority of the issues and transferred title on several properties. The remaining property we deemed to be not worth dealing with and we found the families new homes. In the course of six months, we handled problems that had been present for years. I was able to leverage my relationship with my attorney and my friend's relationship with his attorney to get some much needed work accomplished.

Pro Bono Short Sale

Every once in a while, even agents do pro bono work. You know the deal, the house isn't going to sell for nearly enough to justify the commission you'll need to charge to make it worth your while to do the deal. We had just such an instance when this little old lady with a mobile home came to our office. Her mobile home was worth about $2,500. She owed the bank $4,000. She needed to move. She had no savings. She lived on social security. She wanted to move into a retirement home, but couldn't afford to buy out her mortgage on the mobile home. Renting out the mobile home was more than she could deal with. We were making no money on this deal—guaranteed. But she was a sweet little old lady. We liked her. So this was our designated pro bono deal for the year.

The challenge with mobile homes is that there are only a few companies that finance them. It is a specialized industry and there was only one lender in our area that we knew of. My partner did a lot of mobile-home business and was in direct competition with the other major mobile-home agent in the area. This agent did slightly more business than he did in that market. The relevance of this will become apparent shortly.

We put the house on the market and found a willing buyer. Now all we needed to do was get the approval from the bank for the short sale. The bank initially said "yes," but called back an hour later to say they couldn't do it. We were puzzled for a moment, but then the light dawned. You see, the other mobile-home agent was known as a bit of a hardball player. We were certain that what had happened was that she had called the mortgage lender to find out what was going on with the deal and then threatened to pull her business if they approved the short sale. (You see, she got all of their foreclosure listings.) I was incensed.

I got back on the phone with the lender and told him that I was pretty sure this was what had happened. He didn't say it had, but he didn't deny it either. I told him that if he was going to make this poor little old lady go into foreclosure over a $2,500 mobile home listing then I was going to go to the banking commission and explain that his listing agent was determining his banking practices. I was certain that there was some sort of RESPA violation in that collusion. And even if there wasn't, it was enough to get the banking commission to check out their other deals, and was he sure he wanted to get into this? (I can play hardball myself at times.) We had the short sale approval faxed to us fifteen minutes later.

Had I not been aware of this other agent's tactics, I would not have been in a position to counter them, and my client would have paid the price. Knowing who is in your marketplace and how they do business is the key to getting things done.

The At-Cost Roofing Job

When you're in the business long enough, you develop a lot of contractor relationships. I needed a lot of different jobs done over the years. Most often on the list of items to be repaired or replaced were roofs. I had a lot of work for my roofing contractor. Subsequently, I also had a lot of pull with him when I needed a favor. I had a deal that wasn't going to come together unless I could get a roof replaced for $2,000 or less. We both knew that this was an at-cost job, especially given that there were solar panels on the roof that had to be removed and replaced during the job. But, because I fed him a lot of business, he agreed to do the roof for me at cost and I got the deal done. For the record, with the money I got from the closing, I hired the roofer to replace my roof the following month—at full price.

Our relationships in the industry are the one thing for which there is no substitute. Knowing who we are working with makes all the difference in the deal. Establishing a good reputation in the industry, building good relationships with colleagues and related businesses, can only serve to improve the quality of service we provide to our clients and our effectiveness in the long run.

CHAPTER 20

TIME MANAGEMENT

If we embrace the process of coaching our clients through the transaction, then we put a lot of our personal energy into our businesses. We are required to be more present and to get more involved with our clients. In order to do this on an ongoing basis, we need to be certain that we build a balanced life for ourselves. It is important that we schedule time off and then take it. We need to be careful to play as hard as we work, or we'll burn out in short order.

If we are going to build a balanced life and still do enough business to make our income goals, then we have to learn how to manage our time effectively. Time management is the art of getting more done in the same amount of time. There are several ways to accomplish this task. The first, and probably the most effective of all of them, is to create systems in our businesses.

Systems

One of the biggest time-wasters is being disorganized. We spend time mentally reviewing the same information because we haven't written it down and we want to be sure to remember it. We look at the same piece of paper over and over again because we've put it in a pile and haven't filed it where it belongs. We spend time searching the piles of paper on our desk to find the one page we need. We lose phone numbers and spend fifteen minutes tracking them down before we can make our calls. We call a person twice about the same thing because we're so busy that we forgot we already talked to them. No matter what part of our business is lacking organization, it is damaging our ability to be effective and it's wasting our time.

Putting a system in place in your business keeps you on track. If you refuse to have a stack of papers on your desk, then you are forced to find a place for them. If you keep things in your files in a certain order, clamped to the folder, then you can always find the page you're looking for quickly. If you write down everything you do in the client file, then you never end up doing the same thing twice (and you are better off in the event of a lawsuit). If you keep a running "things to do" list that you carry everywhere with you, then you needn't clog your brain with random things you need to remember. If you keep a pad of paper and a pen by the bed, then you can write down all of the random items running through your head at night and you actually get to sleep at night.

Take an inventory of what systems exist in your business and what ones you could put in place. If you're not good at putting systems in place, then you need to hire someone who is or purchase a system ready-made. Personal Organizers exist everywhere in the country. These people are saviors to those of us who are organizationally challenged or just overwhelmed.

I am actually a great organizer. I've written a complete procedure manual for real estate businesses that brings organization into our decidedly unstructured industry. *(The New Agent's Survival Guide to Real Estate* and *Taking It to the Next Level: Systems for Successful Agents* are both available on my website at www.spartasuccess.com). But *even I* hired a personal organizer recently. Why? Because I had so many projects going on simultaneously that I could no longer even keep what they were in my head much less trying to keep track of the details of each one. I was completely overwhelmed and subsequently, I would come into my office, look at my desk, and my brain would shut down completely. I would sit and stare, trying desperately to figure out where I should start. I knew I had tons of work to do—more than I could ever possibly complete in a year—and yet I couldn't think of a single thing to do.

This is what happens when our brains shut down. We are so overwhelmed by the immense amount of work to do that we go into denial and pretend that it doesn't exist at all. I knew that if I was going to get anything done, I needed help.

This wonderful woman named Kristy Wacek, who runs the company Breathing Room, came into my office. She asked me to list everything I did in my business. Thankfully, I had already done this as part of my business planning for the year. (I think this was when my brain realized the scope of the work on my plate and shut down.) She then set about creating binders for all of my projects and putting all the papers in my bins on my desk into the binders. The binders were placed out of my direct line of sight so that all I could focus on in any given moment was the project in front of me. Once this task was complete, my brain switched back on and I could think again. I still have a lot to do. It's still more than I can do in a year. But now I'm making progress on one project at a time and letting the rest be until I can get to them. I am functional again. In my case, getting systems in place in my business meant the difference between doing business and not.

Exercise

Look at your business. Are there piles of paper on your desk? Can you even see your desk? How long does it take you to find something in your files? Do you have a "things to do" list? Do you wake up in the middle of the night because you just remembered something you forgot to do? Do you have trouble getting to sleep because of all the items running through your brain that you need to do tomorrow? Do you miss deadlines? Do you fail to keep your promises to your clients because you forgot you made them? Are you keeping in touch with your past clients? Do you follow the same procedures for each client? Are those procedures written down in checklist format? What parts of your business are lacking systems? Put a plan in place now to get those systems set up.

Blocking Time

For those of us who are already in over our heads, we need to first carve out the time we need to create our systems to save us time later. We can accomplish this task by blocking our time. We schedule all like items together so that we can move smoothly from one item to another without having to mentally or physically change gears. This means making all of our calls at the same time or running all of our errands at the same time. If we're going to file things away on our desk, then we need to stick with that task until it's done rather than starting it and then getting sidetracked as we find items that need to be dealt with in the pile. As we find these items, we need to set them in a separate pile and continue filing. When we finish filing, then we can take the items that need attention and block those into *like-items*. Then we can deal with those pieces together with the other like-items from the rest of our day.

If we schedule our days to include planning sessions at either the beginning or the end of our days, then we can keep ourselves on track. We can use these times to put all of the day's work into categories. And if we schedule time to do each of the types of categories, then we know what part of the day we will spend doing what. If we know that we are at our best in the morning and that a particular task needs our best effort, then we schedule it for that time slot. And so on.

By simply creating this simple system in our day, we can garner as much as an hour or two of extra time. We can then use that time to create and implement new systems in our business that will create even more free time. This eventually opens up our schedule to allow for (gasp) time off! Yea!

Scheduling Time Off

When we schedule time off, it is important to remember that this means that it is *time off*. This is not a time when we will answer e-mails or check the MLS for new listings or return calls or even answer calls. We are OFF. *Not* working. *Not* available for business. *Relaxing*. Doing something *fun*.

The problem with most agents I meet is that they decide they're going to take time off, but then they don't know what to do with that time off. They do some errands, watch a little TV, get bored and restless and, in the absence of something more interesting to do, end up going online to check the MLS for new listings or returning e-mails or checking their voice mail. In short: They end up working because they had nothing better to do.

The problem with this approach is that they never end up taking time off. They get stressed and they burn out. They forget how to relax. They begin to take work with them on vacation and then end up working even though there obviously *is* something more interesting to do.

The solution to this problem is to create a list of things that we like to do and that we've always wanted to do. The list should be one hundred items long. It can include simple, mundane things like seeing a movie, and it can include items that take more time, like learning to play the piano like Billy Joel. They don't even have to all be totally realistic—my list includes going into space and having a discussion about the nature of the universe with the Dalai Lama. Whatever we put on the list must be something we want to do though—not a chore or something that someone else wants us to do. It is a list of fun.

Once we have this list written out, we then have no excuse to work on our days off. We can pick an item off the list and do it. We don't have to think too hard about it (which is good because we're usually too fried to come up with a creative idea at that time). In this way we will make sure that we renew ourselves each week. We must take time to take care of ourselves so that we can be present for others. Otherwise we're trying to draw water from a dry well. We need to take at least one day off per week, and a vacation—even a short one—at least once a quarter.

So what do we do with our clients while we're taking this time off? Nothing. Obviously, if there is a time crunch to get something accomplished, then we need to get someone to cover for us. But otherwise, the clients can wait. And they won't even mind waiting if we train them in the beginning of our relationship that we do take days off.

Give Your Client a Schedule

Just as we talked about in Chapter 1, it is important to set our clients' expectations early in this process. At the initial meeting with our clients we need to give them a copy of our ideal schedule. This schedule should include days off, the times at night after which they should not call, a block each morning or evening for our planning sessions, and the best times to reach us by phone during the day. We can explain to the client that this is an ideal, and that obviously our business needs to be flexible because of its nature. But they need to understand that we will be taking at least one day off each week to recharge and that we do not intend to take or return any calls or e-mails during this time. We will be unavailable for one day each week. If there is an emergency, they can call the office and someone will help them, but we will not be available.

Once we set this rule with our clients, we then need to enforce it. If we have given out our cell phone number to clients, then we should check the caller ID before answering. If it's not a personal friend calling, we don't answer it. If our voice mail forwards to our cell phone, then we turn off that forwarding for the day we're off. If our clients e-mail us, then we don't check e-mail that day. And we certainly don't call into the office for messages, nor do we take calls from the office on our days off. We need to enforce our boundaries, or the people in our business will walk all over them and it will be our fault for letting it happen.

Now I know that some of you are baulking at this concept. You're thinking that you need to be available to your clients 24/7 because if you don't do it, then someone else will. For a small percentage of clients in the marketplace, you are correct. But these clients are also the biggest wasters of your time and energy. They are not good clients. It's OK if they go away. They will free up enough time for you to help two or three good clients. Plus, when you're not available 24/7, you're telling your clients that you are a professional. Think about it for a minute. How many doctors and lawyers and other professionals do you know who give you a home phone number and tell you to call anytime? Not many. Do you resent them for it? No. It's expected that they have business hours during which they are available. And you can too. Now, being agents and given the nature of our business, our business hours will be longer than the average professional's, but there should still be limits.

E-Mail: The Great Time Saver

Since the advent of the Internet, e-mail has become more and more prevalent in our society. Many buyers and sellers prefer to communicate this
way. And still more are OK with it if we prefer to use e-mail. E-mail is
great. We can say everything we need to, without interruption. We don't
have to do the small talk thing just to pass along a piece of information.
And if it's 3:00 A.M., we can still get the message to our client without
waking them up.

Before e-mail got popular, I had a set of sellers who lived on an early
morning schedule. They were up at 5:00 A.M., at work by 7:00 A.M., and
in bed by 7:00 to 8:00 P.M. Now I am a night person. I'm happiest when
I'm up at 7:30 to 8:00 A.M. and in bed by midnight. Obviously, our schedules didn't work together. But, through the creative use of technology, we
still stayed in touch. I had a voice mail system that didn't ring anywhere,
so they could call and leave messages at 5:00 A.M. without waking me. I
left messages back for them on their answering machine at home while
they were at work and they retrieved them at night before they went to
bed. I had very few actual conversations with them during the course of
their listing, but we kept in touch constantly. E-mail works much the
same way today.

WARNING! The one problem with e-mail over the exchange of voice
mails is the lack of tonality in the written word. I have seen instances
where something that was written with the intention of just being infor-
mative was perceived by the recipient to be angry and insulting. When
there are no tonality, body language, or other cues about the sender's state
of mind or intentions around the e-mail, it is often easy to misconstrue
the other person's meaning. Be very careful using this medium for just
this reason. If the issue being addressed is at all sticky emotionally, a
phone call is far more appropriate.

What to Do When Our Brains Turn Off

As I am writing this book, I am looking forward to the next month's
business. I've recently realized that if I don't finish the book this week, I
will not make my deadline by mid-month next month for the editing. As
of this morning, I was fifty pages into what is supposed to be a 240-page
book. Talk about overwhelming. So I took today to plow through a couple
of chapters. The first chapter went well, but when I went to start the
second one, my brain began to fuzz over. I realized I'd been sitting at the
computer screen for over two hours typing away. I was tired. My brain

needed a break. And not just doing something else in front of the computer, I needed to get up.

So I went out into my office and began to clean up from my class I had a couple days ago. Then I decided it was time to finally wire up the stereo that's been sitting in my office for almost a year. I moved around and did some physical labor for a while and it allowed my brain to reset.

There is only so long we can work on something before we need a break. Trying to work past that point only reduces our effectiveness and increases the chances of mistakes. When our brains turn off, it's an indicator that it's time to take a break and do something else. When we can step away from a task and take a breather, we can then come back to it again with renewed energy and enthusiasm later.

The moral: Don't work too hard. It's not good for you and it's not worth it in the end.

CHAPTER 21

NEGOTIATION SKILLS

Negotiation is a hard skill to learn. It takes a keen understanding of your opponent and nerves of steel to get the best results. You need to be able to see not only your own side of the negotiations, but also the other person's side. Significant progress can be made only when each side understands and respects the other's position.

In order to get everyone to the point of agreement, you must first have an understanding of the issues yourself. You need to know what is going into the decision-making process for your client. If you have done your work up front, then this should not be an issue. You should already be aware of what issues are in play. Then it simply becomes a matter of finding out the other side's issues.

Finding out what is important to the other side can often be a challenge. This is especially true when you are dealing with good negotiators on the other side of the equation. A good negotiator gives away only as much information as is necessary to get the end result without giving up enough to damage his clients' negotiating position. A good negotiator will also ask questions to get information from the other side. Knowing how to handle these questions is key—whether you are the one giving the information or asking the questions.

Questions

The first rule of negotiations is: The quality of the answers you receive is in direct proportion to the quality of the questions you ask. If you ask poor questions, then you get poor answers. Open-ended questions are your best bets. This way if the agent on the other side is not free to give you the information that you want, then you leave them an opening to give you something else they do feel comfortable revealing. Here are some examples of good questions to ask.

Questions to Ask a Listing Agent

- *Why are your clients selling?* This question opens a multitude of doors. Depending on the skill of the agent on the receiving side of this question, we may get next to no response ("They want to move"), or we may get the whole enchilada ("They're getting a divorce").

- *What is your client's time frame for moving?* This may give us a hint as to the seller's motivation. If it's a short time frame, perhaps he is more open to negotiating on the price. If it's a long one, then perhaps he would be open to a lower price if the buyer were willing to be patient. Of course, a good negotiator would answer this question with, "He's negotiable. Why? What is your client's time frame?"

- *How motivated are your clients?* This is a hard question to answer, but it will often elicit a response when others will not. For agents who do not have good negotiation skills, asking the same question in different ways may eventually break down their defenses. From those who do have good skills, you'll probably get "they are motivated enough to have listed their home for sale" or "they're motivated enough to have made you an offer" as a non-informational response.

Here's an example of a few ways to phrase this question:

- How motivated are your clients?
- How serious are your clients?
- If we do X, then can you guarantee that they will do Y?
- How sure do you feel that this deal will go through?
- What do you think, is this going to happen?
- Give me a hint, are we just spinning our wheels here?

- *It looks like they just finished renovating. Why are they moving now? They obviously intended to stay.* Sometimes you can tell a little about the motivation of the other side by the circumstances you see in front of you. If you can convince the other side that the information is obvious, then you can often get them to tell you the details. The good negotiator would answer that question with "They decided to move," or "Their circumstances changed," or "They renovated to improve the value of the home." Let's face it. For all you know, the sellers may have done the upgrades to put the house on the market. But by assuming that they didn't, you put the listing agent in a position to either confirm or deny your comment—thereby giving you more information.

The goal of all of these questions is to get information. Information is king when negotiating. When you get blocked in one direction, you need to snake around and try another direction. At each feint you are hoping to squeeze out a bit of something that could be useful to you. Don't give up! Even the best negotiators get tired. That next question may be the one where the agent cracks.

Questions to Ask a Buyer's Agent

- *Why did your buyers choose this home? What was it about this house that appealed to them?* This question works well to identify items of interest to the buyers. It helps you, as the listing agent, to determine whether the features the buyers are making their decisions upon are readily available in other homes. If they aren't, then you have a little more wiggle room.

- *Is the buyer planning to owner-occupy?* This is a good question because it gives you the buyer's motivation. Investors are generally far less motivated than owner-occupants. They are not emotionally attached to the property and therefore are less likely to pay more for a house than an owner-occupant. If the buyer is buying to live there, then it is possible that she is in love with the property and will buy it for any price for which she can get financing.

- *What is your client's ideal time frame for closing?* If the buyer must move quickly, then you may be able to leverage that information to get your seller a higher price.

When We Have to Give Information

There are times when you will have to eke out a little information to keep the process moving. If it seems like the negotiations are going nowhere, you may wish to throw in a little bit of motivational info to sweeten the pot.

"You know, the buyers really love this home."

"The sellers like what they see, but they just can't come to that price. Is there anything we can do?"

And so on. As long as both parties are talking, you are in a position to put the deal together. When they stop talking, you're in trouble. The key to this process is to care about the outcome, but still be willing to walk away if you need to. When you are not willing to walk away, you lose most of your negotiation power. When the other side realizes that you are not willing to walk away, then you've lost all of your power.

Closings

The final question in any negotiation must be a closing question. The question effectively asks, "So, do we have a deal?" You may ask this question directly, such as I did just now, or it can be more obliquely stated. Below are several closing techniques for getting the deal done. Each has its own merits and many can be combined together. The best negotiators use all of these techniques at some point or another.

The Assumptive Close

In this closing, we assume the result that we desire—such as "When you list your house with me, I will . . ." or "So should we meet on Monday at 9:00 or Tuesday at 4:00?" We do not give the other person the opportunity to say "no." We assume that he will go along with us. By phrasing our comments in this way, the other person has to work harder to get out of the plan we are putting forth. We have not given him the option to say "no," so if that's what he wants to do, then he has to create that option for himself.

The Take Away

If buyers or sellers refuse to be reasonable about something, we offer to remove the offending object from their view. For example, if the buyers ask for too many items on a home inspection to be repaired by the seller, I tell them, "OK, I'll start pulling some new listings for you to see." At which point they ask why I'm doing that. I tell them that obviously they don't want this house since they're not being reasonable about the repairs, so let's just skip negotiating over the repairs and go right on to the next house.

When we are negotiating with the other agent in a deal, then the take away is a threat to walk away from the house sale. Most of the time, we will want this threat to be implied rather than implicit. We will want to say that the buyer said this issue was a deal breaker. Or we will want to sound very dubious when we respond to the other agent's questions about whether our client is willing to negotiate further. We may say something like, "I'll try, but my client is really running out of patience with this deal."

Whether we are telling a buyer that we should start looking for other houses or another agent that we are walking away from the deal, we need to be prepared for the possibility that they may agree with us. We may kill the deal in hand. There is always a risk in using this approach, but it is a great litmus test of how the parties are feeling. If they are not committed to the process, then the deal may fall apart later anyway. It's best to know now.

The Benjamin Franklin Close

Benjamin Franklin used a technique of writing down a list of the pros and cons in a situation when he couldn't decide what to do. We can suggest this same technique for a client who has a problem making a decision. It takes the problem out of his head and puts it onto the table in front of him where we can help him sort through it. For people who have problems making decisions, this technique is a godsend.

Silence is Golden

One of the biggest mistakes made by agents in the negotiation process is not being able to shut up. We must ask for what we want and then wait for an answer. No matter how uncomfortable the silence makes us, we must wait it out. We should realize that the silence is making the other person uncomfortable too. We need to wait, be patient, and bite our tongues. If we talk first, then we will undo all the good we did in asking the closing question in the first place.

In my marketplace, there was an attorney who had a well-known policy. He felt that his job was to make sure that the transaction closed if it was at all possible. His opinion was that no one's interests were served if the house ended up back on the market, and that most situations could be negotiated at the closing table for less money than it would cost his client to go through the process again. This perspective made him very popular with agents. To accomplish this goal, his rule was, "he who speaks first loses." If there was a problem at the closing table and an issue that cost money was being addressed, the agents knew that they needed to shut up. This attorney's policy was to drop the issue on the table by saying something like, "OK, so the buyer needs a refrigerator," and then wait to see who couldn't take the heat. The first person to speak after he made his comment was the person he would expect to pay to fix it. Sometimes, we would sit in silence for several minutes before someone spoke. Sometimes it was only seconds. Someone always broke the silence and someone always paid.

Every agent who worked with him knew this. And yet, one of the biggest producers he worked with was completely unable to avoid paying for things. She was not capable of keeping her mouth shut when these comments happened. She knew that it would cost her to open her mouth, but she just couldn't help herself. She laughed every time she came out of the closing room having paid for something new. She shook her head and put it down to another lesson in negotiations. She considered it an education she was paying for. I thought she should have switched to another attorney who didn't have that policy.

Keep Your Eye on the Goal

We need to know what motivates our client. If we put that goal in front of them and remind them of what they are shooting for, then we have a much better chance of getting them to move in the direction of agreement. People often get distracted and make emotional decisions that are based on issues other than what gets them closer to what they want. Our job is to get them back on track and to put things in perspective.

This issue comes into play most often with sellers, although we can run across it with buyers and with other agents too. Sellers can often get wrapped up in the emotion of the sale, especially if they have lived in the home for a long time and are still emotionally attached to the home.

If the sellers receive a low-ball offer from a buyer, they can often react badly, assuming that the buyer is devaluing their home and, by association, the life they lived in it. The sellers don't understand that the buyer is just trying to get the best deal and by starting low, he is setting his mind at ease that he tried his best. In this case, it helps to do two things.

First, explain the buyer's motivations to the seller (even if we don't know them, we can talk about how buyers want to know they got the best deal and didn't start negotiating too high, etc.). Then, we need to refocus the sellers on the goal. They want to move. This is no longer their house, it is a product they have for sale. They need to detach a little and at least counter the offer—even if it's just to come down $1,000.

If the sellers are moving long distance, then we can bring them a copy of a brochure for the area they are moving to. If they are moving locally and have already located their new place, then a picture of that home works nicely. Either way, the items serve as a reminder of the goal. We attach the brochure or the picture to the offer and explain that one begets the other, so we don't want to be too hasty in turning the offer down.

Too Many Choices

Just a note. Buyers can get overwhelmed if we show them too many properties. We need to be careful when a buyer wants to see a lot of properties, that they don't get stuck in the "what ifs." They need to be able to make a decision. What this means to us is that we need to help them narrow the field. If they see a house and they don't like it, then we must take the listing sheet away from them. We should have them crumple it up immediately and throw it in the backseat of our car. This way, the only sheets they keep in their possession are the ones that are still in the running. Periodically, we should weed this list down with them too. They should never have more than three properties on the list at once.

If they are still reluctant to buy, then we need to talk to them about why. Perhaps they are afraid of making a mistake and not picking the right house. They need to understand that there is no "perfect" house. All houses will represent a compromise of some sort or another. If there is one on their list that they can live with, could even potentially be happy in, then they should place an offer. We need to give them permission to act.

Once, I was showing one of my listings to a buyer's agent and her clients. This agent was fairly new in the business and as she walked in the front door, she proudly announced that this was the 100th house she had shown them. I was stunned. I looked at the buyers and said, "Wow, you must be so tired."

They said that they were tired.

"How long have you been looking?" I asked.

They said, "Six months."

"Oh my gosh. Well, no worries," I responded. "You're going to love this house. I'm sure it will be the one you buy. Why don't you two take a look around while I talk to your agent for a minute?"

I pulled the agent aside and told her that showing any buyers 100 homes was not something to brag about. She had done them a disservice, either by showing them a lot of homes they definitely wouldn't like or couldn't afford, or by not giving her buyers permission to buy something.

I gave the buyers permission to buy my listing. I planted the thought in their heads that they could buy this house and be done with looking. They put in the offer that day.

Push Hard: Then Run Away, Shouting, "Don't Shoot the Messenger!"

Sometimes it's hard to get our clients to budge on a particular issue. They want to dig in. They want to be right. They want it their way—whether it's in their best interests or not. At this time, we need to have courage and determination. We need to make our points more forcefully. We need to keep talking after they've told us to stop. This is shaky ground we're walking on and it takes nimble feet to traverse it without falling.

The first rule of thumb when employing this technique is to not be afraid to go a little past the boundaries we know are in place. *A little past.* Not a football field, just a few steps. Just enough for them to realize that there are parts to the picture that they haven't let us show them.

Then, when they get upset that we have exceeded their boundaries, we run backwards, saying something like, "I know you don't want to talk about it anymore, but I thought it was important for you to know this before you made your final decision. It's your decision, not mine. I just want to be certain that you are well informed when you make it." In essence, we are saying, "Don't shoot the messenger."

When we accomplish this task well, the clients stop and think about what we just told them. (They didn't register what we had said before—only that we had crossed their boundaries to say it.) They begin to notice that we had something of value to say. And, grudgingly, they will allow us to continue our conversation.

We may have to use this technique several times with some clients. Some people are more stubborn than others. But if we master the art of running away while saying, "Don't shoot the messenger—I'm just looking out for you!" then we are sure to get to the end of the negotiations in one piece.

Don't Get Upset

This is a stressful process. We should strive to maintain control at all times. We are the voice of reason. We speak from a rational perspective. This is our job. Even when using the techniques above (including "I Get to Be Upset"), we do not actually get emotionally out of hand. We always keep in mind that this is not our house, and it is not our life. We need to keep our perspective. We cannot adequately maintain a balance in our lives and the lives of our clients without maintaining a certain distance. We cannot emotionally invest in the process and remain objective. We can be supportive and empathetic, but if we get emotionally invested, then we will lose our focus.

I can't tell you how many times the other agent in the transaction was more of a liability than an asset to the transaction. Often this was because she didn't understand the difference between understanding and advocating for her client and actually standing in the client's emotional shoes. She would get emotionally invested in the situation and lose her objective perspective. At that time, I would then have to do my best to manage the agent's emotions as well as the transaction. It would have been much easier to deal directly with her client instead of her at these times because she was not being rational. As agents, we do a disservice to our clients if we become too emotionally involved.

CHAPTER 22

NETWORKING YOUR
WAY TO SUCCESS

Now that you have your unique selling proposition and negotiating skills in place, you are ready to head out into the world and network. It is time to let people know who you are, what you do, and why they should care. But before you go racing out just yet, you need to know the rules of the game for networking.

Where to Network

You know that you need to network, and you'd like to start, but you're not sure how or where to do it. Never fear. There are many networking opportunities available in the world.

The first place to look for networking opportunities is within your target market. You know who your target market is, now all you have to do is figure out where they gather. You can go to sporting events, classes, meetings, etc. Wherever you are likely to find the people in your target market—that's where you want to be.

Another option is to go to Chamber of Commerce events. The "Business After Hours" and "Business Breakfast" events are usually open to the public as recruiting events for the Chamber. For a small event fee (usually about $15), we can get in the door, have some finger foods and a drink, and mingle our way to more business. We need to be careful when scoping out these events though. There are often many other agents that attend and who are therefore competition for us. This is why having our Elevator Pitch and Creative Answer down cold is so important (see Chapter 13). We have to be able to sell the person we are speaking to on why we are better than the other agents they've talked to that evening.

Another way that people network is through community service groups like Rotary, Kiwanis, or Lions Club. These groups are usually made up of people who are members of the business community. They are prime targets for our services. The downside to these groups is that we often get roped into doing a lot of work for the group and there is no guarantee of a return on our time invested. However, if we are careful about what we volunteer for, we can finagle these chores into additional chances to meet new people. The more people we meet, the better are our chances of finding someone looking to buy or sell real estate.

One of my favorite places to find business is the supermarket. If we spend a couple hours a week in the supermarket wearing our nametags we can kill two birds with one stone. We can get our shopping done for the week and we give people who are interested in hearing about the business a chance to speak with us. In fact, we should seriously consider wearing our name tag everywhere we go. It's a walking advertisement that tells the people around us to ask us about real estate. And (if we're relatively considerate drivers) we should put signs on our cars to do the same thing. The more we give people the opportunity to know who we are and what we do, the more likely we are to find someone interested in utilizing our services.

One of the best sources of networking events are the networking groups set up specifically for this purpose. Business Networking International, LeTip, and others are groups designed around one common purpose—to pass referral business back and forth among their members. Unfortunately, the real estate seat in these groups is often one of the most coveted slots and they are hard to come by. But we have the option of starting our own group and building it up with people we think would be good referral sources.

Setting Up Our Own Group

If you choose to start your own group, then you want to recruit people who are good at both bringing in business and at bringing in additional members to the group. These people are the Kings and Queens of networking. They are the people who know everyone and who have large rolodexes to prove it. It's important that you look for these type of people when recruiting for your group because they can mean the difference between a group that gets off the ground and one that doesn't. And for all the work that goes into setting up one of the groups—you need it to get off the ground.

Networking Rule #1: Talk to People

If you don't talk to people at a networking event, then you aren't networking. It's not sufficient to just show up, you have to open your mouth too.

When you talk to people, you want to interact with them on a business level. If you don't mention what you do and don't give your Elevator Pitch, then you can't expect to get any business from the encounter.

Make a Good Impression

So what do you say to these people when you meet them? First, you're going to greet them with a smile and a firm handshake. (Not too firm, men, or we ladies will feel the pain of having our rings crushed into our fingers. Ladies, please no limp-fish or fingertips-only handshakes. They imply a lack of desire to touch the person you are speaking with and make him feel that you find him distasteful.) Introduce yourself clearly (your name only), and ask the other person who he is and what he does. When he finishes talking, he will ask you what you do and then you can launch into your Creative Answer and Elevator Pitch.

Offer to Help Them

The rule in life is that you have to give to get. So you want to listen to what the other person is saying about his business when he is talking. Remember your deeper listening skills and apply them here. Also be referencing your mental database to determine whether what he does would work for anyone you know.

This is my favorite part of the process. I love to make connections between people. I keep a mental note of all of the people I know and I see how I can creatively put them together. This works well both for the two people we are putting together as well as for us, since they will want to pay us back by finding referrals for us.

Don't overlook the possibility that you may have something of value to offer the person in front of you that *isn't* a referral. Often there are ways in which we can cross-market our businesses that we hadn't anticipated. Perhaps you are talking to a CPA and you can't think of anyone who might need his services. Instead, you might offer him an opportunity. You might suggest that he write a quick little set of tips for homeowners booklet or report that you could send to your client base (with his name on it as the author of course). This is a way to send him business. And don't forget that you may have several free reports on home buying and selling sitting around that might be good information for his clients. Just because there isn't an immediate connection doesn't mean that there isn't room to find one. Think out of the box.

And if the networking event we are attending is more of a community event, then the offer of the free report becomes even more important. Having something of value to offer the potential client (something more than just putting them onto the MLS property finder search—everyone does that) is critical to getting them in the door to speak with you.

Ask for Business

It's all well and fine to tell people our Elevator Pitch and give them our Creative Answer, but if we don't ask for business at the end, then we are not likely to get it. People don't know that we need their help finding business unless we tell them. If we can feed the other person a referral, that's even better. And even if we can't come up with one, simply saying that we are trying to will spur the person in front of us to try to think of a referral for us too. Make it a practice to ask for business. If you are truly giving people something of value, it won't seem out of place. Here are some suggestions for how to ask for business:

- "Here's my card—actually here's two—one for you and one for a friend. If I can be of help to you or anyone you know I'd love to hear from you."

- "Can I have your card? I'd like to have it on hand in case I come across anyone who needs your services. By the way—who do you know who might be looking to buy or sell a house?" (*Remember to ask, "Who do you know?" not "Do you know anyone?" The first question makes them try to think of a name. The second gives them an opportunity to simply say "no" without thinking about it.*)

- "Hey, it was great to meet you. I really enjoyed our conversation. While I'm thinking about it, who do you know who might be looking to buy or sell a home? I'd really love to be able to help them out."

- "Great! I'll send you that free report tomorrow. While I'm sending reports out, is there anyone else you know who might want one of these reports too? I'd be happy to mail it to them when I send yours out."

You will want to ask for business at the end of the conversation—after you have built rapport and tried to offer a referral to that person as well.

Networking Rule #2: Hand Out Cards—Two of Them

At the end of any discussion at a networking event, we should offer the person we are speaking with our business card. Actually, we should offer her two cards. When we give her the cards, we tell her that one card is for her and the other is for a friend who might need our services. In this way, we ask the person to send us business and we give her the means to do so.

Networking Rule #3: Mingle

The Creative Answer and Elevator Pitch will only get you so far. You also need to be able to make your services applicable to the person you are talking to. This means that you need to know what his needs are before you can even begin to sell to him. When people ask me what I can do for them, I immediately respond with the question, "What do you need? Tell me a little about your business. What are you happy with? What are you unhappy with?" When I get the answers to those questions, I'm in a better position to respond. I can speak to the person's desires rather than telling him what I think he would want to hear.

The goal of these conversations is to make a positive impression on the person and be able to exchange cards (and possibly referrals). A secondary goal would be to acquire new business directly from the person we are speaking with. I list them in this order because I find that when agents go in with the intention of finding business they tend to come off as *needy* to the people they meet. Remember, networking and sales are much like dating—people don't want to be around you if you're desperate or needy. You have to look like you don't *need* the business, but you *want* it.

Don't Get Stuck!

One of the challenges that we can face when going to a networking event is getting stuck talking with someone who wants to spend the entire evening talking to us. You want to chat with people, but you don't want to have in-depth conversations. Focus your attention on the people who are interested in your services right away. If they aren't, don't spend too long with them—you can always come back to them if you have the time.

If they express an interest in talking further with you, then it is time to schedule another time to get together to discuss business and then move on. The purpose of this event is to network and you won't get to do much of that if you spend the entire time with one person. There will be plenty of time later to have an in-depth conversation. Tell the person, "You know, I'd love to talk with you further about this, but I'd really like to do it when we have some time to sit down in a quiet space. Can we schedule this conversation for another time? Perhaps Monday at 3:00 p.m.? I'd be happy to come to your office."

These conversations should last no more than five minutes each—preferably less. I've had some great initial conversations that lasted about thirty seconds. The better the networker you are speaking with, the more efficient the conversation will be.

Networking Rule #4: Follow-Up

Once you have met and exchanged business cards with people at a networking event, there is more still left to be done. Add those people to your mailing list so that they receive your hints and tips about home ownership and buying and selling. Follow up immediately after the event with a Thank You note. These notes can be done on computer if it was a large event, or they can be handwritten. A handwritten note is preferable since it is the most personal form of communication in the business world. It shows you valued your interaction with that person enough to take time to buy a card, write out the note, stamp it, and mail it. It makes her feel valued and respected. And this will hopefully impress her enough to send you referrals in the future. She'll certainly remember you.

EPILOGUE

Now that you understand the basics of coaching your clients to success both in their real estate transactions and in their lives, what do you do with it? The first thing you need to do is to let the consumers know that these services exist. Today, many people are of the opinion that they don't need us. They think that they can use the Internet to find all the houses that are available (and they can with www.realtor.com), so why would they possibly call us?

We have been so good at doing our jobs for so long that buyers and sellers don't realize all the work we do for them. They don't see all the details that we handle behind the scenes. They don't see half of the problems that we solve in the course of a day's work. They don't know how hard getting a real estate deal done can be.

It's our fault really. We've been so good at handling the problems and keeping the client unaware of them that we have problem-solved our way right out of being a necessity in the clients' minds. Sometimes being too efficient is a bad thing.

But there is hope. Begin to let your clients in on all the work you do for them. We can let them see behind the scenes into the details of the transaction. In doing this, you can foster a higher level of appreciation for the work that you do.

You can also help your clients on a deeper level. Your clients are almost always going through a major life transition. In this process, they are dealing with stress, grief, anger, depression, feeling out of control, and being overwhelmed. All of these feelings are normal, you see them all of the time. And, because you are the person who sees these feelings all of the time, you are in a unique position to be able to serve not only as agent, but as coach for your clients. You can help them by offering tools that allow them to process through these feelings. You can give them perspective on their personal situations. You can offer hope that there is an end to the process. And you can offer comfort by quantifying that process and explaining the steps. The more information you can offer, the more validation of your clients feelings you can do, the more sense of stability you can provide in a time when they feel totally off balance, the more valuable you become to them in the long run.

Your clients need you. You *know* that. Now it's time for you to teach them that as well. In offering a level of service that goes beyond the transaction, you set yourself apart from the rest of the real estate community. This is a value proposition that is unbeatable in the industry. Why compete on price, commission, or reputation, when you can change the rules and engage on a completely new level? Bring this new approach to your business and you will not only set yourself apart from the competition—you will create a business for yourself that is fulfilling, rewarding, and ultimately more profitable than you could have imagined.

INDEX